Y0-DDO-137

365 PROMISES AND PRAYERS

FOR DEALING WITH

ANXIETY

AND

FEAR

SMITH FREEMAN
Publishing

Copyright 2022 by Smith-Freeman Publishing

365 Promises and Prayers for Dealing with Anxiety and Fear

Bible verses were taken from the following translations:

Scripture quotations marked HCSB are taken from the Holman Christian Standard Bible®, Used by Permission HCSB © 1999, 2000, 2002, 2003, 2009 Holman Bible Publishers. Holman Christian Standard Bible®, Holman CSB®, and HCSB® are federally registered trademarks of Holman Bible Publishers.

Scripture quotations marked (KJV) are from the King James Version. Public domain.

Scripture quotations marked MSG are taken from *THE MESSAGE*, copyright © 1993, 2002, 2018 by Eugene H. Peterson. Used by permission of NavPress. All rights reserved. Represented by Tyndale House Publishers Inc.

Scripture quotations marked (NASB) are from the New American Standard Bible® (NASB), Copyright © 1960, 1962, 1963,1968, 1971, 1972, 1973, 1975, 1977, 1995 by The Lockman Foundation. Used by permission. www.Lockman.org.

Scripture quotations marked (NCV) are taken from the New Century Version®. Copyright © 2005 by Thomas Nelson. Used by permission. All rights reserved.

Scripture quotations marked (NIV) are taken from the Holy Bible, New International Version®, NIV®. Copyright © 1973, 1978, 1984, 2011 by Biblica, Inc.™ Used by permission of Zondervan. All rights reserved worldwide. www.zondervan.com The "NIV" and "New International Version" are trademarks registered in the United States Patent and Trademark Office by Biblica, Inc.™

Scripture quotations marked (NKJV) are taken from the New King James Version®. Copyright © 1982 by Thomas Nelson. Used by permission. All rights reserved.

Scripture quotations marked (NLT) are taken from the Holy Bible, New Living Translation, copyright © 1996, 2004, 2015 by Tyndale House Foundation. Used by permission of Tyndale House Publishers, a Division of Tyndale House Ministries, Carol Stream, Illinois 60188. All rights reserved.

Cover design by Kim Russell | Wahoo Designs

ISBN: 978-1-7378946-3-6

Peace I leave with you, My peace I give to you;
not as the world gives do I give to you.
Let not your heart be troubled, neither let it be afraid.

JOHN 14:27 NKJV

A MESSAGE TO READERS

Anxiety and fear. These two emotional reactions have the power to invade our lives and hijack our thoughts. And there's no question that as citizens of the twenty-first century, we are continually subjected to a steady stream of anxiety-producing, fear-provoking messages that can leave us breathless. So what should we do in response? For starters, we should turn to God's Word for guidance and comfort.

This book contains 365 devotional readings that are intended to help you deal with anxiety, with fear, and with other negative emotions that have the potential to do you harm. If you find yourself focusing on your fears instead of God's promises, the ideas on these pages will provide the wisdom, the courage, and the practical advice you'll need to manage your thoughts and improve your outlook.

The Lord has given you a guidebook for spiritual, emotional, physical, and psychological health. That book, of course, is the Holy Bible. The Bible is a priceless gift, an infallible tool that God intends for you to use every day, in good times and in hard times. Your intentions should be the same.

When you weave the Lord's messages into the fabric of your day—when you learn to focus more intently on His promises and less intently on your fears—you'll quickly discover that God's Word has the power to change everything, including your emotions. So if you sincerely desire to find better strategies for dealing with anxiety and fear, keep searching for direction—God's direction. When you do, you'll discover the courage, the comfort, the peace that only He can give.

YOU ARE NOT ALONE

If your life has been impacted by feelings of anxiety or fear, you are not alone. Please consider the following:

- Anxiety disorders are the most common mental illness in the United States.
- An estimated 19 percent of US adults have experienced an anxiety disorder during the past year.
- An estimated 31 percent of US adults will experience an anxiety disorder at some time in their lives.
- Anxiety disorders are highly treatable, yet only about 37 percent of those suffering receive treatment.*

So what should these statistics mean to you? For starters, the fact that feelings of anxiety and fear are commonplace means that treatment options are commonplace too. So if you're feeling anxious, worried, fretful or afraid, you need not suffer alone. Help is readily available.

Furthermore, the fact that almost one-third of your fellow citizens will experience an anxiety disorder at some point in their lives means that you can feel free to talk openly about your situation. When you share your anxious feelings with others, you'll undoubtedly be speaking to people who have either experienced anxiety themselves or have seen its impact on close friends or family members.

Finally, and most importantly, you must remember that even in your darkest moments, God is with you. He never leaves you; He never stops loving you, and He always keeps His promises. So when you walk through life's darkest valleys, you can be certain that you will never walk alone. The Lord will be with you.

As you consider ways to deal with anxiety and fear, please remember that you don't have to find solutions by yourself. You can seek help from family, from friends, from your pastor, from your physician, or from all of them. And while you're at it, you can ask God to guide you and protect you. When you do these things, you can rest assured that help is on the way.

*Sources: The National Institute of Mental Health *and the Anxiety and Depression Association of America.*

TEN ESSENTIAL STEPS FOR DEALING WITH ANXIETY AND FEAR

Accept the Fact That Chronic Negative Emotions Such as Anxiety and Fear Can Be Dangerous to Your Mental, Spiritual, and Physical Health. God wants you to experience the abundant life described in John 10:10. To achieve it, you must guard your heart and mind against irrational worries, anxieties, and fears.

Understand That It's Possible to Control Irrational Fears and Anxieties. If you believe that you have no control over your anxieties and fears, you're wrong. It may take training, education, practice, and, in some cases, medication. But if you sincerely desire to gain better control over these negative emotions, you can do it. With God, all things are possible.

When You Experience a Major Life-altering Change or a Significant Loss, Express Your Feelings Honestly. If you're experiencing a life-changing event, or if you're recovering from a recent loss, don't keep everything bottled up inside. Talk to people you can trust and express your feelings. And while you're at it, remember that God promises to heal the brokenhearted. In time, He will heal your heart and dry your tears if you let Him. So if you haven't already allowed Him to begin His healing process, today is a perfect day to start.

Understand That Negative Emotions Are Highly Contagious. Unless you make the conscious effort to take control of your thoughts and emotions, other people's outbursts can add to your fears and anxieties. If you find yourself in a situation where another person's negative emotions are continually infecting yours, ask God to help you guard your heart. And while you're at it, establish as much physical and psychological distance as you can by establishing clear boundaries between yourself and the difficult person.

Identify Any Stimulants or Medications That May Be Contributing to Your Anxiety. Sometimes anxieties and irrational fears can be triggered by chemical substances. For example, high-caffeine drinks, when consumed in sufficient quantities, can make you feel anxious even when you have little or nothing to feel anxious about. Additionally, many medications have side-effects that can cause fearful or anxious feelings. So if you're taking medication—or if you're consuming large amounts of caffeine or high-energy drinks—please understand that the chemicals in those substances may be contributing to your emotional distress.

Monitor Your Media Intake. Traditional media and social media share a common goal: to capture your attention and keep you engaged on their platforms. Various media outlets may use disturbing content, anger-inducing narratives, inappropriate images, gratuitous violence, or sensationalized news to keep you tuned in. So whether you realize it or not, the media may be adding to your anxieties and fears. The answer to this dilemma, of course, is to monitor your media intake and to act accordingly.

Avoid the Pitfalls of Procrastination. Procrastination breeds worry; worry breeds anxiety; anxiety breeds fear; fear breeds more procrastination, and the cycle continues. If you're constantly putting off until tomorrow what should be done today, you're actually manufacturing things to worry about. A far better strategy is undoubtedly this: tackle today's problems *today so that you don't have to worry about them tomorrow.*

Forgive Everybody. Hate and peace cannot coexist in the same human heart. God's Word makes it clear that if you want to experience the peace that passes all understanding—His peace—you must learn how to forgive, and you must learn how to move on with your life. So the sooner you forgive everybody—including yourself—the sooner you'll begin feeling better about yourself and your world.

Get Plenty of Rest. Most adults need about eight hours of sleep each night. If you're constantly depriving yourself of much-needed sleep, you may be harming your overall health while manufacturing needless stress and anxiety. So if you've acquired the habit of staying up late and robbing yourself of sleep, it's time to establish a new (and better) habit by turning off your devices and going to bed. But what if you're simply too anxious or too worried to fall asleep or to stay asleep? If you can't sleep, talk with your physician about your sleeping patterns, your situation, your habits, and your emotional state. Why? Because you need a good night's sleep to think clearly and realistically about your life, your blessings, your future, and your calling.

If Your Emotions—or the Emotions of Someone You Love—Begin to Spiral Out of Control, Seek Professional Help Immediately: Small emotional swings are an inevitable part of everyday life. But dramatic emotional swings—such as intense feelings of anxiety, despair, panic, or fear—are dangerous. So don't be embarrassed to seek professional help. Mental health professionals have numerous tools at their disposal to help you deal with emotional swings and anxiety disorders. Since help is available, you should ask for it as soon as you detect a problem.

1

ANXIETY AND FEAR ARE TEMPORARY; GOD'S LOVE ENDURES FOREVER.

So humble yourselves under the mighty power of God,
and at the right time he will lift you up in honor.
Give all your worries and cares to God, for he cares about you.

1 PETER 5:6–7 NLT

Ours is an anxious generation. Never before have so many people been inundated with so much information that has the potential to create so much fear, so much anxiety, and so much dread. But when we experience the inevitable frustrations and anxieties of everyday life, we must remember that the Lord is, indeed, our shepherd.

God loves you and wants the best for you. He sent His Son so that you might experience the gift of eternal life. And during your sojourn from cradle to grave, He remains constant, never leaving you. The Lord is always present, always attentive, and always available. When you're feeling anxious or afraid, you can take your concerns to Him in prayer.

So the next time you're feeling nervous, edgy, or worse, remember that anxiety and panic are temporary conditions that you and God, working together, can manage. That's a promise.

What you trust to Him you must not worry over nor feel anxious about.
Trust and worry cannot go together.

HANNAH WHITALL SMITH

Dear Lord, sometimes my problems are simply too big for me, but they are never too big for You. Today and every day, I will turn my anxieties and concerns over to You. I will trust You, Father, now and forever. Amen.

2

DON'T BE AFRAID TO ASK FOR HELP

*Get all the advice and instruction you can,
so you will be wise the rest of your life.*

PROVERBS 19:20 NLT

If you're experiencing intense feelings of anxiety or fear, you don't have to suffer alone. Help is always available, and you should ask for it. No matter how much you think you know about your emotional state, it never hurts to hear an informed opinion from a knowledgeable professional. By expressing your feelings to a pastoral counselor, to a therapist, to a psychologist, or to your physician, you can gain knowledge about your condition, and you can learn better ways to deal with your feelings and your fears.

When you talk to someone who understands the physical and psychological triggers that are causing your emotional pain, you can learn better coping strategies, better ways to react to the world around you, and better ways to think about your circumstances and your future.

The Roman playwright Plautus said, "None of us are wise enough by ourselves." What was true in 200 BC is still true today. In our complicated world, we all need good counsel, informed opinions, and honest advice, especially when we're dealing with painful emotions.

Timely Tip: If you're experiencing anxiety or fear, don't be embarrassed to ask for help. Find people you can talk to and/or seek help from a trained mental-health professional. When you need help, the best time to ask for it is now, not later.

Dear Lord, when I need help, give me the wisdom to ask for it. And when I receive offers of help, let me accept them. Amen.

3

SPEND TIME
WITH GOD EVERY DAY

He said to him, "Love the Lord your God with all your heart,
with all your soul, and with all your mind.
This is the greatest and most important command."

MATTHEW 22:37–38 HCSB

When it comes to spending time with God, are you a "squeezer" or a "pleaser"? Do you squeeze God into your schedule with a prayer before meals (and maybe, if you've got the time, with a quick visit to church on Sunday)? Or do you please God by talking to Him far more often than that? If you're wise, you'll form the habit of spending time with God every day.

When you begin each day with your head bowed and your heart lifted, you remind yourself of God's love, His protection, and His commandments. And if you are wise, you will use your morning prayer time to align your priorities for the coming day with the teachings of God's holy Word.

This book asks that you give your undivided attention to the Lord at least once a day every day. And make no mistake about it: the emphasis in the previous sentence should be placed on the words "at least." Even if you're the busiest person on planet Earth, you can still carve out time for God.

Are you weak? Weary? Confused? Troubled? Pressured? How is your
relationship with God? Is it held in its place of priority? I believe the greater
the pressure, the greater your need for time alone with Him.

KAY ARTHUR

Dear Lord, let Your priorities be my priorities. Let Your will be my will. Let Your Word be my guide, and let me grow in faith and in wisdom this day and every day. Amen.

4

GOD IS RIGHT HERE,
AND YOU ARE PROTECTED

*This is the confidence we have in approaching God:
that if we ask anything according to his will, he hears us.*

1 JOHN 5:14 NIV

Sometimes, amid the demands and the frustrations of everyday life, we forget to slow ourselves down long enough to talk with our Creator. Instead of turning our thoughts and prayers to Him, we rely upon our own resources. Instead of praying for emotional strength and courage, we seek to manufacture these things by ourselves. Instead of asking God for guidance, we depend only upon our own limited wisdom. Instead of trusting Him completely, we look elsewhere for assurance.

The Lord has made many promises, and He intends to keep every one of them. Our job, simply put, is to trust and obey.

So the next time you find your courage tested to the limit, lean upon God's promises. Remember that God is always near and that He is your protector and your deliverer. When you are worried, anxious, or afraid, call upon Him. God can handle your troubles infinitely better than you can. Remember that your heavenly Father rules both mountaintops and valleys—with limitless wisdom and love—now and forever.

*Faith is the assurance that the thing which God has said in His word is true,
and that God will act according to what He has said.*

GEORGE MUELLER

Dear Lord, You are my Savior and my Sustainer. I will be safe with You in heaven, and I am safe with You here on earth. Today, I will face my challenges with faith and trust—faith in You and trust in Your promises. Amen.

5

MAINTAIN THE
RIGHT KIND OF ATTITUDE

You must have the same attitude that Christ Jesus had.
PHILIPPIANS 2:5 NLT

Attitudes are the mental filters through which we view and interpret the world around us. Positive attitudes produce positive emotions; negative attitudes don't.

The quality of your attitudes will help determine the quality of your life, so you must guard your thoughts accordingly. If you make up your mind to approach life with a healthy mixture of realism and optimism, you'll be rewarded. But if you allow yourself to fall into the unfortunate habit of chronic negative thinking, you will, in all likelihood, doom yourself to unhappiness or mediocrity or worse.

So the next time you find yourself dwelling upon the negative aspects of your life, refocus your attention on things positive. The next time you find yourself falling prey to the blight of pessimism, stop yourself and turn your thoughts around. The next time you're tempted to waste valuable time gossiping, complaining, or revisiting past misfortunes, resist those temptations. Count your blessings instead of your hardships. And thank the Giver of all things good for gifts that are simply too numerous to count.

We choose what attitudes we have right now. And it's a continuing choice.
JOHN MAXWELL

Dear Lord, today I pray for an attitude that reflects my trust in You. As I face the inevitable challenges of everyday life, let me remember that nothing will happen today that You and I, working together, cannot handle. Amen.

6

TAKE YOUR WORRIES TO THE LORD

Therefore do not worry about tomorrow, for tomorrow will worry about its own things. Sufficient for the day is its own trouble.

MATTHEW 6:34 NKJV

Perhaps you are concerned about your future, your relationships, or your finances. Or perhaps you are simply a "worrier" by nature. If so, choose to make Matthew 6:34 a regular part of your daily Bible reading. This beautiful verse will remind you to live in day-tight compartments and to leave everything else up to God.

When we face the inevitable difficulties of life here on earth, God stands ready to protect us. Our responsibility, of course, is to ask Him for protection. When we call upon Him in heartfelt prayer, He will answer—in His own time and according to His own plan—and He will heal us. And while we are waiting for the Lord's plans to unfold and for His healing touch to restore us, we can be comforted in the knowledge that our Creator can overcome any obstacle, even if we cannot.

Pray, and let God worry.

MARTIN LUTHER

Do not worry about tomorrow. This is not a suggestion, but a command.

SARAH YOUNG

Dear Lord, when I am fearful or worried or anxious, help me trust You more. Let me trust Your promises, and let me live courageously this day and every day. Amen.

7

AVOID BURNOUT

But those who wait on the Lord shall renew their strength;
they shall mount up with wings like eagles,
they shall run and not be weary, they shall walk and not faint.

ISAIAH 40:31 NKJV

Has the busy pace of life robbed you of the peace that might otherwise be yours through Jesus Christ? If so, you are simply too busy for your own good, and you're in danger of experiencing a full-blown case of burnout.

Through His only begotten Son, the Lord offers you a peace that passes human understanding, but He won't force His peace upon you; in order to experience it, you must slow down long enough to sense His presence and His love.

Today, take a personal inventory and ask yourself, "Am I trying to do too much?" If the answer to that question is yes, ask God for the wisdom to slow down, to rearrange your priorities, and to focus more intently on the things that matter most: your spiritual, emotional, and physical health.

There are many burned-out people who think more
is always better, who deem it unspiritual to say no.

SARAH YOUNG

Beware of having so much to do that you really do nothing at all.

C. H. SPURGEON

Dear Lord, when I am weighed down by the demands of the day, You are always with me, protecting me from harm and encouraging me to persevere. Whatever today may bring, I thank You, Father, for Your love, for Your guidance, and for Your strength. Amen.

8

LEARN TO DEAL WITH EMOTIONAL UPS AND DOWNS

Should we accept only good things from the hand of God and never anything bad?

JOB 2:10 NLT

From time to time, all of us experience emotional swings. Even the most even-tempered among us experience natural human emotions such as happiness and love, anger, sadness, anxiety, and fear. Since we cannot eliminate these emotional highs and lows, we should seek to understand them. And we must learn to control our negative emotions before they control us.

When you encounter unfortunate circumstances that you cannot change, here's a proven way to retain your sanity: accept those circumstances (no matter how unpleasant), and trust God. The American theologian Reinhold Niebuhr composed a profoundly simple verse that came to be known as the Serenity Prayer: "God, grant me the serenity to accept the things I cannot change, the courage to change the things I can, and the wisdom to know the difference." Niebuhr's words are far easier to recite than they are to live by. Why? Because most of us want life to unfold in accordance with our own wishes and timetables. But sometimes God has other plans. And if we learn to wait patiently for His plans to unfold—and if we learn to accept the things we simply cannot change—we'll deal more effectively with the ups and downs of life.

When we trust God completely, we discover that our emotional swings are less dramatic. We can be comforted in the knowledge that our Creator is both loving and wise, and He understands His plans perfectly, even when we do not.

Dear Lord, as I journey through this day, I may encounter events that cause me emotional distress. When I am troubled, let me turn to You. Keep me steady, Father, and in those uncomfortable moments, renew a right spirit inside my heart. Amen.

9

FOCUS ON BLESSINGS, NOT BURDENS

Blessings crown the head of the righteous.
PROVERBS 10:6 NIV

When you're feeling anxious or fearful, it's easy to focus on your problems, not your blessings. A far better strategy, of course, is to focus on your blessings, not your burdens. If you tried to count all your blessings, how long would it take? A very, very, long time. After all, you've been given the priceless gift of life here on earth and the promise of life eternal in heaven. And you've been given so much more.

Billy Graham noted: "We should think of the blessings we so easily take for granted: Life itself; preservation from danger; every bit of health we enjoy; every hour of liberty; the ability to see, to hear, to speak, to think, and to imagine all this comes from the hand of God." That's sound advice for believers—followers of the One from Galilee—who have so much to be thankful for.

Your blessings, which are gifts from above, are too numerous to count. Even when times are tough, it's always the right time to say thanks to the Giver for the gifts you can count, and all the other ones too.

God is the giver, and we are the receivers. And His richest gifts
are bestowed not upon those who do the greatest things,
but upon those who accept His abundance and His grace.
HANNAH WHITALL SMITH

Dear Lord, You have given me so much, and I will be eternally grateful for Your blessings and Your love. Help me focus, Father, on Your blessings and Your Son, today and every day. Amen.

10
DON'T PANIC!

So we can say with confidence, "The LORD is my helper,
so I will have no fear. What can mere people do to me?"

HEBREWS 13:6 NLT

If you've ever experienced a full-blown panic attack, you can attest to the fact that it is a terrifying experience. Your heart beats faster; you can't catch your breath; your emotions are screaming, and you feel frightened beyond words, yet your mind tells you there's nothing to be afraid of. To make matters worse, after you've experienced your first attack, you may develop an ongoing fear of having another one.

Panic attacks occur when we experience an exaggerated physical response to a situation that shouldn't be so threatening. Researchers have confirmed that these are physiological events that include dramatic increases in both heart rate and adrenaline levels. Fortunately, these attacks are highly treatable with counseling, medicine, or both.

So if you've found yourself paralyzed by fear without good reason, don't suffer in silence. Instead, talk to your doctor—or to a trained mental-help professional who specializes in panic disorders—and develop a recovery plan. God wants you to experience His joyful abundance, but untreated panic disorders can get in the way. So don't be afraid or embarrassed to ask for help. It's the surest way to say no to panic and yes to peace.

Timely Tip: If you experience a full-blown panic attack, don't try to handle it on your own. Instead, talk to your physician. Medical professionals and knowledgeable counselors can offer solutions, but they won't offer them to you unless they're asked.

Dear Lord, You give me peace. When I am panicked or afraid, I will be mindful of your promises. And if I find myself in need of professional counseling or medical assistance, I will accept it and be grateful. Amen.

11

THE TIME TO CELEBRATE IS NOW

Rejoice always, pray without ceasing, in everything give thanks;
for this is the will of God in Christ Jesus for you.

1 Thessalonians 5:16–18 NKJV

Today is a nonrenewable resource—once it's gone, it's gone forever. Our responsibility, as thoughtful believers, is to use this day in the service of God's will and in the service of His people. When we do so, we enrich our own lives and the lives of those whom we love.

God has richly blessed us, and He wants you to rejoice in His gifts. That's why every day should be a time of prayer and celebration as we consider the good news of God's free gift: the gift of eternal life through Jesus Christ.

What do you expect from the day ahead? Are you expecting the Lord to do wonderful things, or are you living beneath a cloud of apprehension and doubt? Today, celebrate the life that God has given you. Today, put a smile on your face, kind words on your lips, and a song in your heart. Be generous with your praise and free with your encouragement. And then, when you have celebrated life to the full, invite your friends to do likewise. After all, this is God's day, and He has given us clear instructions for its use. We are commanded to rejoice and be glad. So with no further ado, let the celebration begin.

Joy is the direct result of having God's perspective on our daily lives and the effect of loving our Lord enough to obey His commands and trust His promises.

Bill Bright

Heavenly Father, today, I will join in the celebration of life. I will be a joyful Christian, and I will share my joy with all those who cross my path. You have given me countless blessings, Lord, and today I will celebrate them. Amen.

12

RECOGNIZE THE PROBLEM AND SEEK TREATMENT

Wisdom calls out in the street; she raises her voice in the public squares. She cries out above the commotion; she speaks at the entrance of the city gates.

PROVERBS 1:20–21 HCSB

If you've experienced prolonged periods of severe anxiety, debilitating panic, or irrational fear, you may be wondering if you'll ever recover. Perhaps you've tried to solve the problem on your own, without much success. If so, you may have convinced yourself that your condition is permanent. But that sort of negative thinking won't help you find a solution that works for you. So it's now time to replace negativity with a healthy dose of reality. And the truth is simply this: if you understand the problem and seek help, things are going to get better.

Anxiety disorders are so common. Thankfully, the strategies for treating anxiety and panic disorders are straightforward. And as it turns out, talk therapy, medication, or a combination of the two have proven remarkably effective for most sufferers. So if you're feeling helpless or hopeless, it's time to ask for help. Don't give up, don't be discouraged, and don't suffer alone. Instead, keep working with your healthcare professionals until you find the best treatment for you.

Dear Lord, I thank You for the healers: the people who serve and counsel and care for those who need their help. When I am troubled, let me turn to them for guidance, for comfort, for treatment, and for wisdom. And Father, let me be a caring friend and a knowledgeable mentor to family and friends who need my help. Amen.

13

WHY DO BAD THINGS HAPPEN?

They won't be afraid of bad news;
*their hearts are steady because they trust the L*ORD*.*

PSALM 112:7 NCV

If God is good, and if He made the world, why do bad things happen? Part of that question is easy to answer, and part of it isn't. Let's get to the easy part first: sometimes bad things happen because people disobey God's commandments and invite sadness and heartache into God's beautiful world.

But on other occasions, bad things happen, and it's nobody's fault. So who is to blame? Sometimes nobody is to blame. Sometimes things just happen, and we simply cannot know why. Thankfully, all our questions will be answered . . . some day. The Bible promises that in heaven we will understand all the reasons behind God's plans. But until then, we must simply trust that God is good, and that, in the end, He will make things right.

Never yield to gloomy anticipation. Place your hope
and confidence in God. He has no record of failure.

LETTIE COWMAN

On the darkest day of your life, God is still in charge. Take comfort in that.

MARIE T. FREEMAN

Dear Lord, give me courage in every circumstance and in every stage of life. Give me the wisdom, Father, to place my hope and my trust in Your perfect plan and Your boundless love. Amen.

14

WHEN YOUR HEART IS TROUBLED, HAVE COURAGE

For God has not given us a spirit of fearfulness,
but one of power, love, and sound judgment.

2 TIMOTHY 1:7 HCSB

Every person's life is a tapestry of events: some wonderful, some not-so-wonderful, and some downright disastrous. When we visit the mountaintops of life, praising God isn't hard—in fact, it's easy. In our moments of triumph, we can bow our heads and thank God for our victories. But when we fail to reach the mountaintops, when we endure the inevitable losses that are a part of every person's life, we find it much tougher to give God the praise He deserves. Yet wherever we find ourselves, whether on the mountaintops of life or in life's darkest valleys, we must still offer thanks to God, giving thanks in all circumstances.

God is not a distant being. He is not absent from our world, nor is He absent from your world. God is not "out there"; He is "right here," continuously reshaping His universe, and continuously reshaping the lives of those who dwell in it.

The Lord is with you always, listening to your thoughts and prayers, watching over your every move. If the demands of everyday life weigh down upon you, you may be tempted to ignore God's presence or—worse yet—to lose faith in His promises. But when you quiet yourself and acknowledge His presence, God will touch your heart and restore your courage.

Dear Lord, sometimes I face challenges and setbacks that leave me worried and afraid. When I am fearful, let me seek Your strength. And keep me mindful, Father, that You are with me today, tomorrow and forever. Amen.

15

EXPECT GOD'S ABUNDANCE

Ask, and God will give to you. Search, and you will find. Knock, and the door will open for you. Yes, everyone who asks will receive. Everyone who searches will find. And everyone who knocks will have the door opened.

MATTHEW 7:7–8 NCV

In the familiar words of John 10:10, Jesus promises, "I have come that they may have life, and that they may have it more abundantly" (NKJV). And in John 15:11, He states, "These things I have spoken to you, that My joy may remain in you, and that your joy may be full." These passages make it clear: our Lord intends that we experience lives of joyful abundance through Him. Our duty, as grateful believers, is to do everything we can to receive the joy and abundance that can be ours in Christ—and the term "everything" includes appropriate medical treatment when necessary.

Some days are light and happy, and some days are not. When we face the inevitable dark days of life, we must choose how we will respond. Will we allow ourselves to sink even more deeply into our own sadness, or will we do the difficult work of pulling ourselves out? We bring light to the dark days of life by turning first to God, and then to trusted family members, to friends, and, in some cases, to medical professionals. When we do, the clouds will eventually part, and the sun will shine once more upon our souls.

Perhaps the greatest psychological, spiritual, and medical need that all people have is the need for hope.

BILLY GRAHAM

Heavenly Father, let my hopes begin and end with You. When I am discouraged, I will turn to You. When I am weak, I will find strength in You. You are my Father, and I will place my faith, my trust, and my hopes in You, this day and forever. Amen.

25

16

TOUGH TIMES NEVER LAST, BUT TOUGH PEOPLE DO

*God blesses those who patiently endure testing
and temptation. Afterward they will receive the
crown of life that God has promised to those who love him.*

JAMES 1:12 NLT

The times that try men's and women's souls are also the times when character is forged on the anvil of adversity. But the character-building is never easy. Overcoming tough times requires, strength, prayer, insight, and perseverance.

During difficult times, we are tempted to complain, to worry, to blame other people, and to do little else. Usually, complaints and worries change nothing; intelligent action, on the other hand, can change everything.

If you find yourself enduring difficult circumstances—or if you're paralyzed by doubts about your faith or your future—remember that God remains in His heaven. He is a God of possibility, not negativity. So the next time you feel anxious or fearful or worried, turn those negative emotions over to God. He will guide you through your difficulties and beyond them. And then, with a renewed spirit of optimism and hope, you can thank the Giver of all things good, for gifts that are too profound to fully comprehend and too numerous to count.

Timely Tip: Perhaps, because of tough times, you're being forced to step outside your comfort zone. If so, consider it an opportunity to grow spiritually and emotionally. Your challenge is to trust yourself, to trust God, and to follow His lead.

Heavenly Father, in good times and hard times, I will praise You. I know that You understand the wisdom of Your perfect plan, and I will trust that plan. Today is the day that You have made. I will rejoice and be glad in it. Amen.

17

DEAL WITH CONSTANT CHANGE

*To every thing there is a season,
and a time to every purpose under the heaven.*

ECCLESIASTES 3:1 KJV

Our world is in a state of constant change. God is not. At times, the world seems to be trembling beneath our feet. But we can be comforted in the knowledge that our heavenly Father is the rock that cannot be shaken.

Is the world spinning a little too fast for your liking? Are you facing difficult circumstances or unwelcome changes? If so, please remember that God is far bigger than any problem you may face. So instead of worrying about life's inevitable challenges, put your faith in the Father and His only begotten Son. After all, "Jesus Christ is the same yesterday, today, and forever" (Hebrews 13:8 NKJV). And it is precisely because your Savior does not change that you can face your challenges with courage for today and hope for tomorrow.

Timely Tip: Change is inevitable; growth is not. God will come to your doorstep on countless occasions with opportunities to learn and to grow. And He will knock. Your challenge, of course, is to open the door.

Heavenly Father, our world is constantly changing. When I face the inevitable transitions of life, I will turn to You for strength and assurance. Thank You, Father, for love that is unchanging and everlasting. Amen.

18

DIFFICULT PEOPLE CAN THREATEN TO HIJACK YOUR EMOTIONS

Bad temper is contagious—don't get infected.
PROVERBS 22:25 MSG

Sometimes people can be cruel, discourteous, untruthful, or rude. When other people do or say things that are hurtful, you may become anxious or angry. So you may be tempted to strike back with a verbal salvo of your own. But before you say words that can never be unsaid, slow down, say a quiet prayer and remember this: God corrects other people's behaviors in His own way, and He doesn't need your help (even if you're totally convinced you're in the right).

The Bible teaches us to be self-controlled, thoughtful, and mature. But the world often tempts us to behave otherwise. Everywhere we turn, or so it seems, we see undisciplined, unruly role models who behave impulsively yet experience few, if any, negative consequences. So it's not surprising that when we meet folks whose personalities conflict with our own, we're tempted to respond in undisciplined, unruly ways. But there's a catch: if we fall prey to immaturity or impulsivity, those behaviors inevitably cause more problems than they solve.

So when other people behave cruelly, foolishly, or impulsively, don't allow yourself to become caught up in their emotional distress. Instead, speak up for yourself as politely as you can and, if necessary, walk away. Next, forgive everybody as quickly as you can. Then get on with your life, and leave the rest up to God.

Heavenly Father, give me a forgiving heart. And let me share Your love with everyone, even with those who make mistakes or behave badly. Let me forgive others, just as You have forgiven me. Amen.

19

YOU WILL EXPERIENCE SETBACKS BUT STAY ON COURSE

For though the righteous fall seven times, they rise again.
PROVERBS 24:16 NIV

If you want to combat negative emotions like anxiety and fear, you must learn how to deal with failure. Why? Because all of us face setbacks from time to time. We all experience occasional disappointments that are simply the price we pay for being dues-paying members of the human race.

Hebrews 10:36 advises, "Patient endurance is what you need now, so that you will continue to do God's will. Then you will receive all that he has promised" (NLT). These words remind us that when we persevere, we will eventually receive the rewards that God has promised us. What's required is perseverance, not perfection.

When we face hardships, God stands ready to protect us. When we call upon Him in heartfelt prayer, He will answer—in His own time and according to His own plan—and He will do His part to heal us. We, of course, must do our part too. And while we are waiting for God's plans to unfold and for His healing touch to restore us, we can be comforted in the knowledge that our Creator can overcome any obstacle, even if we cannot.

No amount of falls will really undo us
if we keep picking ourselves up after each one.
C. S. LEWIS

Dear Lord, when I experience setbacks and disappointments, keep me mindful that You are in control. Let me resist the temptation to give up or give in, even if my soul is troubled. And let me follow Your Son, Jesus Christ, this day and forever. Amen.

20

UNDERSTAND DEPRESSION

He heals the brokenhearted and binds up their wounds.

PSALM 147:3 HCSB

It has been said, and with good reason, that depression is the common cold of mental illness. Why? Because depression is such a common malady. But make no mistake: depression is a serious condition that, if untreated, can take a terrible toll on individuals and families alike.

The sadness that accompanies any significant loss is an inescapable fact of life. Throughout our lives, all of us must endure the kinds of deep personal losses that leave us struggling to find hope. But in time, we move beyond our grief as the sadness runs its course and gradually abates. Depression, on the other hand, is a physical and emotional condition that is, in almost all cases, treatable with medication and counseling. Depression is not a disease to be taken lightly. Left untreated, it presents real dangers to patients' physical health and to their emotional well-being.

Here are a few simple guidelines to consider as you make decisions about possible medical treatment:

- If you have persistent urges toward self-destructive behavior or feel as though you have lost the will to live, consult a professional counselor or physician immediately.
- If someone you trust urges you to seek counseling, schedule a session with a professionally trained counselor to evaluate your condition.
- If you experience persistent and prolonged changes in sleep patterns, or if you experience a significant change in weight (either gain or loss), consult your physician.

- If you are plagued by consistent, prolonged, severe feelings of hopelessness, consult a physician, a professional counselor, or your pastor.

Dear Lord, You have promised to lift me up from my despair. If the darkness envelops me, Father, remind me of Your promises. And let me accept help from those You have placed along my path. Amen.

21

TO REDUCE STRESS AND ANXIETY, TAKE GOOD CARE OF THE BODY GOD HAS GIVEN YOU

You should know that your body is a temple for the Holy Spirit
who is in you. You have received the Holy Spirit from God.
So you do not belong to yourselves, because you were
bought by God for a price. So honor God with your bodies.

1 CORINTHIANS 6:19–20 NCV

As adults, each of us bears a personal responsibility for the general state of our own physical health. Certainly, various aspects of health are beyond our control: illness sometimes strikes even the healthiest men and women. But for most of us, physical health is a choice: it is the result of hundreds of small decisions that we make every day of our lives. If we make decisions that promote good health, our bodies respond.

Poor physical health and stress often go hand in hand. That's one reason that you should place a high priority on caring for the only body that you'll ever own. If your approach to your physical or emotional health has, up to this point, been undisciplined, pray for the strength to do what you know is right.

Our body is a portable sanctuary through which
we are daily experiencing the presence of God.

RICHARD FOSTER

Dear Lord, Your Word teaches me that my body is, indeed, a priceless gift from You. Guide my steps, Father, and help me treat my body with care today and every day of my life. Amen.

22

TRUST HIM IN
EVERY CIRCUMSTANCE

*Trust in him at all times, you people; pour out
your hearts to him, for God is our refuge.*

PSALM 62:8 NIV

Every human life (including yours) is a tapestry of events: some grand, some not so grand, and some downright disheartening. When we reach the mountaintops of life, praising God is easy. But when the storm clouds form overhead and we find ourselves in the dark valley of despair, our faith is stretched, sometimes to the breaking point. As Christians, we can be comforted: wherever we find ourselves, whether at the top of the mountain or the depths of the valley, God is there, and because He cares for us, we can live courageously.

Psalm 147 promises, "He heals the brokenhearted" (v. 3, NIV), but Psalm 147 doesn't say that His healing is instantaneous. Usually, it takes time (and maybe even a little help from you) for God to fix things. So if you're facing tough times, face them with God by your side. If you find yourself in any kind of trouble, pray about it and ask God for help. And be patient. God will work things out, just as He has promised, but He will do it in His own way and in His own time.

Timely Tip: No circumstances are too tough for God, and no problems are too big for Him. When times are tough, cast your burden upon Him, and He will give you the strength and courage you need to face any situation.

Heavenly Father, sometimes, this world can be a fearful place, but You have promised that You are with me always. Today, Lord, I will live confidently as I place my trust in Your everlasting power and my faith in Your everlasting love. Amen.

23

THANK GOD FOR
THE JOYS OF FRIENDSHIP

I give thanks to my God for every remembrance of you.
PHILIPPIANS 1:3 HCSB

What is a friend? The dictionary defines the word friend as "a person who is attached to another by feelings of affection or personal regard." This definition is accurate, as far as it goes, but when we examine the deeper meaning of friendship, so many more descriptors come to mind: trustworthiness, loyalty, helpfulness, kindness, encouragement, humor, and cheerfulness, to mention but a few.

Today, as you consider the many blessings that God has given you, remember to thank Him for the friends He has chosen to place along your path. May you be a blessing to them, and may they richly bless you today, tomorrow, and every day that you live.

Friendship, of itself a holy tie, is made more sacred by adversity.
JOHN DRYDEN

A friend is one who makes me do my best.
OSWALD CHAMBERS

Dear Lord, I thank you for my friends. You have brought wonderful Christian friends into my life. Let our friendships honor You as we walk in the footsteps of Your Son. Amen.

24

WHEN YOU'RE DISAPPOINTED, GOD CAN HEAL YOUR HEART

Then they cried out to the LORD in their trouble,
and He saved them out of their distresses.

PSALM 107:13 NKJV

From time to time, all of us face life-altering, anxiety-increasing disappointments that leave us breathless. Oftentimes these disappointments come unexpectedly, leaving us with more questions than answers. But even when we don't have all the answers—or, for that matter, even when we don't seem to have *any* of the answers—God does. Whatever our circumstances, whether we stand atop the highest mountain or wander through the darkest valley, God is ready to protect us, to comfort us, and to heal us. Our task is to let Him.

When we are disheartened—on those cloudy days when our strength is sapped and our hope is shaken—there exists a source from which we can draw perspective and courage. That source is God. When we turn everything over to Him, we find that He is sufficient to meet our needs. No problem is too big for Him.

So the next time you feel discouraged or fearful, slow down long enough to have a serious talk with your Creator. Pray for guidance, strength, and the wisdom to trust your heavenly Father. Your troubles are temporary; His love is not.

Timely Tip: When you're discouraged, disappointed, or hurt, don't spend too much time asking, "Why me, Lord?" Instead, ask, "What now, Lord?" and then get busy. When you do, you'll feel better, stronger, and more confident.

Dear Lord, When I face the inevitable disappointments of life, remind me that You are in control. You are the Giver of all good things, Father, and You will bless me today, tomorrow, and forever. Amen.

25

GOD DESERVES
FIRST PLACE

You must not have any other gods except me.
EXODUS 20:3 NCV

In the twentieth chapter of Exodus, the Lord commands us to place Him first in our lives. Not second, or third, or on Sunday mornings when the church doors open. Our heavenly Father commands us to focus first and foremost on His promises, His commandments, and His only begotten Son.

God deserves first place in your heart, and you deserve the experience of putting Him there *and* keeping Him there. So don't let troublesome circumstances or irrational fears monopolize your thoughts. Put God first. When you do, everything else has a way of falling into place.

*The most important thing you must decide
to do every day is put the Lord first.*
ELIZABETH GEORGE

Even the most routine part of your day can be a spiritual act of worship.
SARAH YOUNG

Christ is either Lord of all, or He is not Lord at all.
HUDSON TAYLOR

Heavenly Father, You have given me so many blessings, and I will strive to put You first in my life. Today and every day, I will praise You with my thoughts, my prayers, and my service as I follow in the footsteps of Your only begotten Son. Amen.

26

KEEP STUDYING GOD'S WORD

*All scripture is given by inspiration of God, and is profitable for doctrine,
for reproof, for correction, for instruction in righteousness.*

2 TIMOTHY 3:16 KJV

If you're dealing with anxiety or fear, there's a book for that. It's called the Holy Bible. God's Word is unlike any other book. The words of Matthew 4:4 remind us that, "Man shall not live by bread alone, but by every word that proceedeth out of the mouth of God." (KJV).

As believers, we are instructed to study the Bible and meditate upon its meaning for our lives, yet far too many Bibles are laid aside by well-intentioned believers who would like to study the Bible if they could "just find the time."

Warren Wiersbe observed, "When the child of God looks into the Word of God, he sees the Son of God. And, he is transformed by the Spirit of God to share in the glory of God." God's holy Word is, indeed, a transforming, life-changing, one-of-a-kind treasure. And it's up to you—and only you—to use it that way.

*Do you want your faith to grow?
Then let the Bible began to saturate your mind and soul.*

BILLY GRAHAM

Timely Tip: The Bible is God's guidebook for every situation you'll ever face. Even if you've studied the Bible for many years, you've still got lots to learn. Bible study should be a lifelong endeavor. Make it your lifelong endeavor.

Dear Lord, You have given me instructions for life here on earth and for life eternal. I will use the Bible as my guide, and I will trust Your holy Word today and every day. Amen.

27

BEWARE: EMOTIONS ARE CONTAGIOUS

Bad temper is contagious—don't get infected.
PROVERBS 22:25 MSG

Emotional highs and lows are contagious. When we're surrounded by people with positive attitudes, we tend to think positively. But when we're surrounded by people whose emotions are negative, we get infected. Negative feelings can rob us of the peace and abundance that would otherwise be ours through Christ. When fear or anxiety separates us from the spiritual blessings that God has in store, we must rethink our priorities. And we must place faith above feelings.

Human emotions are highly variable, decidedly unpredictable, and often unreliable. Our emotions are like the weather, only sometimes far more fickle. As a consequence, we must learn to live by faith, not by the ups and downs of our neighbors' emotional roller coasters. So here's a question you should ask yourself: Who's pulling your emotional strings? Are you allowing highly emotional people or highly charged situations to dictate your moods, or are you wiser than that?

Sometime during the coming day, you may encounter a tough situation or a difficult person. And as a result, you may be gripped by a strong negative emotion. Distrust it. Reign it in. Test it. And turn it over to God. Your emotions will inevitably change; God will not. So trust Him completely. When you do, you'll be surprised at how quickly those negative feelings can evaporate into thin air.

Timely Tip: The friends you choose can make a profound impact on every aspect of your life. So choose your friends carefully. And remember that you are perfectly within your rights to select friends who contribute to your spiritual and emotional health.

Dear Lord, the Bible teaches us to choose our friends carefully. And that's what I intend to do today and every day of my life. Amen.

BE ENTHUSIASTIC!

Whatever you do, do it enthusiastically,
as something done for the Lord and not for men.

COLOSSIANS 3:23 HCSB

Can you truthfully say that you are enthusiastic about facing the challenges and opportunities you will inevitably encounter as you experience another day of life? Hopefully so. But if you find yourself caught in a web of anxiety and fear, it's time to recharge your spiritual batteries. And that means refocusing your priorities by putting God first.

Are you excited about the possibilities for service that the Lord has placed before you, whether at home, at work, or at church? You should be. Norman Vincent Peale advised, "Get absolutely enthralled with something. Throw yourself into it with abandon. Get out of yourself. Be somebody. Do something." His words apply to you. So don't settle for a lukewarm existence and don't let your fears determine the direction of your life. Instead of sitting on the sidelines, become genuinely involved in life. The world needs your enthusiasm, And so, for that matter, do you.

Two types of voices command your attention today. Negative ones
fill your mind with doubt, bitterness, and fear. Positive ones purvey hope
and strength. Which one will you choose to heed?

MAX LUCADO

Heavenly Father, if the obligations of the day leave me exhausted or discouraged, I will turn to You for strength and for renewal. Today and every day, let Your will be my will, Lord, and let me find strength and courage in You. Amen.

29

FEAR NOT;
GOD WILL PROTECT YOU

Fear not, for I am with you; be not dismayed,
for I am your God. I will strengthen you, yes, I will help you,
I will uphold you with My righteous right hand.

ISAIAH 41:10 NKJV

All of us may find our courage tested by the inevitable disappointments and tragedies of life. After all, ours is a world filled with uncertainty, hardship, sickness, and danger. Old Man Trouble, it seems, is never too far from the front door.

When we focus upon our fears and our doubts, we may find many reasons to lie awake at night and fret about the uncertainties of the coming day. A better strategy, of course, is to focus not upon our fears, but instead upon our God.

God is as near as your next breath, and He is in control. He offers salvation to all His children, including you. The Lord is your shield and your strength; you are His forever. So don't focus your thoughts upon the fears of the day. Instead, trust God's plan and His eternal love for you. And remember: God is good, and He has the last word.

The presence of fear does not mean you have no faith.
Fear visits everyone. But make your fear a visitor and not a resident.

MAX LUCADO

Dear Lord, when this world becomes a fearful place, give me faith. When I am filled with uncertainty and doubt, give me faith. In the dark moments, help me to remember that You are always near and that You can overcome any challenge. And in the joyous moments, keep me mindful that every gift comes from You. Amen.

30

FAITH MAKES
THE DIFFERENCE

And he said unto her, Daughter, thy faith hath made thee whole;
go in peace, and be whole.

MARK 5:34 KJV

Because we live in a demanding world, all of us have mountains to climb and mountains to move. Moving those mountains requires faith. And the experience of trying, with God's help, to move mountains builds character.

Faith, like a tender seedling, can be nurtured or neglected. When we nurture our faith through prayer, meditation, and worship, the Lord blesses our lives and lifts our spirits.

When you place your faith, your trust, indeed your life in the hands of Christ Jesus, you'll be amazed at the marvelous things He can do with you and through you. So strengthen your faith through praise, through worship, through Bible study, and through prayer. And trust God's plans. With Him, all things are possible, and He stands ready to open a world of possibilities to you *if* you have faith.

Shout the shout of faith. Nothing can withstand
the triumphant faith that links itself to omnipotence.
The secret of all successful living lies in this shout of faith.

HANNAH WHITALL SMITH

Dear Lord, in the darkness of uncertainty, give me faith. In those moments when I am afraid, give me faith. When I am discouraged or confused, strengthen my faith in You. You are the Good Shepherd, let me trust in the perfection of Your plan and in the salvation of Your Son, this day and every day of my life. Amen.

31

BE PASSIONATE FOR LIFE

Never be lazy, but work hard and serve the Lord enthusiastically..
ROMANS 12:11 NLT

Are you passionate about your life, your loved ones, your work, and your faith? As a believer who has been saved by a risen Christ, you should be.

As a thoughtful Christian, you have every reason to be enthusiastic about life, but sometimes the inevitable struggles of life may cause you to feel decidedly unenthusiastic. If you feel that your enthusiasm is slowly fading away, it's time to slow down, to rest, to count your blessings, and to pray. When you feel worried or weary, you must pray fervently for God to renew your sense of wonderment and excitement. Life with God can be—and should be—a glorious adventure. Revel in it. When you do, God will most certainly smile upon your work and your life.

Timely Tip: Involve yourself in activities that you can support wholeheartedly and enthusiastically. It's easier to celebrate life when you're passionately involved in life.

Dear Lord, the life that I live and the words that I speak bear testimony to my faith. Make me a faithful and passionate servant of Your Son, and let my testimony be worthy of You. Let my words be sure and true, Lord, and let my actions point others to You. Amen.

32

RECOGNIZE THE IMPORTANCE OF PRAYER

Be anxious for nothing, but in everything by prayer and supplication, with thanksgiving, let your requests be made known to God.

<small>PHILIPPIANS 4:6 NKJV</small>

Prayer is powerful tool for communicating with our Creator; it is an opportunity to commune with the Giver of all things good. Prayer is not a thing to be taken lightly or to be used infrequently. Prayer should never be reserved for mealtimes or for bedtimes; it should be an ever-present focus in our daily lives.

Daily prayer and meditation is a matter of will and habit. You must willingly organize your time by carving out quiet moments with God, and you must form the habit of daily worship. When you do, you'll discover that no time is more precious than the silent moments you spend with your heavenly Father.

Prayer is of transcendent importance. Prayer is the mightiest agent to advance God's work. Praying hearts and hands only can do God's work. Prayer succeeds when all else fails.

<small>E. M. BOUNDS</small>

Dear Lord, make me a prayerful Christian. In good times and in bad times, in whatever state I find myself, let me turn my prayers to You. You always hear my prayers, God; let *me* always pray them! Amen.

33

DON'T LET THE FEAR OF FAILURE HOLD YOU BACK

For though the righteous fall seven times, they rise again..
PROVERBS 24:16 NIV

As we consider the uncertainties of the future, we are confronted with a powerful temptation: the temptation to play it safe. Unwilling to move mountains, we fret over molehills. Unwilling to entertain great hopes for tomorrow, we focus on the unfairness of the today. Unwilling to trust God completely, we take timid half-steps when God intends that we make giant leaps. Why are we willing to settle for baby steps when God wants us to leap tall buildings in a single bound? Because we are fearful that we might fail.

The occasional disappointments and failures of life are inevitable. Such setbacks are simply the price that we must occasionally pay for our willingness to take risks as we follow our dreams. But even when we encounter bitter disappointments, we must never lose faith. And we must remember that in the game of life, we never hit a home run unless we are willing to step up to the plate and swing.

Failure is one of life's most powerful teachers. How we handle our failures determines whether we're going to simply "get by" in life or "press on."
BETH MOORE

Heavenly Father, when I encounter disappointments and setbacks, keep me mindful that You are in control. Let me persevere—even when I am fearful or discouraged—and let me trust Your promises this day and every day. Amen.

34

DON'T BE TOO HARD ON YOURSELF

He who covers his sins will not prosper,
but whoever confesses and forsakes them will have mercy.

PROVERBS 28:13 NKJV

Everybody makes mistakes, and so will you. In fact, Winston Churchill once observed, "Success is going from failure to failure without loss of enthusiasm." What was good for Churchill is also good for you. You should expect to make mistakes—plenty of mistakes—but you should not allow those missteps to rob you of the enthusiasm you need to fulfill God's plan for your life.

We are imperfect people living in an imperfect world; occasional blunders are simply part of the price we pay for being here. But even though mistakes are an inevitable part of life's journey, repeated mistakes should not be. When we commit those inevitable missteps, we must correct them, learn from them, and pray for the wisdom not to repeat them. When we do, our mistakes become lessons, and our lives become adventures in growth, not stagnation.

Have you made a mistake, or two, or three? Of course you have. But here's the big question: Have you used your mistakes as stumbling blocks or stepping stones? The answer to that question will determine the quality of your day *and* the quality of your life.

God is able to take mistakes, when they are committed to Him,
and make of them something for our good and for His glory.

RUTH BELL GRAHAM

Heavenly Father, I know that I am imperfect and that mistakes are an inevitable part of life. Thank You for Your forgiveness and for Your unconditional love. And let me grow each day in wisdom, in faith, and in my love for You. Amen.

35

YOU CAN'T PLEASE
EVERYBODY
(NOR SHOULD YOU TRY)

*For am I now trying to win the favor of people, or God?
Or am I striving to please people? If I were still trying to please people,
I would not be a slave of Christ.*

GALATIANS 1:10 HCSB

If you're like most people, you'd like to gain the admiration of your neighbors, your coworkers, and, most importantly, your family members. Some people, however, are impossible to please, and other people want you to please them by doing things that are contrary to your faith. It's perfectly natural to want to please other people, but you should never allow the fear of their rejection to overshadow your eagerness to please God.

Would you like a time-tested formula for successful relationships? Here is a formula that is proven and true: In every relationship you establish, seek God's approval first. Does this sound too simple? Perhaps it is simple, but it is also the only way to reap the marvelous riches that the Lord has in store for you.

Pride opens the door to every other sin, for once we are more concerned with our reputation than our character, there is no end to the things we will do just to make ourselves "look good" before others.

WARREN WIERSBE

Dear Lord, today I will strive to honor You with my thoughts, actions, and prayers. And I will focus less on pleasing other people and more on pleasing You. Amen.

36

ENTRUST YOUR FUTURE TO GOD

For I know the thoughts that I think toward you, says the LORD,
thoughts of peace and not of evil, to give you a future and a hope.
Then you will call upon Me and go and pray to Me, and I will listen to you.
JEREMIAH 29:11–12 NKJV

Sometimes, when the future seems daunting, we are gripped by unfounded fears and unwarranted anxieties. We lose sight, at least temporarily, of the fact that God's promises never fail and that we, His children, are protected.

It is inevitable that we will face disappointments and failures while we are here on earth, but these are only temporary defeats. This world can be a place of trials and tribulations, but when we place our trust in the Giver of all things good, we are secure. God has promised us peace, joy, and eternal life. And God keeps His promises today, tomorrow, and forever.

Today, as you live in the present and look to the future, remember that God has a plan for you. Act—and believe—accordingly.

Never be afraid to trust an unknown future to a known God.
CORRIE TEN BOOM

Knowing that your future is absolutely assured
can free you to live abundantly today.
SARAH YOUNG

Heavenly Father, as I consider my future, I will place my trust in You. If I become discouraged, I will turn to You. If I am afraid, I will seek strength in You. Because You are with me always, Lord, I can live courageously today, tomorrow, and every day of my life. Amen.

37

HE WANTS YOU TO FOLLOW HIM

Then He said to them all, "If anyone wants to come with Me,
he must deny himself, take up his cross daily, and follow Me."
Luke 9:23 HCSB

Whom will you walk with today? Are you going to walk with people who worship the ways of the world? Or are you going to walk with the Son of God? Jesus walks with you. Are you walking with Him? Hopefully, you will choose to walk with Him today and every day of your life.

The nineteenth-century writer Hannah Whitall Smith observed, "The crucial question for each of us is this: What do you think of Jesus, and do you yet have a personal acquaintance with Him?" Indeed, the answer to that question determines the quality, the course, and the direction of our lives today and for all eternity.

Today provides another glorious opportunity to place yourself in the service of the One from Galilee. May you seek His will, may you trust His word, and may you walk in His footsteps now and forever.

A disciple is a follower of Christ. That means you take
on His priorities as your own. His agenda becomes
your agenda. His mission becomes your mission.
Charles Stanley

Heavenly Father, I know that You sent Jesus to save the world and to save me. I thank You, Father, for Your Son, and I will do my best to follow Him, today and forever. Amen.

LISTEN CAREFULLY TO YOUR CONSCIENCE

So I strive always to keep my conscience clear before God and man.

ACTS 24:16 NIV

Few things in life torment us more than a guilty conscience. And few things in life provide more contentment than the knowledge that we are obeying God's commandments. A clear conscience is one of the rewards we earn when we obey God's Word and follow His will. When we follow God's will and accept His gift of salvation, our earthly rewards are never ceasing, and our heavenly rewards are everlasting.

We can sometimes keep secrets from other people, but we can never keep secrets from God. The Lord knows what we think and what we do. And if we want to please Him, we must start with good intentions, with a pure heart, and with a clear conscience.

If you sincerely desire to live a life that is pleasing to God, you must strive to follow His commandments. When you do, you'll soon discover that your anxieties and fears will begin to subside. And your clear conscience will be an additional blessing because you'll never need to look over your shoulder to see who—besides God—is watching.

The conscience is a built-in warning system that signals us when something we have done is wrong.

JOHN MACARTHUR

Dear Lord, You speak to me through the Bible, through the words of others, and through that still, small voice within. Through my conscience, You reveal Your will and Your way for my life. In these quiet moments, show me Your plan for this day, heavenly Father, that I might serve You. Amen.

39

BE QUICK TO FORGIVE

Above all, love each other deeply, because love covers a multitude of sins.
1 PETER 4:8 NIV

The world holds few if any rewards for those who remain angrily focused upon the past. Still, the act of forgiveness is difficult for all but the most saintly men and women. Are you mired in the emotional quicksand of bitterness or regret? If so, you are not only disobeying God's Word, you are also wasting your time.

Being frail, fallible, imperfect human beings, most of us are quick to anger, quick to blame, slow to forgive, and even slower to forget. Yet as Christians, we are commanded to forgive others, just as we, too, have been forgiven.

If there exists even one person—alive or dead—against whom you hold bitter feelings, it's time to forgive. Or if you are embittered against yourself for some past mistake or shortcoming, it's finally time to forgive yourself and move on. Hatred, bitterness, and regret are not part of God's plan for your life. Forgiveness is.

Forgiveness is one of the most beautiful words
in the human vocabulary. How much pain could
be avoided if we all learned the meaning of this word!
BILLY GRAHAM

Dear Lord, when I am bitter, You can soften my heart. When I am slow to forgive, Your Word reminds me that forgiveness is an integral part of your plan for my life. Let me be Your obedient servant, Lord, and let me forgive others just as You have forgiven me. Amen.

40

GOD WANTS YOU TO LIVE ABUNDANTLY

*I have come that they may have life,
and that they may have it more abundantly.*

JOHN 10:10 NKJV

The Lord has a plan for every facet of your life, and His plan includes provisions for your spiritual, physical, and emotional health. But He expects you to do your fair share of the work.

When you encounter a prickly personality or a sticky situation, you may find it all too easy to respond impulsively, thus making matters even worse. A far better strategy, of course, is to ask for God's guidance. And you can be sure that whenever you ask for the Lord's help, He will give it.

God's Word promises that He will support you in good times and comfort you in hard times. The Creator of the universe stands ready to give you the strength to meet any challenge and the courage to deal effectively with difficult circumstances. When you ask for God's help, He responds in His own way and at His own appointed hour. But make no mistake: He always responds.

Today, as you encounter the challenges of everyday life, remember that your heavenly Father never leaves you, not even for a moment. He's always available, always ready to listen, always ready to lead. When you make a habit of talking to Him early and often, He'll guide you and comfort you every day of your life.

Timely Tip: God's blessings are always available. The Lord is constantly offering you His abundance and His peace. So remember that you can still find peace amid the storm if you guard your thoughts, do your best, and leave the rest up to Him.

Dear Lord, You have offered me the gift of abundance through Your Son. Thank You, Father, for the abundant life that is mine through Christ Jesus. Let me accept His gifts and use them always to glorify You. Amen.

41

LET GOD BE YOUR GUIDE

Trust in the Lord with all your heart, and lean not on your own understanding; in all your ways acknowledge Him, and He shall direct your paths.

PROVERBS 3:5–6 NKJV

If you're dealing with anxiety, irrational fears, or other negative emotions, you need God's guidance. And of this you can be sure: if you seek His guidance, He will give it.

C. S. Lewis observed, "I don't doubt that the Holy Spirit guides your decisions from within when you make them with the intention of pleasing God. The error would be to think that He speaks only within, whereas in reality He speaks also through Scripture, the Church, Christian friends, and books." These words remind us that God has many ways to make Himself known. Our challenge is to make ourselves open to His instruction.

If you're wise, you'll form the habit of speaking to God early and often. But you won't stop there—you'll also study God's Word, you'll obey God's commandments, and you'll associate with people who do likewise. So if you're unsure of your next step, lean upon God's promises and lift your prayers to Him. Remember that God is always near—always trying to get His message through. Open yourself to Him every day, and trust Him to guide your path. When you do, you'll be protected today, tomorrow, and forever.

Timely Tip: Need direction? Let God be your guide. When your emotions are frayed—or if you feel like you're losing control—call time out and pray for guidance. When you seek it, God will give it.

Dear Lord, thank You for You constant presence and Your constant love. I draw near to You this day with the confidence that You are ready to guide me. Help me walk closely with Your Son, and help me share Your good news with all who cross my path. Amen.

42

LET GOD CREATE A NEW AND IMPROVED YOU

For I hold you by your right hand—I, the LORD your God.
And I say to you, "Don't be afraid. I am here to help you."

ISAIAH 41:13 NLT

God can make all things new, including you. When you are anxious or fearful, He can renew your spirit and restore your strength. Your job, of course, is to let Him.

The Lord has a plan for your life, a combination of skills, tools and opportunities that are uniquely yours. If you've already discovered your special calling, say a prayer of thanks. But if you're still searching for answers, start spending more time talking to God. When you have questions, He has answers. And if you're looking for a fresh start, He can provide that too.

Are you weak? Weary? Confused? Troubled? Pressured? How is your relationship with God? Is it held in its place of priority? I believe the greater the pressure, the greater your need for time alone with Him.

KAY ARTHUR

God specializes in giving people a fresh start.

RICK WARREN

Dear Lord, sometimes the demands of the day leave me discouraged and frustrated. Renew my strength, Father, and give me patience and perspective. Today and every day, let me draw comfort and courage from Your promises, from Your love, and from Your Son. Amen.

43

GOD IS ALWAYS WITH YOU

Draw near to God, and He will draw near to you.

JAMES 4:8 HCSB

If God is everywhere, why does He sometimes seem so far away? The answer to that question, of course, has nothing to do with God and everything to do with us. When we begin each day on our knees, in praise and worship to Him, God often seems very near indeed. But if we ignore God's presence or—worse yet—rebel against it altogether, the world in which we live can become a spiritual and emotional wasteland.

Are you tired, discouraged or fearful? Be comforted because God is with you. Are you anxious or confused? Listen to the quiet voice of your heavenly Father. Are you bitter? Talk with God and seek His guidance. Are you celebrating a great victory? Thank God and praise Him. He is the Giver of all things good.

In whatever condition you find yourself, wherever you are, whether you are happy or sad, victorious or vanquished, troubled or triumphant, celebrate God's presence. And be comforted. God is not just near. He is here.

Timely Tip: The next time you feel a flood of negative emotions coming on, take a deep breath and remind yourself that God isn't far away. He's right here, right now. And He's willing to talk to you right here, right now.

Dear Lord, I know that You are always with me and that You are always listening. Help me feel Your presence in every situation and in every circumstance. Today and every day, Father, let me feel the presence of Your love, Your power, and Your Son. Amen.

44

TRUST GOD'S PROMISES

As for God, his way is perfect: the word of the Lord is tried:
he is a buckler to all those that trust in him.

PSALM 18:30 KJV

In the eighteenth Psalm, David teaches us that God is trustworthy. Simply put, when God makes a promise, He keeps it.

So what do you expect from the day ahead? Are you willing to trust God completely or are you living beneath a cloud of doubt and fear? God's Word makes it clear: you should trust Him and His promises, and when you do, you can live courageously.

For thoughtful Christians, every day begins and ends with God's Son and God's promises. When we accept Christ into our hearts, God promises us the opportunity for earthy peace and spiritual abundance. But more importantly, God promises us the priceless gift of eternal life.

Timely Tip: God has made many promises to you, and He will keep every single one of them. Your job is to trust God's Word and to live accordingly.

Heavenly Father, You have promised to protect me, and I will trust You. Today, I will live courageously as I place my hopes, my faith, and life in Your hands. Let my life be a testimony to the transforming power of Your love, Your grace, and Your Son. Amen.

45

THE LORD IS OUR SHEPHERD IN GOOD TIMES AND DIFFICULT TIMES

The LORD is my shepherd, I shall not want. He makes me lie down in green pastures; He leads me beside quiet waters. He restores my soul.

PSALM 23:1–3 NASB

God knows everything about His creation *and* His children. Whether we're enjoying happy days or challenging ones, the Creator watches over us and protects us.

The Lord is our greatest refuge. When every earthly support system fails, He remains steadfast, and His love remains unchanged. When we encounter life's inevitable disappointments and setbacks, the Father remains faithful. When we experience anxieties or fear, He is always with us, always ready to respond to our prayers, always working in us and through us to turn trouble into triumph.

Thankfully, even when there's nowhere else to turn, we can turn our thoughts and prayers to the Lord, and He will respond. Even during life's most difficult days, God stands by us. Our job, of course, is to return the favor and stand by Him.

Measure the size of the obstacles against the size of God.

BETH MOORE

Heavenly Father, You are my shepherd. You care for me; You comfort me; and You watch over me. I will praise You, Father, for Your glorious works, for Your protection, for Your love, and for Your Son. Amen.

46

TRUST GOD'S TIMING

Therefore humble yourselves under the mighty hand of God,
that He may exalt you in due time.

1 PETER 5:6 NKJV

If you're experiencing tough times, you're undoubtedly eager for things to improve. Perhaps you've prayed about your situation but seen no results. If so, keep praying, keep working, and be patient.

The Bible teaches us to trust God's timing in all matters, but we are sorely tempted to do otherwise, especially when our hearts are breaking. We pray (and trust) that we will find peace someday, and we want it now. God, however, works on His own timetable, and His schedule does not always coincide with ours.

God's plans are perfect; ours most certainly are not. Thus we must learn to trust the Father in good times and hard times. So today, as you meet the challenges of everyday life, do your best to turn everything over to God. Whatever your problem, He can solve it. And you can be sure that He will solve it when the time is right.

We must learn to move according to the timetable
of the Timeless One, and to be at peace.

ELISABETH ELLIOT

Dear Lord, Your wisdom is infinite, and the timing of Your heavenly plan is perfect. You have a plan for my life that is grander than I can imagine. When I am impatient, remind me that You are never early or late. You are always on time, Father, so let me trust in You. Amen.

47

WHEN YOU GRIEVE, HE OFFERS COMFORT

Weeping may endure for a night, but joy comes in the morning.

PSALM 30:5 NKJV

Grief visits all of us who live long and love deeply. When we lose a loved one, or when we experience any other profound loss, darkness overwhelms us for a while, and it seems as if our purpose for living has vanished.

God intends that you have an abundant life, but He expects you to do your part in claiming those blessings. So as you work through your grief, you will find it helpful to utilize all the resources that God has placed along your path. God makes help available, but it's up to you to find it and then to accept it. First and foremost, you should lean upon the love, help, and support of family members, friends, fellow church members, and your pastor. Other resources include:

- Various local counseling services including, but not limited to, pastoral counselors, psychologists, and community mental health facilities
- Group counseling programs which may deal with your specific loss
- Your personal physician
- The local bookstore or library

If you are experiencing the intense pain of a recent loss, or if you are still mourning a loss from long ago, perhaps you are now ready to begin the next stage of your journey with God. If so, remember this: as a wounded survivor, you will have countless opportunities to serve others. And by serving others, you will bring purpose and meaning to the suffering you've endured.

Heavenly Father, You have promised to lift me out of my grief and despair. You have put a new song on my lips. I thank You, Lord, for sustaining me in my days of sorrow. Restore me, and heal me, and use me as You will. Amen.

48

GOD WANTS YOU TO GUARD YOUR HEART

Guard your heart above all else, for it is the source of life.
PROVERBS 4:23 HCSB

You live in world filled with high-anxiety messages that can promote fear and discouragement. Whether you're standing in line at the checkout counter or checking your updates on social media, you're bombarded by a near-endless stream of distractions and subtle temptations are seem to be woven into the fabric of everyday life. Yet God's Word is clear: we are to guard our hearts "above all else." So how should we respond to the difficult people and troubling circumstances that complicate our lives and rouse our emotions? We must react fairly, honestly, maturely, and we must never betray our Christian beliefs.

Do you seek God's peace and His blessings? Then guard your heart. When you're tempted to lash out in anger, hold your tongue. When you're faced with a difficult choice or a powerful temptation, seek the Lord's counsel and trust the counsel He gives. When you're anxious or afraid, take a deep breath, calm yourself, and follow in the footsteps of God's only begotten Son. Invite God into your heart and live according to His commandments. When you do, you will be blessed today, and tomorrow, and forever.

The insight that relates to God comes from purity of heart,
not from clearness of intellect.
OSWALD CHAMBERS

Dear Lord, today I will guard my heart against the evils, the temptations, and the distractions of this world. I will focus, instead, upon Your love, Your blessings, and Your Son. Amen.

49

DON'T LET GUILT RULE YOUR LIFE

*Blessed are those who don't feel guilty
for doing something they have decided is right..*

ROMANS 14:22 NLT

All of us have sinned. Sometimes our sins result from our own stubborn rebellion against God's commandments. And sometimes we are swept up in events that are beyond our abilities to control. Under either set of circumstances, we may experience intense feelings of guilt. But God has an answer for the guilt that we feel. That answer, of course, is His forgiveness. When we confess our wrongdoings and repent from them, we are forgiven by the One who created us.

Are you troubled by feelings of guilt or regret? Are you focused so intently on yesterday that your vision of today is clouded? If so you still have work to do—spiritual work. You must atone for your mistakes as best you can, and you must ask your heavenly Father for His forgiveness. When you do so, He will forgive you completely and without reservation. Then, you must forgive yourself just as the Lord has forgiven you: thoroughly and unconditionally.

God's forgiveness is permanent. And if He, in His infinite wisdom, has forgiven your sins, how then can you withhold forgiveness from yourself? The answer, of course, is that once God has forgiven you, you should forgive yourself too. When you forgive yourself once and for all, you'll stop investing energy in those most useless of emotions: bitterness, regret, and self-recrimination. Then you can get busy making the world a better place, and that's as it should be. After all, since God has forgiven you, isn't it about time that you demonstrate your gratitude by serving Him?

Heavenly Father, when I ask for forgiveness, You give it. Today and every day, help me confess my wrongdoings, help me accept Your forgiveness, and help me renew my passion to serve You. Amen.

50

YES, YOU CAN BE HAPPY

Those who listen to instruction will prosper;
those who trust the LORD will be joyful.

PROVERBS 16:20 NLT

Do you seek happiness, abundance, and contentment? And do you want to experience these things now, not later? If so, here's what you should do: love the Lord and depend upon Him for strength; try, to the best of your abilities, to follow God's will; and strive to follow the instructions you find in His holy Word. When you do these things, you'll discover that happiness goes hand in hand with obedience.

The happiest people are not those who resist God's instruction or intentionally rebel against Him; the happiest people are those who love God and obey His commandments. So if you sincerely want to be happy, you should behave accordingly.

What should you expect from the upcoming day? A world full of possibilities (of course it's up to you to seize them), and God's promise of abundance (of course it's up to you to accept it). So as you prepare for the next step in your life's journey, remember this: obedience to God doesn't ensure instant happiness, but disobedience to God always makes genuine happiness impossible.

The truth is that even in the midst of trouble, happy moments swim
by us every day, like shining fish waiting to be caught.

BARBARA JOHNSON

Heavenly Father, today, I choose to rejoice in the day that You have made. I ask that you help me focus on my blessings as I share Your good news with friends, with family, and with the world. Amen.

51

NEVER LOSE HOPE

Let us hold fast the confession of our hope without wavering,
for He who promised is faithful.
HEBREWS 10:23 NASB

On the darkest days of our lives, we may be confronted with an illusion that seems very real indeed—the illusion of hopelessness. Try though we might, we simply can't envision a solution to our problems, and we fall into the darkness of despair. During these times, we may question God—His love, His presence, even His very existence. Despite God's promises, despite Christ's love, and despite our many blessings, we may envision little or no hope for the future. These dark days can be dangerous times for us and for our loved ones.

If you find yourself falling into the spiritual traps of anxiety, fear, and discouragement, seek the encouraging words of fellow Christians, and the healing touch of Jesus. After all, it was Christ who promised, "These things I have spoken unto you, that in me ye might have peace. In the world ye shall have tribulation: but be of good cheer; I have overcome the world" (John 16:33 KJV).

The earth's troubles fade in the light of heaven's hope.
BILLY GRAHAM

Heavenly Father, give me the wisdom to trust Your promises and make me a hope-filled Christian. If I become discouraged, let me turn to You. If I grow weary, let me seek strength in You. In every aspect of my life, I will trust You, Lord, today, tomorrow, and forever. Amen.

52

BE JOYFUL!

Rejoice in the Lord always. Again I will say, rejoice!
PHILIPPIANS 4:4 NKJV

Joy does not depend upon your circumstances; it depends upon your thoughts and upon your relationship with God. Every day, the Lord gives you many reasons to rejoice. The gifts are His, but the rejoicing is up to you. If you have decided to follow in the footsteps of God's only begotten Son, today can, and should, be a celebration of your life, your faith, and your future. The Lord has made many promises to you, and He intends to keep every single one of them. So with no further ado, let the rejoicing begin. And as you're celebrating God's blessings, consider these words of wisdom:

Joy is the great note all throughout the Bible.
OSWALD CHAMBERS

Joy is the settled assurance that God is in control of all the details of my life, the quiet confidence that ultimately everything is going to be all right, and the determined choice to praise God in all things.
KAY WARREN

Joy comes not from what we have but what we are.
C. H. SPURGEON

Heavenly Father, You have instructed me to give thanks always and to rejoice in Your marvelous creation. Let me be a joyful Christian, Lord, and let me focus my thoughts upon Your blessings and Your Love. Help me make this day and every day a cause for celebration as I share the good news of Your Son Jesus. Amen.

53

GOD IS TRYING TO GET HIS MESSAGE THROUGH SO LISTEN CAREFULLY

Come to me with your ears wide open. Listen, and you will find life.

Isaiah 55:3 NLT

Sometimes God displays His wishes in ways that are undeniable. But on other occasions, the Lord's messages are much more subtle. Sometimes God speaks to us in quiet tones, and when He does, we are well advised to listen carefully.

Do you take time each day for an extended period of silence? And during those precious moments, do you sincerely open your heart to your Creator? If so, you are wise and you are blessed.

The world can be a noisy place, a place filled to the brim with distractions, interruptions, and frustrations. And if you're not careful, the struggles and stresses of everyday living can rattle your emotions and rob you of the peace that should rightfully be yours because of your personal relationship with Christ. So take time each day to quietly commune with your Savior. When you do, you will most certainly encounter the subtle hand of God, and if you are wise, you will let Him lead you along the path that He has chosen.

If you, too, will learn to wait upon God, to get alone with Him, and remain silent so that you can hear His voice when He is ready to speak to you, what a difference it will make in your life!

Kay Arthur

Dear Lord, You have so much to teach me, and my time here on earth is limited. Today and every day, give me the wisdom to be still so that I can understand your will and hear Your voice. Amen.

54

ARE YOU FEELING LONELY?

I am not alone, because the Father is with me.

JOHN 16:32 KJV

If you're like most people, you've experienced occasional bouts of loneliness. If so, you understand the genuine pain that accompanies those feelings that "nobody cares." In truth, lots of people care about you, but at times, you may hardly notice their presence.

Sometimes, intense feelings of loneliness can be the result of clinical depression. In such cases, it's time to seek professional help. Other times, however, your feelings of loneliness may come as a result of your own hesitation: the hesitation to get out there and make new friends.

The world is literally teeming with people who are looking for new friends. Here are a few tips for finding them and keeping them.

- Remember the first rule of friendship: it's the Golden one, and it starts like this: "Do to others . . . " (Matthew 7:12 NCV).
- If you're trying to make new friends, become interested in them . . . and eventually they'll become interested in you. (Colossians 3:12).
- Take the time to reconnect with old friends; they'll be glad you did, and so, too, will you (Philippians 1:3).
- Become more involved in your church or in community service; they'll welcome your participation, and you'll welcome the chance to connect with more and more people (1 Peter 5:2).

Dear heavenly Father, on those days when I am troubled, You comfort me if I turn my thoughts and prayers to You. When I am afraid, You protect me. When I am lonely or discouraged, You lift me up. You are my unending source of strength, Lord. Let me trust Your plan and Your will for my life. Amen.

55

KEEP THINGS IN PERSPECTIVE

*Since you have been raised to new life with Christ,
set your sights on the realities of heaven, where Christ sits
in the place of honor at God's right hand..*

COLOSSIANS 3:1 NLT

For most of us, life is busy and complicated. Amid the rush and crush of the daily grind, it is easy to lose perspective . . . it's easy, but it's wrong. When our emotions seem to have been hijacked and the world seems to be spinning out of control, we can regain perspective by slowing ourselves down and then turning our thoughts and prayers toward God.

Do you carve out quiet moments each day to offer thanksgiving and praise to your Creator? You should. During these moments of stillness, you will often sense the love and wisdom of our Lord. When you call upon the Lord and prayerfully seek His will, He will give you wisdom and perspective. When you make God's priorities your priorities, He will direct your steps and calm your fears.

So today and every day hereafter, pray for a sense of balance and perspective. And remember: no challenges are too big for God—and that includes yours.

*It is not so much adverse events that make you anxious
as it is your thoughts about those events.*

SARAH YOUNG

Dear Lord, give me wisdom and perspective. Guide me according to Your plans for my life and according to Your commandments. And keep me mindful, dear Lord, and that Your truth is—and will forever be—the ultimate truth. Amen.

56

MAKE PEACE WITH YOUR PAST

One thing I do, forgetting those things which are behind and reaching forward to those things which are ahead, I press toward the goal for the prize of the upward call of God in Christ Jesus.

PHILIPPIANS 3:13–14 NKJV

Because you are human, you may be slow to forget yesterday's disappointments. But if you sincerely seek to focus your hopes and energies on the future, then you must find ways to accept the past, no matter how difficult it may be to do so.

Have you made peace with your past? If so, congratulations. But if you are mired in the quicksand of bitterness or regret, it's time to plan your escape. How can you do so? By accepting what has been and by trusting God for what will be. You must also forgive those who have hurt you and learn the lessons that hard times have taught you.

So if you have not yet made peace with the past, today is the day to declare an end to all hostilities. When you do, you can then turn your thoughts to the wondrous promises of God and to the glorious future He has in store for you.

Trust the past to God's mercy, the present to God's love and the future to God's providence.

ST. AUGUSTINE

Heavenly Father, free me from anger, resentment, and envy. When I am bitter, I cannot feel the peace that You intend for my life. Keep me mindful that forgiveness is Your commandment, and help me accept the past, treasure the present, and trust the future to You. Amen.

57

LEARN TO MANAGE ANXIETY

Cast all your anxiety on him because he cares for you.

1 Peter 5:7 NIV

Ours is an anxious generation. We live in an uncertain world—a world where tragedies can befall the most righteous among us. Yet even on those difficult days when our anxieties threaten to overwhelm us, we can be assured that God stands ready to protect us. Psalm 147 promises "He heals the brokenhearted and bandages their wounds" (v. 3, NCV). So when we are troubled or anxious, we must call upon the Lord, and, in His own time and according to His own plan, He will heal us.

Sometimes our anxieties may stem from physical causes—chemical and physiological responses in the brain that produce severe emotional distress or crippling panic attacks. In such cases, modern medicine offers hope to those who suffer. But oftentimes our anxieties result from spiritual deficits, not physical ones. And when we're spiritually depleted, the best prescription is found not in the medicine cabinet but deep inside the human heart. What we need is a higher daily dose of God's love, God's peace, God's assurance, and God's presence. And how do we acquire these blessings from our Creator? Through prayer, through meditation, through worship, and through trust.

Timely Tip: When feelings become debilitating—or if you're unable to sleep because of racing thoughts or irrational worries—consult your physician. Your anxiety may have physical causes that are contributing to your distress. Help is available. Ask for it.

Heavenly Father, when I am fearful or worried, I will turn to You for strength and comfort. And when my soul is troubled, I will seek help from the friends, the mentors, and the healers You place along my path. Amen.

58

EXPECT A MIRACLE

Is anything too hard for the LORD?

GENESIS 18:14 NKJV

Do you believe in an all-powerful God who can do miraculous things in you and through you? You should. But perhaps, as you have faced the inevitable struggles of life here on earth, you have—without realizing it—placed limitations on God. To do so is a profound mistake. God's power has no such limitations, and He can work mighty miracles in your own life if you let Him.

Do you lack a firm faith in God's power to perform miracles for you and your loved ones? Have you convinced yourself that your anxieties are incurable or your situation is hopeless? If so, you are attempting to place limitations on a God who has none. So instead of doubting your heavenly Father, you must place yourself in His hands. Instead of increasing your anxieties by doubting His power, you must increase your courage by trusting Him. Instead of focusing on your fears and expecting the worst, you must remember that the Lord works miracles.

With God, absolutely nothing is impossible, including an amazing assortment of miracles that He stands ready, willing, and perfectly able to perform for you and yours.

Timely Tip: Nothing is impossible for God. And He's in the business of doing miraculous things. So never be afraid to ask—or to pray—for a miracle.

Dear Lord, Your power is beyond human understanding. With You, Lord, nothing is impossible. Keep me always mindful of Your power, and let me share the glorious message of Your miracles. Today, Lord, let me expect a miracle. Amen.

59

YES, YOU CAN LEARN TO KEEP YOUR EMOTIONS IN CHECK

Grow a wise heart—you'll do yourself a favor;
keep a clear head—you'll find a good life.

PROVERBS 19:8 MSG

Time and again, the Bible instructs us to live by faith. Yet, despite our best intentions, difficult people and the negative feelings they engender can rob us of the peace and abundance that could be ours—and should be ours—through Christ. When anger, frustration, impatience, or anxiety separate us from the spiritual blessings that God has in store, we must rethink our priorities. And we must place faith above feelings.

Who is in charge of your emotions? Is it you, or have you formed the unfortunate habit of letting other people—or troubling situations—determine the quality of your thoughts and the direction of your day? If you're wise—and if you'd like to build a better life for yourself and your loved ones—you'll learn to control your emotions before your emotions control you. So the next time you feel your emotions beginning to fray, take a deep breath, step back from the situation, and collect your thoughts. Then ask yourself if the emotions you're feeling are healthy and productive or harmful and destructive. The answer to that question will help you regain control of your thoughts, your emotions, and your life.

Heavenly Father, You are my strength and my refuge. As I journey through this day, I will encounter events that cause me emotional distress. Lord, when I am troubled, let me turn to You. Keep me steady, Lord, and in those difficult moments, renew a right spirit inside my heart. Amen.

60

HANDLE THE MEDIA WITH CARE

*Therefore, whether you eat or drink, or whatever you do,
do everything for God's glory.*

1 CORINTHIANS 10:31 HCSB

The Bible assures us that God is always with us, which means that we can live courageously. But sometimes, here in the world of lightning-fast news cycles, it's hard to fight the fear mongers. After all, we face an avalanche of negativity from a widening array of media sources that have discovered bad news sells better than good. So anxiety-producing headlines shout about shocking stories while good news often goes unreported.

The media is working around the clock to grab your attention in an attempt to rearrange your priorities. Yet the all-important things in life have little to do with the alarming images that are so common in today's media-driven world. The most important things in your life have to do with your faith, your family, and your future. Period. So here's a question for you: Will you focus on God's messages or the media's messages? The answer should be obvious.

*The media relentlessly proclaim bad news: for breakfast, lunch, and dinner.
A steady diet of their fare will sicken you. Instead of focusing on fickle,
ever-changing news broadcasts, tune in to the living Word.*

SARAH YOUNG

Heavenly Father, I know that the world is filled with countless distractions. Today, help me to focus, not on the world's messages, but instead on the message of Your Son. Let me keep Jesus in my heart as I focus on His good news and follow in His footsteps. Amen.

61

MENTAL HEALTH PROFESSIONALS OFFER HELP

A cheerful disposition is good for your health;
gloom and doom leave you bone-tired.

PROVERBS 17:22 MSG

Although research has clearly proven that many forms of mental illness have physiological causes, far too many people still avoid medical treatment. Instead of seeking help from counselors and physicians, they avoid professional assistance. This failure to seek treatment has consequences that can be unfortunate and, at times, tragic.

So why do so many people avoid the services that mental health professionals can provide? For many sufferers and their families, emotional disorders are still a source of confusion, embarrassment, or shame. Thankfully, the unwarranted stigma of mental illness is fading as more and more people come to understand that proven treatments can be life-altering and, in severe cases, life-saving.

An informed public has become keenly aware that most mental disorders have both medical as well as psychological origins. Consequently, most emotional disorders, including anxiety disorders, are now imminently treatable through counseling, medication, or a combination of the two. So if you suspect that you—or someone you care about—may be suffering from an anxiety disorder or any other psychiatric condition, seek help immediately. By seeking treatment, you'll be managing your mental health, which can sometimes be even more important than managing your physical health.

Heavenly Father, sometimes abundance and peace seem very far away. But Your Word teaches that a cheerful disposition is priceless blessing. So if I need medical or professional assistance to achieve a peaceful spirit as I follow in the footsteps of Your Son, please give me the wisdom to ask for help. Amen.

62

JUST SAY NO TO NEGATIVITY

In my distress I prayed to the LORD,
and the LORD answered me and set me free.

PSALM 118:5 NLT

From experience, we know that it is easier to criticize than to correct; we understand that it is easier to find faults than solutions; and we realize that excessive criticism is usually destructive, not productive. Yet the urge to criticize others remains a powerful temptation for most of us. Our task, as obedient believers, is to break the twin habits of negative thinking and critical speech.

In the book of James, we are issued a clear warning: "Don't criticize one another, brothers" (4:11 HCSB). Undoubtedly, James understood the paralyzing power of chronic negativity, and so must we. Negativity is highly contagious: we give it to others who, in turn, give it back to us. Thankfully, this cycle can be broken by positive thoughts, heartfelt prayers, and encouraging words.

As you examine the quality of your own communications, can you honestly say that you're a booster not a critic? If so, keep up the good words. But if you're occasionally overwhelmed by negativity, and if you pass that negativity along to your neighbors, it's time for a mental housecleaning and verbal makeover. As a thoughtful Christian, you can use the transforming power of Christ's love to break the chains of negativity. And you should.

> *I may not be able to change the world I see around me,*
> *but I can change the way I see the world within me.*
>
> JOHN MAXWELL

Heavenly Father, today I ask You to free me from the negative emotions that have been holding me back. Give me the wisdom to reject bitterness, envy, hatred, and regret. Then, when my heart has been emptied of these needless burdens, fill it with Your love. Amen.

63

GET INVOLVED—AND STAY INVOLVED—IN A LOCAL CHURCH

If two or three people come together in my name, I am there with them.
MATTHEW 18:20 NCV

We live in a world that is teeming with temptations, distractions, and fear-provoking situations—a world where good and evil struggle in a constant battle to win our minds, our hearts, and our souls. Our challenge, of course, is to ensure that we make choices that are pleasing to our Creator. One way that we remain faithful to Him is through the practice of regular, purposeful worship. When we worship the Father faithfully and fervently, we are blessed.

Your participation in a caring fellowship is good for your spiritual, psychological, and emotional health. Your local church needs you, just as importantly, you need your local church, as the following quotations attest:

> *Church-goers are like coals in a fire. When they cling together, they keep the flame aglow; when they separate, they die out.*
> BILLY GRAHAM

> *The church is a hospital for sinners, not a museum for saints.*
> VANCE HAVNER

> *Every believer is commanded to be plugged in to a local church.*
> DAVID JEREMIAH

Heavenly Father, today and every day, I will support Your church, I will help build Your church, and I will remember that church is not only a place, but that it is also a state of mind and a state of grace. Amen.

64

EXPERIENCE CHRIST'S LOVE AND SHARE IT

We love him, because he first loved us.

1 JOHN 4:19 KJV

Hannah Whitall Smith spoke to believers of every generation when she advised, "Keep your face upturned to Christ as the flowers do to the sun. Look, and your soul shall live and grow." But when we're dealing with difficult people, it becomes harder to focus on Christ's love because we overwhelmed by other emotions. It's hard to focus on Jesus, but not impossible. When we turn our hearts to Him we receive His blessings, His peace, and His grace.

Christ is the ultimate Savior of mankind and the personal Savior of those who believe in Him. As his servants, we should place Him at the very center of our lives. And every day that God gives us breath, we should share Christ's love and His message with a world that needs both.

Christ's love changes everything, including you. When you accept His gift of grace, you are transformed, not only for the moment, but also for all eternity. He's waiting patiently for you to invite Him into your heart. Please don't make Him wait a single minute longer.

Timely Tip: Christ's love is meant to be experienced—and shared—by you. If you're feeling anxious or afraid, it's time to remind yourself that your problems are temporary but Christ's love lasts forever.

Dear Lord Jesus, I am humbled by Your love and Your sacrifice. You died that I might have eternal life. Thank You, Jesus, for Your priceless gift, and for Your compassion. You loved me first, Lord, and I will return Your love today and forever. Amen.

IT PAYS TO THINK OPTIMISTICALLY

But if we look forward to something we don't yet have,
we must wait patiently and confidently.

ROMANS 8:25 NLT

As a follower of Christ, you have every reason to be optimistic about your future here on earth and your future in heaven. God is good, and your eternal future is secure, so why not be an optimist?

The following words of wisdom remind us that optimism pays and pessimism doesn't. Read and heed.

The essence of optimism is that it takes no account of the present.
It is a source of vitality and hope where others have resigned.
It enables a man to hold his head high, to claim the future
for himself, and not to abandon it to his enemy.

DIETRICH BONHOEFFER

Avoid arguments, but when a negative attitude is expressed,
counter it with a positive and optimistic opinion.

NORMAN VINCENT PEALE

Take courage. We walk in the wilderness today
and in the Promised Land tomorrow.

D. L. MOODY

Heavenly Father, let me be an expectant Christian. Let me expect the best from You, and let me look for the best in others. If I become discouraged, Father, turn my thoughts and my prayers to You. Let me trust You, Lord, to direct my life. And let me share my faith and optimism with others every day that I live. Amen.

66

RESIST NEGATIVE PEER PRESSURES

Do not be mismatched with unbelievers. For what partnership is there between righteousness and lawlessness? Or what fellowship does light have with darkness?

2 CORINTHIANS 6:14 HCSB

Peer pressure can be a good thing or a bad thing, depending upon your peers. If your peers encourage you to make integrity a habit—and if they encourage you to follow God's will and to obey His commandments—then you'll experience positive peer pressure, and that's good. But if you are involved with people who encourage you to do foolish things, you're facing a different kind of peer pressure: the negative kind. And the more negative peer pressure you experience, the more anxious you'll become.

Rick Warren observed, "Those who follow the crowd usually get lost in it." We know those words to be true, but oftentimes we fail to live by them. Instead of trusting God for guidance, we imitate our friends and suffer the consequences. Instead seeking to please our Father in heaven, we strive to please our peers, with decidedly mixed results. Instead of doing the right thing, we do the "easy" thing or the "popular" thing. And when we do, we pay a high price for our shortsightedness.

> *If you really want to please God and intend to be in full agreement with His will, you can't go wrong.*
>
> FRANCIS MARY PAUL LIBERMANN

Dear Lord, today I will worry less about pleasing other people and more about pleasing You. I will honor You with my thoughts, my actions, and my prayers. And I will worship You, Father, with thanksgiving in my heart, this day and forever. Amen.

67

BE PERFECT IN GOD

Those who wait for perfect weather will never plant seeds;
those who look at every cloud will never harvest crops. . . .
Plant early in the morning, and work until evening, because
you don't know if this or that will succeed. They might both do well.

ECCLESIASTES 11:4,6 NCV

As a citizen of the twenty-first century, you know that demands can be high and expectations even higher. Traditional media outlets, along with their social-media counterparts, deliver an endless stream of messages that tell you how to look, how to behave, how to eat, and how to dress. And that's only the beginning. If you're not careful, you'll find yourself scrambling to keep up with everybody's expectations, which is impossible.

The world's expectations are impossible to meet—God's are not. God doesn't expect you to be perfect, and neither, by the way, should you. So if you're a person who possesses perfectionistic tendencies, here's a word of warning: perfectionism and anxiety are traveling companions. If you're striving to be perfect, you'll inevitably make yourself more anxious than necessary. To combat perfectionism, remember this: the expectations that really matter are God's expectations. Everything else should take a back seat.

> *God is so inconceivably good. He's not looking for perfection.*
> *He already saw it in Christ. He's looking for affection.*
>
> BETH MOORE

Dear Lord, I'm certainly not perfect, but You love me despite my imperfections. Thank You for Your love, and for Your Son. Amen.

68

KEEP PERSEVERING

*Let us not become weary in doing good, for at the proper time
we will reap a harvest if we do not give up.*

GALATIANS 6:9 NIV

If you're trying to rid yourself of anxious thoughts or unfounded fears, you will undoubtedly experience a few setbacks along the way. When you do, don't be discouraged. Keep searching for more effective ways to manage your negative emotions. And while you're at it, remember that God isn't finished with you yet.

The old saying is as true today as it was when it was first spoken: "Life is a marathon, not a sprint." That's why wise travelers select a traveling companion who never tires and never falters. That partner is your heavenly Father.

The next time you find your courage tested by anxious thoughts or unfortunate circumstances, remember that the Lord is as near as your next breath, and remember that He offers strength and comfort to His children. He is your shield and your strength; He is your protector and your deliverer. Call upon Him in your hour of need and be comforted. Whatever your problem, God can handle it. Your job is to keep persevering until He does.

*Everyone gets discouraged. The question is:
Are you going to give up or get up? It's a choice.*

JOHN MAXWELL

Dear Lord, when life is difficult I am sometimes tempted to abandon hope in the future. But You are my God, and I can draw strength from You. When I am exhausted, You energize me. When I am afraid, You give me courage. You are with me, Father, in good times and in hard times. I will persevere in the work that You have placed before me, and I will trust in You forever. Amen.

69

THE LORD HAS PROMISED TO PROTECT YOU: TRUST HIM

The Lord is near all who call out to Him, all who call out to Him with integrity. He fulfills the desires of those who fear Him; He hears their cry for help and saves them.

PSALM 145:18-19 HCSB

The Lord has made many promises to you, and He will keep every single one of them. God has promised that He will never leave you. And He has promised that He will protect you now and forever. So if you're worried or anxious or afraid, pray for guidance and pray for a trusting heart. You need both, and He will give you both *if* you ask.

Earthly security is an illusion. Your only real security comes from the loving heart of God. When you trust Him completely, you can face the inevitable challenges of everyday life with the knowledge that the Creator of the universe is watching over you.

Discipline yourself to stay close to God. He alone is your security.

BILLY GRAHAM

Faith is not merely holding on to God. It is God holding on to you.

CORRIE TEN BOOM

Dear Lord, You have promised to protect me, and I will trust You. Today, I will live courageously as I place my hopes, my faith, and life in Your hands. Let my life be a testimony to the transforming power of Your love, Your grace, and Your Son. Amen.

70

YES, YOU CAN LEARN
TO MANAGE YOUR EMOTIONS

I can do all things through Christ which strengtheneth me.

PHILIPPIANS 4:13 KJV

All of us face difficult days—days when then challenges of everyday life threaten to hijack our emotions. Sometimes even the most optimistic Christians can become discouraged, and you are no exception. If you find yourself enduring difficult circumstances, perhaps it's time for an extreme intellectual makeover. Perhaps it's time to focus more on your strengths and opportunities, and less on the challenges that confront you.

If you believe, even for a moment, that you can never learn to deal with anxiety and fear, you are mistaken. With God, all things are possible. So keep praying, keep thinking good thoughts, and don't be embarrassed to talk with a trained mental health professional if necessary. And while you're at it, keep reminding yourself that better days are ahead.

Every day is filled opportunities to heal, to grow, to serve, to share, and to rise above unfortunate situations. But if you are entangled in a web of anxious thoughts, you may overlook the blessings that God has scattered along your path. So don't give in to pessimism, to doubt, to cynicism, or to fear. Instead, keep your eyes focused upon the possibilities, fix your heart upon the Creator, do your best, and let Him handle the rest.

Timely Tip: Dealing with anxious thoughts and roller-coaster emotions can be painful, but with God's help, you're up to the challenge. Keep praying and keep trying to do the right thing. And remember: with God, all things are possible.

Dear Lord, I want to be a disciplined believer. Let me learn to control negative emotions, let me focus on Your blessings, and let me teach others by the faithfulness of my conduct, today and every day. Amen.

71

PRAY FOR PEACE OF MIND

Be anxious for nothing, but in everything by prayer and supplication, with thanksgiving, let your requests be made known to God.

PHILIPPIANS 4:6 NKJV

When you're enduring difficult circumstances, it's easy to become frustrated. But even in the most difficult situations, God offers His peace if you ask for it. The beautiful words of John 14:27 remind us that Jesus offers us peace, not as the world gives, but as He alone gives: "Peace I leave with you. My peace I give to you. I do not give to you as the world gives. Your heart must not be troubled or fearful" (HCSB). Our challenge is to accept Christ's peace and then, as best we can, to share His peace with our neighbors.

Today, as a gift to yourself, to your family, and to your friends, claim the inner peace that is your spiritual birthright: the peace of Jesus Christ. It is offered freely; it has been paid for in full; it is yours for the asking. So ask. And then share.

Timely Tip: God's peace is available to you this very moment if you place absolute trust in Him. So if you're not feeling peaceful, pray about it. Ask God to bring peace to your soul. And keep praying. The Lord is your shepherd, and He wants to hear from you now. Trust Him today and be blessed.

Heavenly Father, the peace that the world offers is brief, but Your peace, the peace that passes all understanding, is eternal. Let me take my concerns and burdens to You, Father, and let me experience the spiritual abundance that can be mine when I follow in the footsteps of Your Son, the Prince of Peace. Amen.

72

GOD'S TIMING IS BEST

He has made everything beautiful in its time.
He has also set eternity in the human heart; yet no one
can fathom what God has done from beginning to end.

ECCLESIASTES 3:11 NIV

If you're waiting patiently for the Lord to help you resolve a difficult situation, remember this: God is never early or late; He's always on time. Although you don't know precisely what you need—or when you need it—He does. So your assignment, simply put, is to trust His timing.

The quotations that follow are intended to remind us that the Lord doesn't do things by accident. He has a plan that only He can see. And His timing is, indeed, best.

Waiting on God brings us to the journey's end quicker than our feet.

LETTIE COWMAN

Teach us, O Lord, the disciplines of patience,
for to wait is often harder than to work.

PETER MARSHALL

The Christian's journey through life isn't a sprint but a marathon.

BILLY GRAHAM

Heavenly Father, Your timing is seldom my timing, but Your timing is always right for me. You are my Father, and You have a plan for my life that is grander than I can imagine. When I am impatient, remind me that You are never early or late. You are always on time, Lord, and I will trust You today, tomorrow, and every day of my life. Amen.

73

MEASURE YOUR WORDS

A wise heart instructs its mouth and increases learning with its speech.
PROVERBS 16:23 HCSB

God's Word reminds us that "The words of the reckless pierce like swords, but the tongue of the wise brings healing" (Proverbs 12:18 NIV). If you seek to be a source of encouragement to friends, to family members, and to coworkers, then you must measure your words carefully. And that's exactly what the Lord wants you to do.

Today, make this promise to yourself: vow to be an honest, effective, encouraging communicator at work, at home, and everyplace in between. Speak wisely, not impulsively. Use words of kindness and praise, not words of anger or derision. Learn how to be truthful without being cruel. Remember that your have the power to heal others or to injure them; your words have the power to escalate stressful situations or to heal them; your words have the power to lift others up or to hold them back. And when you learn how to lift them up, you'll soon discover that you've lifted yourself up too.

Attitude and the spirit in which we communicate
are as important as the words we say.
CHARLES STANLEY

Dear Lord, You have warned me that I will be judged by the words I speak. Keep me mindful, Lord, that I have influence on many people; make me an influence for good. And may the words that I speak today be worthy of the One who has saved me forever. Amen.

74

THE LORD ALWAYS KEEPS HIS PROMISES

Let us hold fast the confession of our hope without wavering, for He who promised is faithful.

HEBREWS 10:23 NASB

Sometimes, especially when we find ourselves caught in the inevitable entanglements of everyday life, we fail to trust God completely. Instead of reading His Word and trusting His promises, we fall prey to anxiety and fear. We forget, at least temporarily, that the Lord is, indeed, our shepherd, and that He always keeps His promises.

Are you tired? Discouraged? Fearful? Be comforted and trust the promises that God has made to you. Are you worried or anxious? Be confident in God's power. Do you see a difficult future ahead? Be courageous and call upon God. He will protect you and then use you according to His purposes. Are you confused? Listen to the quiet voice of your heavenly Father. He is not a God of confusion. Talk with Him; listen to Him; trust Him, and trust His promises. He is steadfast, and He is your Protector, now and forever.

Let God's promises shine on your problems.

CORRIE TEN BOOM

Dear Lord, Your holy Word contains many promises, and I know that You will keep every one of them. Today and every day, let me trust You completely, and let me follow closely in the footsteps of Your only begotten Son. Amen

75

FIRST THINGS FIRST: SET THE RIGHT PRIORITIES

Seek first God's kingdom and what God wants.
Then all your other needs will be met as well.

MATTHEW 6:33 NCV

First things first." These words are easy to speak but hard to put into practice. For busy people living in a demanding world, placing first things first can be difficult indeed. Why? Because so many people are expecting so many things from us!

If you're anxiously agonizing over a to-do list that seems impossibly long, perhaps you've been trying to organize your life according to your own plans, not God's. A better strategy, of course, is to take your daily obligations and place them in the hands of the One who created you. To do so, you must prioritize your day according to God's commandments, and you must seek His will and His wisdom in all matters. Then you can face the day with the assurance that the same God who created our universe out of nothingness will help you place first things first in your own life.

Do you feel overwhelmed, anxious, or emotionally distraught? If so, turn the concerns of this day over to God—prayerfully, earnestly, and often. Then listen for His answers, and trust the answers He gives.

Energy and time are limited entities. Therefore, we need to
use them wisely, focusing on what is truly important.

SARAH YOUNG

Dear Lord, today and every day, let me focus on doing first things first. Let Your priorities be my priorities. Let Your will be my will. Let Your Word be my guide, and let me follow as closely as I can in the footsteps of Your Son. Amen.

PROBLEM SOLVING 101

People who do what is right may have many problems,
but the LORD will solve them all.

PSALM 34:19 NCV

It's inevitable: the upcoming day will not be problem free. In fact, your life can be viewed as an exercise in problem solving. The question is not whether you will encounter difficult situations or prickly problems; the real question is how you will choose to respond.

When it comes to solving the problems of everyday living, we often know precisely what needs to be done, but we may be slow in doing it—especially if what needs to be done is difficult or uncomfortable. So we put off till tomorrow what should be done today.

The words of Psalm 34 remind us that the Lord solves problems for "people who do what is right." And usually, doing "what is right" means doing the uncomfortable work of confronting our problems sooner rather than later. So with no further ado, let the problem solving begin *now*.

Everyone gets discouraged. The question is:
Are you going to give up or get up? It's a choice.

JOHN MAXWELL

Dear Lord, today I will summon the courage to face my challenges with courage and determination. I will trust that You are working in me and through me to turn problems into opportunities. And I will focus, not on my challenges, but on my opportunities to work, to serve, and to follow in the footsteps of Your Son. Amen.

77

AVOID THE TRAP OF PROCRASTINATION

But prove yourselves doers of the word,
and not merely hearers who delude themselves.

JAMES 1:22 NASB

If you find yourself bound by the chains of procrastination, ask yourself what you're waiting for—or more accurately what you're afraid of—and why. As you examine the emotional roadblocks that have, heretofore, blocked your path, you may discover that you're waiting for the "perfect" moment, that instant in time when you feel neither afraid nor anxious. But in truth, perfect moments like these are few and far between.

So stop waiting for the perfect moment and focus, instead, on finding the right moment to do what needs to be done. Then trust God and get busy. When you do, you'll discover that you and the Father, working together, can accomplish great things . . . and that you can accomplish them sooner rather than later.

Once you acquire the habit of doing what needs to be done when it needs to be done, you will avoid untold trouble, worry, and stress. So how do you acquire that habit? You can learn to overcome procrastination by paying less attention to your fears and more attention to your responsibilities. God has created a world that punishes procrastinators and rewards people who "do it now." In other words, life doesn't procrastinate. Neither should you.

Our grand business is, not to see what lies dimly at a distance,
but to do what lies closely at hand.

THOMAS CARLYLE

Dear Lord, when I am confronted with things that need to be done, give me the courage and the wisdom to do them now, not later. Amen.

78

FIND ABUNDANCE THROUGH CHRIST

A thief comes to steal and kill and destroy,
but I came to give life—life in all its fullness.

JOHN 10:10 NCV

Sometimes, life here on earth can be complicated, demanding, and frustrating. When the demands of life leave us rushing from place to place with scarcely a moment to spare, we may fail to pause and thank our Creator for His gifts. And that's unfortunate because when we turn our minds and lift our prayers to God, He blesses us with an array of spiritual and emotional gifts that can brighten our days and transform our lives.

The words of wisdom that follow are intended to remind us that Jesus came to this earth so that we might live abundantly. It's a message that we must never forget.

Knowing that your future is absolutely assured
can free you to live abundantly today.

SARAH YOUNG

God loves you and wants you to experience
peace and life—abundant and eternal.

BILLY GRAHAM

Thank You, Father, for the abundant life that is mine through Christ Jesus. Guide me according to Your will, and help me to be a worthy servant through all that I say and do. Give me courage, Lord, to claim the rewards You have promised, and when I do, let all the glory be Yours. Amen.

79

FIND STRENGTH IN QUIET MOMENTS

In quietness and in confidence shall be your strength.

ISAIAH 30:15 KJV

The world seems to grow louder day by day, and angry people are using technology to spread negativity far and wide. No wonder our senses seem to be invaded at every turn. If we allow the inevitable distractions of a clamorous society to separate us from God's peace, we do ourselves a profound disservice.

If we sincerely want the peace that passes all understanding, we must carve out time each day for prayer, reflection, and Bible study. When we meet with God in the morning, we can quiet our minds and sense His presence.

Has the hectic pace of everyday life robbed you of the peace that God has promised? If so, it's time to reorder your priorities and rearrange your schedule. Nothing is more important than the time you spend with your heavenly Father. So be still and claim the inner peace that is found in the silent moments you spend with Him.

Timely Tip: You live in a noisy world filled with distractions, interruptions, and occasional frustrations, a world where silence is in short supply. But God wants you to carve out quiet moments with Him. Silence is, indeed, golden. Value yours.

Dear Lord, Your Word is a light unto the world; I will study it and trust your promises. I will come to you, Father, in the quiet moments of the day. And in all that I say and do, I will strive to share the good news of Your perfect Son and Your perfect Word. Amen.

CHANGE CAN BE DIFFICULT

God is our protection and our strength. He always helps in times of trouble.
PSALM 46:1 NCV

Every day we mortals encounter a multitude of changes—some good, some not so good. And on occasion, all of us must endure life-altering personal losses that leave us heartbroken. When we do, our heavenly Father stands ready to comfort us, to guide us, and—in time—to heal us.

Are you anxious about situations that you cannot control? Take your anxieties to God. Are you troubled? Take your troubles to Him. Does your little corner of the universe seem to be trembling beneath your feet? Seek protection from the One who cannot be moved. The same God who created the universe will protect you if you ask Him . . . so ask Him . . . and then serve Him with willing hands and a trusting heart.

Are you on the eve of change? Embrace it. Accept it. Don't resist it. Change is not only a part of life, change is a necessary part of God's strategy. To use us to change the world, he alters our assignments.

MAX LUCADO

Transitions are almost always signs of growth, but they can bring feelings of loss. To get somewhere new, we may have to leave somewhere else behind.

FRED ROGERS

Heavenly Father, our world changes, but You are unchanging. When I face challenges that leave me discouraged or fearful, I will turn to You for strength and assurance. Let my trust in You—like Your love for me—be unchanging and everlasting. Amen.

81

YES, YOU HAVE
THE RIGHT TO SAY NO

Let us lay aside every weight, and the sin which so easily ensnares us,
and let us run with endurance the race that is set before us.

HEBREWS 12:1 NKJV

If you haven't yet learned to say no—to say it politely, firmly, and often—you're inviting untold stress into your life. Why? Because if you can't say no (when appropriate), some people will take advantage of your good nature.

If you have trouble standing up for yourself, perhaps you're afraid that you'll be rejected. But here's a tip: don't worry too much about rejection, especially when you're rejected for doing the right thing.

Pleasing other people is a good thing up to a point. But you must never allow your willingness to please to interfere with your own good judgment or with God's priorities. God gave you a conscience for a reason: to inform you about the things you need to do as well as the things you don't need to do. It's up to you to follow your conscience wherever it may lead, even if it means making unpopular decisions. Your job, simply put, is to be popular with God, not people.

As you live your life, you must localize and define it.
You cannot do everything.

PHILLIPS BROOKS

Dear Lord, when I need to say no, give me the courage, the wisdom, and the strength to say it. Today and every day, help me follow my conscience, not the crowd. Amen.

82

BUILD SELF-CONFIDENCE

You are my hope; O Lord God, You are my confidence.

PSALM 71:5 NASB

Do you believe that you can accomplish big things for your family, for your community, and for your Lord? Or have you convinced yourself that you're a second-tier talent who'll be lucky to finish far back in the pack? Before you answer these questions, remember this: God sent His Son so that you might enjoy the abundant life that Jesus describes in the familiar words of John 10:10. But God's gifts are not guaranteed—it's up to you to claim them.

If you want to achieve the best that life has to offer, you must put the self-fulfilling prophecy to work for you. How? By convincing yourself beyond a shadow of a doubt that you have the ability to earn the rewards you desire. You must become sold on yourself—sold on your skills, sold on your opportunities, sold on your potential, sold on your attitude, and sold on your character. If you're sold on yourself, chances are the world will soon become sold too. And the results will be beautiful.

*If you doubt you can accomplish something,
you can't accomplish it. Instead, you have to be confident
in yourself and you need to be tough enough to follow through.*

ROSALYNN CARTER

Dear Lord, because You have promised to protect me now and forever, I have every reason to be confident about my life and my eternal future with You. Today, I will trust You, Father, and I will strive to be a confident as I follow in the footsteps of Your Son. Amen.

83

USE THE POWER
OF SELF-DISCIPLINE

Rather, he must be hospitable, one who loves what is good,
who is self-controlled, upright, holy and disciplined.

TITUS 1:8 NIV

God's Word reminds us again and again that our Creator expects us to lead disciplined lives. God doesn't reward laziness, misbehavior, or apathy. To the contrary, He expects us to behave with dignity and discipline. But ours is a world in which dignity and discipline are often in short supply.

We live in a world in which leisure is glorified and indifference is often glamorized. But God has other plans. God gives us talents, and He expects us to use them. But it is not always easy to cultivate those talents. Sometimes, we must invest countless hours (or, in some cases, many years) honing our skills. And that's perfectly okay with God, because He understands that self-discipline is a blessing, not a burden.

Life's greatest rewards seldom fall into our laps; to the contrary, our greatest accomplishments usually require work, perseverance, and discipline. May we, as disciplined believers, be willing to work the rewards we so earnestly desire.

Heavenly Father, Your Word teaches us to be diligent and disciplined. You have told us that the fields are ripe and the workers are few. Lead me to Your fields, Lord, and make me a disciplined worker in the service of Your Son, Christ Jesus. When I am weary, give me strength. When I am discouraged, give me hope. Make me a disciplined, courageous, industrious servant for Your kingdom today and forever. Amen.

84

BECOME BETTER ACQUAINTED WITH YOURSELF

*And why worry about a speck in your friend's eye when you have a log
in your own? . . . Hypocrite! First get rid of the log in your own eye;
then you will see well enough to deal with the speck in your friend's eye.*

MATTHEW 7:3, 5 NLT

If you're looking for better ways to manage your emotions, it's tempting to focus exclusively on the stressors around you. But it's also helpful to look at the stressors within you. Perhaps you're overestimating the size of your problems or you're overly pessimistic or you're too hard on others. Or perhaps other issues are stealing your joy.

If you're experiencing hurtful feelings that just won't go away, it's time to schedule an appointment with your pastor, counselor, or mental health professional. These people can help you look inside to discover, and then banish, the hurtful feelings or exaggerated thought patterns that may be holding you back. When you look at your own personal history and your habitual ways of dealing with the world around you, you many decide it's time to make some changes. If so, here's twofold advice: get started now and be patient.

Being patient with other people can be difficult. But sometimes we find it even more difficult to be patient with ourselves. If you happen to be your own worst critic—or if you expect perfection from yourself yourself and others—it's time to reconsider. When you look inward—and upward—you'll discover that life doesn't have to be perfect to be wonderful.

Dear Lord, I have so much to learn and so many ways to improve myself, but You love me just as I am. Thank You, Father, for Your love and for Your Son. Help me to become the person that You want me to become. Amen.

85

MOVE BEYOND SHAME AND GUILT

Let us come near to God with a sincere heart and a sure faith,
because we have been made free from a guilty conscience,
and our bodies have been washed with pure water.

HEBREWS 10:22 NCV

Have you done things you're ashamed of? If so, welcome to a very large club. Even the most honorable people on the planet have done things that only God can forgive. But the good news is this: whenever we admit our shortcomings to the Lord and ask for His forgiveness, He gives them.

There's nothing any of us can do to redeem ourselves from sin; that's something only God can do. So what can we do? We can allow God's Son into our hearts and allow Him to do what we cannot.

Shame is a form of spiritual cancer; it can be deadly, but it is treatable. The treatment begins when we acknowledge our sins and ask for God's mercy. But it doesn't end there. Once God forgives us, we still have work to do: we must forgive ourselves.

The Lord knows all your imperfections, all your faults, and all your shortcomings . . . and He loves you anyway. And because God loves you, you can—and should—feel good about the person you see when you look into the mirror. God's love is bigger and more powerful than anybody (including you) can imagine, but His love is very real. So do yourself a favor right now: accept God's love with open arms. And while you're at it, remember this: even when you don't love yourself very much, God loves you. And God is always right.

Dear Lord, I thank You for the guilt that I feel when I disobey You. Help me confess my wrongdoings, help me accept Your forgiveness, and help me renew my passion to serve You. Amen.

WHEN IN DOUBT, SIMPLIFY YOUR LIFE

*A simple life in the Fear-of-God is better than
a rich life with a ton of headaches.*

PROVERBS 15:16 MSG

Want to reduce stress? Here's a simple solution: simplify your life. Unfortunately, simplification is easier said than done. After all, you live in a world where simplicity is in short supply.

Think for a moment about the complexity of your everyday life and compare it to the lives of your ancestors. Certainly, you are the beneficiary of many technological innovations, but those innovations have come at a price: in all likelihood, your world is highly complex. Unless you take firm control of your time and your life, you may be overwhelmed by an anxiety-producing, stress-inducing tidal wave of obligations that leave you spiritually and emotionally drained.

Time and again God's Word warns us against the trap of materialism. And as Proverbs 15:16 reminds us, a simple life with God is vastly superior to its materialistic alternative. So do yourself and your loved ones a favor: keep your life as simple as possible. Simplicity is, indeed, genius. By simplifying your life, you are destined to improve it.

The characteristic of the life of a saint is essentially elemental simplicity.

OSWALD CHAMBERS

Dear Lord, life is complicated enough without my adding to the confusion. Help me understand the wisdom of simplicity. Wherever I happen to be, help me to keep it simple—very simple. And help me focus on your will for my life and on your never-ending love for me. Amen.

87

ARE YOU GETTING ENOUGH REST?

The Lord shall give thee rest from thy sorrow, and from thy fear.
ISAIAH 14:3 KJV

You inhabit an interconnected world that never slows down and never shuts off. The world tempts you to stay up late watching the news or surfing the Internet or checking out social media or gaming, or doing countless other activities that gobble up your time and distract you from more important tasks. But too much late-night screen time robs you of something you need very badly: sleep.

Are you going to bed at a reasonable hour and sleeping through the night? If so, you're both wise and blessed. But if you're staying up late with your eyes glued to a screen, you may be increasing your anxiety level, and you're most certainly putting your long-term health at risk. To make matters worse, you may be wasting lots of time too.

So the next time you're tempted to engage in late-night, time-gobbling activities, resist the temptation. Instead, turn your thoughts and prayers to God. And when you're finished, turn off the lights and go to bed. You need rest more than you need entertainment.

> *Think in the morning. Act in the noon.*
> *Eat in the evening. Sleep in the night.*
> WILLIAM BLAKE

Heavenly Father, when the day is done, give me the wisdom to rest. And when the day draws to a close, give me the wisdom to say a prayer, to turn out the lights, and go to sleep. Amen.

SEIZE EVERY OPPORTUNITY FOR SPIRITUAL GROWTH

I remind you to fan into flames the spiritual gift God gave you.
2 TIMOTHY 1:6 NLT

The path to spiritual maturity unfolds day by day, through good times and hard times. Each day offers the opportunity to worship God and to be blessed by the richness of our relationship with Him.

In those quiet moments when we open our hearts to the Father, the One who made us keeps remaking us. He gives us direction, hope, perspective, and courage. And the appropriate moment to accept those spiritual gifts is always the present one.

Are you feeling anxious? Are you fearful? Are you enduring tough times that have left your head spinning? If so, you can be certain that God still has important lessons to teach you. So ask yourself this: What lesson is God trying to teach me today? And then go about the business of learning it.

God's ultimate goal for your life on earth is not comfort, but character development. He wants you to grow up spiritually and become like Christ.
RICK WARREN

Dear Lord, when I feel overwhelmed with anxiety or fear or sadness, I will turn to You. Help me to live according to Your Word, Father, and let me grow in my faith every day that I live. Amen.

YOU CAN START OVER

*Then the One seated on the throne said,
"Look! I am making everything new."*

REVELATION 21:5 HCSB

If you're experiencing tough times—or if you're starting over from scratch—you may feel like you're entering an entirely new phase of life. If so, congratulations. Your fresh start is an occasion to be celebrated. God has a perfect plan for your life, and He has the power to make all things new.

As you think about your future—and as you consider the countless opportunities that will be woven into the fabric of the days ahead—be sure to include God in your plans. When you do, He will guide your steps and light your path.

Perhaps you want to change the direction of your life, or perhaps you're determined to make major modifications in the way you live or the way you think. If so, you and God, working together, can do it. But don't expect change to be easy or instant. God expects you to do your fair share of the work, and that's as it should be.

If you're graduating into a new phase of life, be sure to make God your partner. When you do, He'll guide your steps; He'll help carry your burdens; and He'll help you focus on the opportunities of the future, not the losses of the past.

*Whoever you are, wherever you are, whatever you've
been through, it's never too late to begin again.*

JOYCE MEYER

Heavenly Father, conform me to Your image. Create in me a new heart—a heart reflects the love that You lavish upon me. When I need to change, Lord, change me, and make me new again. Amen.

90

GOD OFFERS EMOTIONAL STRENGTH

He gives strength to the weary,
and to him who lacks might He increases power.

Isaiah 40:29 NASB

God's love and support never changes. From the cradle to the grave, God has promised to give you the strength to meet any challenge. God has promised to lift you up and guide your steps if you let Him. God has promised that when you entrust your life to Him completely and without reservation, He will give you the courage to face any trial and the wisdom to live in His righteousness.

Are you an energized Christian? You should be. But if you're not, you must seek emotional strength from the source that will never fail. That source, of course, is your heavenly Father. And rest assured: when you sincerely petition Him, He will give you all the strength you need to live victoriously for Him.

God has promised to protect us. In a world filled with dangers and temptations, the Lord is the ultimate armor. In a world filled with misleading messages, God's Word is the ultimate truth. In a world filled with more frustrations than we can count, God offers us the ultimate peace. When we turn to the Lord for strength and perspective, He never fails us.

God is in control. He may not take away trials or make detours
for us, but He strengthens us through them.

Billy Graham

Dear Lord, whenever I feel discouraged or tired, I will turn to You for strength. I know that when I open my heart to You, Father, You will renew my strength and my enthusiasm. Let Your will be my will, Lord, and let me find my strength in You. Amen.

91

MANAGE STRESS

Come unto me, all ye that labour and are heavy laden, and I will give you rest.
MATTHEW 11:28 KJV

Stressful days are an inevitable fact of modern life. And how do we best cope with the challenges of our demanding, twenty-first-century world? By turning our days and our lives over to God. Elisabeth Elliot writes, "If my life is surrendered to God, all is well. Let me not grab it back, as though it were in peril in His hand but would be safer in mine!" Yet even the most devout Christians may, at times, seek to grab the reins and proclaim, "I'm in charge!" To do so is foolish, prideful, and stress-inducing.

When we seek to impose our own wills upon the world—or upon other people—we invite stress into our lives . . . needlessly. But when we turn our lives and our hearts over to God—when we accept His will instead of seeking vainly to impose our own—we discover the inner peace that can be ours through Him.

Do you feel overwhelmed by the stresses of daily life? Turn your concerns and your prayers over to the Lord. Trust Him. Trust Him completely. Trust Him today. Trust Him always. Whatever your concerns, whatever your challenges, hand them over to God completely and without reservation. He knows your needs and will meet those needs in His own way and in His own time. He's always with you, always in your corner ready to help. And the rest is up to you.

Timely Tip: If you're serious about beating stress, reducing anxiety, and overcoming fear, you should form the habit of talking to God first thing every morning. He's available. Are you?

Dear Lord, sometimes the stresses of the day leave me tired and frustrated. Renew my energy, Father, and give me perspective and peace. Let me draw comfort and courage from Your promises, from Your love, and from Your Son. Amen.

92

ARE YOU SUFFERING?

And the God of all grace, who called you to his eternal glory in Christ,
after you have suffered a little while, will himself restore you
and make you strong, firm and steadfast.

1 PETER 5:10 NIV

All of us face times of hardship and emotional strain. When we face the inevitable difficulties of life here on earth, we can seek help from family, from friends, and from God . . . but not necessarily in that order.

Barbara Johnson writes, "There is no way around suffering. We have to go through it to get to the other side." And the best way "to get to the other side" of suffering is to get there with God. When we turn open hearts to Him in heartfelt prayer, He will answer—in His own time and according to His own plan—and He will heal us.

If you are experiencing the intense pain of a recent loss, or if you are still mourning a loss from long ago, perhaps you are now ready to begin the next stage of your journey with God. If so, be mindful of this fact: the loving heart of God is sufficient to meet any challenge, including yours.

The promises of God's Word sustain us in our suffering, and we know
Jesus sympathizes and empathizes with us in our darkest hour.

BILL BRIGHT

Dear Lord, Your Word promises that You will not give us more than we can bear; You have promised to give us rest from our sorrows and deliverance from our pain. Today, Father, I pray for those who suffer and for those who mourn. And I thank You for sustaining us in our days of sorrow. May we trust You always and praise You forever. Amen.

93

BE OBEDIENT NOW

And hereby we do know that we know him,
if we keep his commandments.

1 JOHN 2:3 KJV

In order to enjoy a deeper relationship with God, you need to live in accordance with His commandments. But there's a problem: you live in a world that seeks to snare your attention and lead you away from the Lord.

Because you are an imperfect mortal being, you cannot be perfectly obedient, nor does God expect you to be. What is required, however, is a sincere desire to be obedient coupled with an awareness of sin and a willingness to distance yourself from it as soon as you encounter it.

Are you willing to conform your behavior to God's rules? Hopefully, you can answer that question with a resounding yes. Otherwise, you'll never experience a full measure of the emotional and spiritual blessings that the Creator gives to those who obey Him.

Above all else, the Christian life is a love affair of the heart.

JOHN ELDREDGE

Heavenly Father, I want to grow closer to You each day. I know that obedience to Your will strengthens my relationship with You, so help me to follow Your commandments and obey Your Word today . . . and every day of my life. Amen.

94

DON'T BE AFRAID

Don't be afraid, because I am your God. I will make you strong and will help you; I will support you with my right hand that saves you.

ISAIAH 41:10 NCV

The Bible promises this: tough times are temporary but God's love is not—God's love lasts forever. So what does that mean to you? Just this: from time to time, everybody faces tough times, and so will you. When those tough times arrive, you need not be afraid because the Lord always stands ready to protect you and heal you.

The next time you're faced with a difficult situation or an unfortunate set of circumstance, don't fall prey to fear. Instead, trust God's promises, follow closely in the footsteps of His Son, and pay careful attention to these words of wisdom:

Jesus did not promise to change the circumstances around us. He promised great peace and pure joy to those who would learn to believe that God actually controls all things.

CORRIE TEN BOOM

Don't let obstacles along the road to eternity shake your confidence in God's promises.

DAVID JEREMIAH

No time is too hard for God, no situation too difficult.

NORMAN VINCENT PEALE

Heavenly Father, I will turn to You today for courage and for strength. When I am fearful, I will focus on Your promises. When I am anxious, I will turn my thoughts and prayers to You. Dear Lord, I know that You are with me always, and I know that You are my shepherd now and forever. Amen.

95

POINT YOUR THOUGHTS
IN THE RIGHT DIRECTION

Finally, brothers and sisters,, whatever is true, whatever is noble, whatever is right, whatever is pure, whatever is lovely, whatever is admirable— if anything is excellent or praiseworthy—think about such things.

PHILIPPIANS 4:8 NIV

How will you direct your thoughts today? Will you obey the words of Philippians 4:8 by dwelling upon those things that are noble, pure, and admirable? Or will you allow your thoughts to be hijacked by the general negativity that seems to dominate our troubled world?

Are you feeling fearful, angry, frustrated, or anxious? Are you so preoccupied with the concerns of this day that you fail to thank God for the promise of eternity? Are you confused, bitter, or pessimistic? If so, God wants to have a little talk with you.

God intends that you be an ambassador for Him, an enthusiastic, hope-filled Christian. But God won't force you to adopt a positive attitude. It's up to you to do think positively about your blessings and your opportunities. When you do so, your positive thoughts will generate positive emotions.

So today and every day hereafter, celebrate this life that God has given you by focusing your thoughts and your energies upon things that are excellent and praiseworthy. It's the best way to think and the best way to live.

It is the thoughts and intents of the heart that shape a person's life.

JOHN ELDREDGE

Dear Lord, help me focus on things that are good, things that are true, and things that are right. And as I face the inevitable ups and downs of everyday life, help me direct my thoughts in ways that are pleasing to You. Amen.

REMEMBER THAT EVERY DAY IS PRECIOUS

So teach us to number our days,
that we may present to You a heart of wisdom.

PSALM 90:12 NASB

This day is a blessed gift from God. And as Christians, we have countless reasons to rejoice. Yet on some days, when we experience unwelcome emotions—or when the demands of daily life threaten to overwhelm us—we don't feel much like rejoicing. Instead of celebrating God's glorious creation, we may find ourselves discouraged by the frustrations of today and worried about the uncertainties of tomorrow.

C. H. Spurgeon, the renowned nineteenth-century English clergymen, advised, "Rejoicing is clearly a spiritual command. To ignore it, I need to remind you, is disobedience." As Christians, we are called by our Creator to live abundantly, prayerfully, and joyfully. To do otherwise is to squander His spiritual gifts.

If you're a thoughtful Christian, you're a thankful Christian. Because of your faith, you can face the inevitable challenges and disappointments of each day armed with the joy of Christ and the promise of eternal life. So whatever this day holds for you, begin it and end it with God as your partner and Christ as your Savior. Treasure the time that the Lord has given you. And search for the hidden possibilities that He has placed along your path. This day is a priceless gift from your Creator; use it joyfully and productively. After all, night is coming when no one can work.

Dear Lord, I thank You for the gift of life, and I thank You for another day that is filled with opportunities to serve You and to follow in the footsteps of Your Son. Guide my steps, Father, and help me celebrate Your blessings today and every day. Amen.

WHEN YOUR COURAGE IS TESTED, TRUST GOD

Indeed, God is my salvation; I will trust Him and not be afraid.

ISAIAH 12:2 HCSB

God's instructions to mankind are contained in a book like no other: the Holy Bible. When we obey God's commandments and listen carefully to the conscience He has placed in our hearts, we are secure. But if we disobey our Creator, if we choose to ignore the teachings and the warnings of His Word, we do so at great peril.

If we believe in God, we should also trust in God. Yet sometimes, when we are besieged by fears and doubts, trusting God is hard indeed. Trusting God means entrusting Him with every aspect of our lives as we follow His commandments and pray for His guidance. When we experience the pains of life here on earth, we must accept His will and seek His healing touch. And at times, we must be willing to wait patiently for the Lord to reveal plans that only He can see.

The next time you find your courage tested to the limit, lean upon God's promises. Trust His Son. Remember that God is always near and that He is your protector and your deliverer. God can handle your troubles infinitely better than you can, so turn them over to Him. Remember that Lord rules both mountaintops and valleys—with limitless wisdom and love—now and forever.

Once God leads you to make a decision, don't draw back. Instead, trust His leading and believe He goes before you–because He does.

BILLY GRAHAM

Today, Lord, I will trust You and seek Your will for my life. You have a plan for me, Father. Let me discover it and live it, knowing that when I trust in You, I am eternally blessed. Amen.

98

THE WISDOM
OF MODERATION

Patience is better than power,
and controlling one's temper, than capturing a city.

PROVERBS 16:32 HCSB

Moderation and wisdom are traveling companions. If we are wise, we must learn to temper our appetites, our desires, and our impulses. When we do, we are blessed, in part, because God has created a world in which temperance is rewarded and intemperance is inevitably punished.

Would you like to improve your life and reduce your stress? Then harness your appetites and restrain your impulses. Moderation is difficult, of course; it is especially difficult in a prosperous society such as ours. But the rewards of moderation are numerous and long-lasting. Claim those rewards today. No one can force you to moderate your appetites. The decision to live temperately (and wisely) is yours and yours alone. And so are the consequences.

Virtue—even attempted virtue—brings light; indulgence brings fog.

C. S. LEWIS

Dear Lord, give me the wisdom to be moderate and self-disciplined. Let me strive to do Your will here on earth, and as I do, let me find contentment and balance. Let me be a disciplined person, today and every day. Amen.

99

YOU CAN'T PLEASE EVERYBODY, AND IT'S BETTER NOT TO TRY

Do you think I am trying to make people accept me?
No, God is the One I am trying to please. Am I trying to please people?
If I still wanted to please people, I would not be a servant of Christ.
GALATIANS 1:10 NCV

As you seek to discover God's purpose for your life, you will inevitably confront the expectations and demands of life here on earth. Perhaps the pressures of caring for your family or the stresses of building your career have placed a heavy weight upon your shoulders. Whatever your circumstances, remember this: your first responsibility is to trust God and to obey His commandments. Obedience to Him is determined, not by words, but by deeds. Talking about righteousness is easy; living righteously and responsibly is far more difficult, especially in today's temptation-filled world.

If you are burdened with a people-pleasing personality, it's now officially time to outgrow it. In other words, it's time to realize that you can't please all of the people all of the time, nor should you attempt to.

If pleasing people is your goal, you will be enslaved to them.
People can be harsh taskmasters when you give them this power over you.
SARAH YOUNG

Dear Lord, today I will focus, not on pleasing other people; I will focus on pleasing You. You have given me more blessings than I can count. Today and every day I will try to please You with my thoughts, my actions, and my prayers. Amen.

100

TAKE YOUR WORRIES TO GOD, AND LEAVE THEM THERE

Cast your burden on the LORD, and He shall sustain you;
He shall never permit the righteous to be moved.

PSALM 55:22 NKJV

Because we are fallible human beings struggling through the inevitable challenges of life here on earth, we worry. Even though we, as Christians, have been promised the gift of eternal life—even though we are blessed by God's love and protection—we find ourselves fretting over the inevitable frustrations of everyday life.

Where is the best place to take your worries? Take them to God. Take your concerns to Him; take your fears to Him; take your doubts to Him; take your weaknesses to Him; take your sorrows to Him . . . and leave them all there. Seek protection from the Creator and build your spiritual house upon the Rock that cannot be moved. Remind yourself that God still sits in His heaven and that you are His beloved child. Then, perhaps, you will worry less and trust Him a more. And that's as it should be because the Lord is trustworthy, and you are protected.

Knowing that God is faithful really helps me to not be captivated by worry.

JOSH MCDOWELL

Heavenly Father, You understand my worries and my fears. And You forgive me when I am weak. When my faith begins to wane, help me, Lord, to trust You more. Then, with Your holy Word on my lips and with the love of Your Son in my heart, let me live courageously, faithfully, prayerfully, and thankfully today and every day. Amen.

101

KEEP YOUR FOCUS ON GOD

Cast your burden upon the LORD and He will sustain you;
He will never allow the righteous to be shaken.

PSALM 55:22 NASB

On average, adults consume approximately five times more information each day than did their counterparts 50 years ago. In fact, a recent survey found that the typical American spends over 11 hours per day listening to, watching, reading, or interacting with some form of media. No wonder so many of us feel like anxious observers, watching helplessly as the world spins out of control.

Sometimes our anxieties and fears also have physiological origins. Too much caffeine, for example, can heighten anxious feelings. And sometimes medications can have unintended side-effects that can make us feel nervous. Exercise, diet, and sleep can also affect our emotions. Regular exercise can reduce stress; a sensible diet promotes good overall health; and common-sense sleep habits have numerous benefits that impact both mind and body.

So, if you're serious about dealing with anxiety and fear, you should monitor your media consumption, your medications, your sleep, and your diet. You should also determine the level of exercise that's right for you. But that's not the end of the story. If you're seeking permanent peace—God's peace—then you must learn to focus, not on the temporary challenges of everyday life but, instead, upon His never-ending love for you.

Preoccupy my thoughts with your praise beginning today..

JONI EARECKSON TADA

Dear Lord, I want to experience the peace that passes all understanding: Your peace. Give me the wisdom to trust Your promises and follow in the footsteps of Your Son today, tomorrow, and forever. Amen.

HELP IS ALWAYS AVAILABLE

The wise are glad to be instructed.

PROVERBS 10:8 NLT

It's a truism: advice is cheap. And sometimes advice is worth exactly what you pay for it: zero. Some people simply don't possess the insight or the wisdom to provide you with the counsel you need to deal with anxiety and fear. That's why it's so important to find friends, mentors, counselors, and medical professionals whose advice you can trust. And then, once you've received their advice, you should be wise enough to take it.

Are you actively seeking sound, reliable, informed advice about your mental, physical, and spiritual health? If so, you're actively building a better life for yourself and your loved ones. And, just as importantly, are you spending time with wise men and women whose advice you trust and whose character admire? If you genuinely seek to walk with God, you will walk with wise people, and you will listen carefully to their words

Do not be inaccessible. None is so perfect that
he does not need at times the advice of others.

BALTASAR GRACIÁN

Heavenly Father, give me the courage to share Your wisdom with others. And when I receive godly advice from friends, family members, and knowledgeable professionals, give me the wisdom to accept their guidance, today and every day. Amen.

103

MAKE YOUR LIFE'S JOURNEY WITH GOD

*For it is God who is working in you, enabling you
both to desire and to work out His good purpose.*

PHILIPPIANS 2:13 HCSB

Your life is a journey, and every step of the way, God is with you. Sometimes God's plans seem obvious. But other times, you may find yourself struggling with lots of questions and very few answers. When you are unsure of your next step—or when you're fretting about an uncertain future that only the Lord can see—pray about it. Pray for patience; pray for guidance; pray for courage; and pray for the peace of mind that only God can give.

The Lord has a plan for your life. The decision to seek His plan and to follow it is yours and yours alone. The consequences of that decision have implications that are both profound and eternal, so choose carefully.

*When the dream of our heart is one that God has planted there,
a strange happiness flows into us. At that moment, all of the spiritual
resources of the universe are released to help us. Our praying
is then at one with the will of God and becomes a channel
for the Creator's purposes for us and our world.*

CATHERINE MARSHALL

Heavenly Father, You created me for a reason. Give me the wisdom to follow Your direction for my life's journey. Let me do Your work here on earth by seeking Your will and living it, knowing that when I trust in You, Father, I am eternally blessed. Amen.

104

WHEN YOU ASK FOR GOD'S HELP, HE WILL ANSWER YOU

Ask, and it will be given to you; seek, and you will find;
knock, and it will be opened to you. For everyone who asks receives,
and he who seeks finds, and to him who knocks it will be opened.

MATTHEW 7:7–8 NASB

If you're dealing with rollercoaster emotions, you need God's help. And if you ask Him, He will most certainly provide the help you need. So how often do you ask the Lord for His help and His wisdom? Occasionally? Intermittently? Whenever you experience a crisis? Hopefully not. Hopefully, you've acquired the habit of asking for God's assistance early and often. And hopefully, you have learned to seek His guidance in every aspect of your life.

Jesus made it clear to His disciples: they should ask for God's help. So should you. Heartfelt prayer produces powerful changes in you and in your world. God can do great things through you if you have the courage to ask Him (and the determination to keep asking Him). But don't expect Him to do all the work. When you do your part, He will do His part—and when He does, you can expect miracles to happen.

Timely Tip: If you're experiencing anxieties or fears, ask for God's help. And remember that if you have questions, God has answers. So when in doubt, pray. And keep praying until the answers arrive.

Dear Lord, today and every day, I will ask You for the things I need. In every situation and in every circumstance, I will come to you in prayer. And I will trust the answers that you give. Amen.

105

ADOPT THE RIGHT ATTITUDE

A merry heart makes a cheerful countenance.

PROVERBS 15:13 NKJV

As a Christian, you have every reason on earth—and in heaven—to have a positive attitude. After all, God is in charge; He loves you; and He's prepared a place for you to live eternally with Him. These promises should give you comfort, but sometimes you may find yourself plagued by negativity or pessimism.

When life seems to be spiraling out of control, you can improve your attitude by focusing more intently on the Lord's blessings, which are eternal, and less on your challenges, which are not. A positive attitude is its own blessing. It is through gratitude, not grumpiness, that you will claim the best that life has to offer.

Those who are the happiest are not necessarily those for whom life has been the easiest. Emotional stability is an attitude.

JAMES DOBSON

It's your choice: you can either count your blessings or recount your disappointments.

JIM GALLERY

Dear Lord, today and every day give me a happy heart and a positive attitude. Make me a person whose thoughts are Christlike and whose hopes are worthy of the One who has given me so much. Amen.

106

AVOID DEAD-END ARGUMENTS

Avoiding a fight is a mark of honor; only fools insist on quarreling.

PROVERBS 20:3 NLT

Time and again, God's Word warns us against angry outbursts and needless arguments. Arguments are seldom won but often lost, so when we acquire the unfortunate habit of habitual bickering, we do harm to our friends, to our families, to our coworkers, and to ourselves. When we engage in petty squabbles, our losses usually outpace our gains.

If you're dealing with a difficult person, you may be tempted to take the bait and argue over matters great and small. If you find yourself in that predicament, take a deep breath, say a silent prayer, and calm yourself down. Arguments are a monumental waste of time and energy. And since you're unlikely to win the argument anyway, there's no rational reason to participate.

An argument seldom convinces anyone contrary to his inclinations.

THOMAS FULLER

Timely Tip: Arguments usually cause more problems than they solve. And if you're dealing with a highly emotional person, you probably won't win the argument anyway. So don't be afraid to leave the scene of an argument rather than engage in a debate that cannot be won. Dead-end arguments tend to increase stress and heighten anxiety, so you're better off avoiding them.

Heavenly Father, when I am tempted to be argumentative, keep me calm. When I am gripped by irrational anger, give me serenity. Let me show my thankfulness to You by offering forgiveness to others. And when I do, may others see Your love reflected through my words and my deeds. Amen.

107

WHEN YOU TRUST THE LORD, HE WILL DIRECT YOUR PATH

The LORD says, "I will guide you along the best pathway for your life. I will advise you and watch over you."

PSALM 32:8 NLT

When our dreams come true and our plans prove successful, we find it easy to thank our Creator and easy to trust His divine providence. But in times of sorrow or hardship, we may find ourselves questioning God's plans for our lives.

On occasion, you will confront circumstances that trouble you to the very core of your soul. It is during these difficult days that you must find the wisdom and the courage to trust your heavenly Father despite your circumstances.

Are you a person who seeks God's blessings for yourself and your family? Then trust Him. Trust Him with your relationships. Trust Him with your priorities. Follow His commandments and pray for His guidance. Trust Your heavenly Father day by day and moment by moment—in good times and in trying times. Then, wait patiently for God's revelations. And prepare yourself for the abundance and peace that will most certainly be yours when you do.

Trust God's Word and His power more than you trust your own feelings and experiences. Remember, your Rock is Christ, and it is the sea that ebbs and flows with the tides, not Him.

LETTIE COWMAN

Dear Lord, You have promised that I will be safe with You in heaven. And you have promised that I am safe with You here on earth. Today, I will trust in Your promises, and I will be a confident, obedient, purposeful servant to Your Son. Amen.

108

MANAGE TIME WISELY

Teach us how short our lives really are so that we may be wise.
PSALM 90:12 NCV

Time is a nonrenewable gift from above. How will you use it? You know from experience that you should invest some time each day in yourself, but finding time to do so is easier said than done. As a busy citizen of the twenty-first century, you may have difficulty investing large blocks of time in much-needed thought and self-reflection. If so, it may be time to reorder your priorities.

If you don't prioritize your day, other people will. Before you know it, you'll be taking on lots of new commitments, doing many things but doing few things well. God, on the other hand, encourages you to slow down, to quiet yourself, and to spend time with Him. And you can be sure that God's way is best.

How will you organize your life? Will you carve out quiet moments with the Creator? And while you're at it, will you focus your energies and your resources on only the most important tasks on your to-do list? Will you summon the strength to say no when it's appropriate, or will you max out your schedule, leaving much of your most important work undone? Today, slow yourself down, commit more time to God, and spend less time on low-priority tasks. When you do, you'll be amazed at how the Father can revolutionize your life.

Timely Tip: Feeling overwhelmed? Perhaps you're not doing a very good job of setting priorities—or perhaps you're allowing other people to set your priorities for you. In either case, perhaps it's time for a change.

Heavenly Father, every day presents me with the opportunity to do Your will and to honor Your Son. Today, give me the wisdom to know what needs to be done and the courage to do it. Amen.

109

BE JOYFUL

I have told you these things so that you can have the same joy
I have and so that your joy will be the fullest possible joy.

JOHN 15:11 NCV

Oswald Chambers correctly observed, "Joy is the great note all throughout the Bible." E. Stanley Jones echoed that thought when he wrote "Christ and joy go together." But even the most dedicated believers can, on occasion, forget to celebrate each day for what it is: a priceless gift from God.

God's plan for you and your family includes heaping helpings of abundance and joy. Claim them. And remember that Christ offers you and your family priceless gifts: His abundance, His peace, and His joy. Accept those gifts and share them freely, just as Christ has freely shared Himself with you. And as you're sharing His good news, be sure to share these good ideas too:

The greatest honor you can give Almighty God is to live gladly
and joyfully because of the knowledge of His love.

JULIANA OF NORWICH

Every day we live is a priceless gift of God, loaded with possibilities
to learn something new, to gain fresh insights.

DALE EVANS ROGERS

Joy is the direct result of having God's perspective on our daily lives and the
effect of loving our Lord enough to obey His commands and trust His promises.

BILL BRIGHT

Heavenly Father, make me a joyful believer. Today and every day, I have so many reasons to celebrate life. Let me experience Your joy and share it with family, with friends, and with the world. Amen.

110

GET INVOLVED
IN YOUR CHURCH

*Be on guard for yourselves and for all the flock that the
Holy Spirit has appointed you to as overseers, to shepherd
the church of God, which He purchased with His own blood..*

ACTS 20:28 HCSB

The Bible teaches that we should worship God in our hearts and in our churches. We have clear instructions to "feed the church of God" and to worship our Creator in the presence of fellow believers (Acts 20:28 KJV).

Are you an active member of your own fellowship? Are you a builder of bridges inside the four walls of your church and outside it? Do you contribute to God's glory by contributing your time and your talents to a close-knit band of believers? Hopefully so. The fellowship of believers is intended to be a powerful tool for spreading God's good news and uplifting His children. And God intends for you to be a fully contributing member of that fellowship. Your intentions should be the same.

Timely Tip: What you put into church determines what you get out of it. Your attitude towards worship is vitally important to your spiritual and emotional health, so attend church regularly and celebrate accordingly.

Heavenly Father, I thank You for Your church. Today and every day, help me feed Your flock by building my faith community so that others too, might experience Your perfect love and Your eternal grace. Amen.

111

GOD WANTS YOU
TO CELEBRATE LIFE

This is the day the LORD has made; let us rejoice and be glad in it.
PSALM 118:24 HCSB

The familiar words of Psalm 118:24 promises us that every day is a gift from God. Yet on some days, we don't feel much like celebrating. When the obligations of everyday living seem to overwhelm us, we may find ourselves frustrated by the demands of the present and worried by the uncertainty of the future.

How will you invest this day? Will you treat your time as a commodity too precious to be squandered? Will you carve out time during the day to serve God by serving His children? Will you celebrate God's gifts and obey His commandments? And will you share words of encouragement with the people who cross your path? The answers to these questions will determine, to a surprising extent, the quality of your day and the quality of your life.

So wherever you find yourself today, take time to celebrate and give thanks for another priceless gift from the Father. The present moment is precious. Treat it that way.

Today is mine. Tomorrow is none of my business.
If I peer anxiously into the fog of the future, I will strain my
spiritual eyes so that I will not see clearly what is required of me now.
ELISABETH ELLIOT

Heavenly Father, today, I will celebrate the precious gift of life. I will rejoice in tasks you have given me, and I will celebrate the lives of my friends and family. Thank You, Lord, for Your love. Let me treasure Your blessings and share them this day and forever. Amen.

112

BE OPTIMISTIC!

We have this hope as an anchor for the soul, sure and strong.
It enters behind the curtain in the Most Holy Place in heaven.

HEBREWS 6:19 NCV

Are you a passionate Christian who expects God to do big things in your life and in the lives of those around you? If you're a thinking Christian, you have every reason to be confident about your future here on earth and your eternal future in heaven. As English clergyman William Ralph Inge observed, "No Christian should be a pessimist, for Christianity is a system of radical optimism." Inge's observation is true, of course, but sometimes, you may find yourself caught up in the inevitable complications of everyday living. When you find yourself fretting about the ups and downs of life here on earth, it's time to slow down, collect yourself, refocus your thoughts, and count your blessings.

God has made promises to you, and He will keep every one. So you have every reason to be an optimist and no legitimate reason to ever abandon hope.

Today, trust your hopes, not your fears. And while you're at it, take time to celebrate God's blessings. His gifts are too numerous to calculate and too glorious to imagine. But it never hurts to try.

All things work together for good. Fret not, nor fear!

LETTIE COWMAN

Heavenly Father, You love me, You care for me, and You protect me. You have given me the priceless gift of eternal life through the sacrifice that Christ made on the cross at Calvary. Because of You, Father, and because of Your Son, I can live each day with celebration in my heart and praise on my lips. Let me always be thankful, and let me share the good news of Jesus as I turn my thoughts to You this day and every day. Amen.

113

PRAY ABOUT YOUR ANXIETIES

*Therefore I say to you, whatever things you ask when you pray,
believe that you receive them, and you will have them.*

MARK 11:24 NKJV

Want an easy-to-use, highly reliable, readily available antidote to anxiety and stress? Well, here it is: it's called prayer.

Is prayer an integral part of your daily life, or is it a hit-or-miss habit? Do you "pray without ceasing," or is your prayer life an afterthought? Do you regularly pray in the solitude of the early morning darkness, or do you lower your head only when others are watching? The answer to these questions will determine both the direction of your day and the way that you deal with the inevitable stressors of everyday life.

So instead of trying to do everything on your own, form the habit of asking God for His help. Begin your prayers early in the morning and continue them throughout the day. And remember this: God does answer your prayers, but He's not likely to answer those prayers until you've prayed them.

Timely Tip: If you need something, don't ask for God's help in general terms. Ask specifically for the things you need. The Lord already knows what you need, but He wants you to have the experience of asking Him.

Dear Lord, when I pray, let me feel Your presence. When I worship You, let me feel Your love. In the quiet moments of the day, I will open my heart to You, Almighty God. And I know that You are with me always and that You will always hear my prayers. Amen.

114

LET GOD
BE YOUR GUIDE

Do not be anxious about anything,
but in every situation, by prayer and petition,
with thanksgiving, present your requests to God.

PHILIPPIANS 4:6 NIV

The Bible promises that God will guide you if you let Him. Your job is to let Him. But sometimes you will be tempted to do otherwise. Sometimes you'll be tempted to go along with the crowd, even when the crowd is heading in the wrong direction. Other times, you'll be tempted to do things your way, not God's way. When you feel those temptations, resist them. Instead, ask the Lord to lead you, to protect you, and to correct you. Then trust the answers He gives.

God stands at the door and waits. When you knock, He opens. When you ask, He answers. Your task, of course, to make God a full partner in every aspect of your life—and to seek His guidance prayerfully, confidently, and often.

God will help us become the people
we are meant to be, if only we will ask Him.

HANNAH WHITALL SMITH

Dear Lord, You created me, and You have called me to do Your work here on earth. Today, I choose to seek Your will and to live it, knowing that when I trust in You, I am eternally blessed. Amen.

WHOM WILL YOU TRY TO PLEASE?

Obviously, I'm not trying to win the approval of people, but of God.
If pleasing people were my goal, I would not be Christ's servant.
GALATIANS 1:10 NLT

The nineteenth-century reformer Margaret Fuller warned, "Beware of over-great pleasure in being popular or even beloved." And her words still ring true. Few things in life are more futile than trying to please other people for the wrong reasons. When we place God in a position of secondary importance, we do ourselves great harm. But when we imitate Jesus and place the Lord in His rightful place—at the center of our lives—then we claim spiritual treasures that will endure forever.

Who will you try to please today: God or man? Your primary obligation is not to please imperfect men and women. Your obligation is to strive diligently to meet the expectations of an all-knowing and perfect God. Trust Him always. Love Him always. Praise Him always. And seek to please Him. Always.

Popularity is far more dangerous for the Christian than persecution.
BILLY GRAHAM

The major problem with letting others define you is that it borders on idolatry.
Your concern to please others dampens your desire to please your Creator.
SARAH YOUNG

Heavenly Father, today I will honor You with my thoughts, my actions, and my prayers. I will seek to please You, and I will strive to serve You. Because I have been so richly blessed, I will worship You, Father, with thanksgiving in my heart and praise on my lips, this day and forever. Amen.

116

IT PAYS TO PERSEVERE

But endurance must do its complete work,
so that you may be mature and complete, lacking nothing.
JAMES 1:4 HCSB

When you're experiencing anxious thoughts or unfounded fears, you may be tempted to give in to negativity and doubt. Resist the temptation. When you are tested, don't quit at the first sign of trouble. Instead, call upon God. He can give you the strength to persevere, and that's exactly what you should ask Him to do.

The ideas below are intended to remind you that perseverance pays. And more often than not, it pays very, very well.

Perseverance is more than endurance. It is endurance combined with absolute assurance and certainty that what we are looking for is going to happen.
OSWALD CHAMBERS

You may have to fight a battle more than once to win it.
MARGARET THATCHER

Character consists of what you do on the third and fourth tries.
JAMES MICHENER

Heavenly Father, Your Word teaches me that life is not a sprint, but a marathon. When the pace of my life becomes frantic, slow me down and give me perspective. Keep me steady and sure. When I become weary, let me persevere so that, in Your time, I might finish my work here on earth, and that You might then say, "Well done my good and faithful servant." Amen.

117

YOU CAN HAVE ABUNDANT LIFE, ETERNAL LIFE

My cup runs over. Surely goodness and mercy shall follow me all the days of my life; and I will dwell in the house of the LORD forever.

PSALM 23:5–6 NKJV

God's Word is clear: Christ came in order that we might have life that is both abundant *and* eternal. Eternal life is priceless possession of all who invite Christ into their hearts, but God's abundance is optional: He does not force it upon us.

Do you sincerely seek the riches that our Savior offers to those who give themselves to Him? Then follow Him completely and obey Him without reservation. When you do, you will receive the love and the abundance that He has promised. Seek first the salvation that is available through a personal relationship with Jesus Christ, and then claim His joy, His peace, and His abundance.

Jesus intended for us to be overwhelmed by the blessings of regular days. He said it was the reason he had come: "I am come that they might have life, and that they might have it more abundantly."

GLORIA GAITHER

Good Shepherd, thank You for the abundant life that is mine through Christ Jesus. Guide me according to Your will, and help me to be a worthy servant in all that I say and do. Give me courage, Lord, to claim the rewards You have promised, and when I do, let the glory be Yours. Amen.

118

SETBACKS ARE NOT PERMANENT

And my God shall supply all your need
according to His riches in glory by Christ Jesus.
PHILIPPIANS 4:19 NKJV

All of us experience adversity, disappointments, and hardship. Sometimes we bring these hardships upon ourselves, and sometimes we are victimized by circumstances that we cannot control and cannot fully understand. As human beings with limited insight, we can never completely comprehend the will of our Father in heaven. But as believers in a benevolent God, we must always trust His providence.

Have you been touched by personal tragedy that you did not deserve and cannot understand? If so, it's time to make peace with life. It's time to forgive others, and, if necessary, to forgive yourself. It's time to accept the unchangeable past, to embrace the priceless present, and to have faith in the promise of tomorrow. It's time to trust God completely. And it's time to reclaim the peace—His peace—that can and should be yours.

Measure the size of the obstacles against the size of God.
BETH MOORE

Dear Lord, I will seek Your plan for my life. Even when I don't understand why things happen, I will trust You. Even when I am uncertain of my next step, I will trust You. There are many things that I cannot do, Lord, and there are many things that I cannot understand. But one thing I can do is to trust You always. And I will. Amen.

119

BE A PRACTICAL CHRISTIAN

Therefore, with your minds ready for action,
be serious and set your hope completely on the grace
to be brought to you at the revelation of Jesus Christ.

1 PETER 1:13 HCSB

As Christians, we must do our best to ensure that our actions are accurate reflections of our beliefs. Our theology must be demonstrated, not only by our words but, more importantly, by our actions. In short, we should be practical believers, quick to act whenever we see an opportunity to serve God.

The Christian faith offers powerful solutions to the stressors of everyday life. Are you a practical Christian who is willing to dig in and do what needs to be done when it needs to be done? If so, congratulations: God acknowledges your service and blesses it. But if you find yourself more interested in the fine points of theology than in the needs of your neighbors, it's time to rearrange your priorities. God needs believers who are willing to roll up their sleeves and go to work for Him. Count yourself among that number. Theology is a good thing unless it interferes with God's work. And it's up to you to make certain that your theology doesn't.

Christianity is not a spectator sport, it is something
in which we become totally involved.

BILLY GRAHAM

Heavenly Father, I believe in You, and I believe in Your Word. Help me to live in such a way that my actions validate my beliefs—and let the glory be Yours forever. Amen.

120

RELY ON GOD WHEN THE JOURNEY IS DIFFICULT

For whatever is born of God overcomes the world.
And this is the victory that has overcome the world—our faith.

1 JOHN 5:4 NKJV

All of us face times of adversity. On occasion, we all must endure the disappointments and tragedies that befall believers and nonbelievers alike. And sometimes we experience setbacks that leave us wondering if we'll ever recover. But even when we cannot see solutions to our problems, God can. His plans for us extend throughout all eternity, and He knows that our challenges are temporary, but His love endures forever.

The reassuring words of 1 John 5:4 remind us that when we accept God's grace, we overcome the passing hardships of this world by relying upon His strength, His love, and His promise of eternal life.

Crisis brings us face to face with our inadequacy and our inadequacy
in turn leads us to the inexhaustible sufficiency of God.

CATHERINE MARSHALL

Dear Heavenly Father, when I am troubled, You heal me. When I am afraid, You protect me. When I am discouraged, You lift me up. In times of adversity, let me trust Your plan and Your will for my life. And whatever my circumstances, Lord, let me always give the thanks and the glory to You. Amen.

121

SERVE OTHERS WITH A LOVING HEART AND WILLING HANDS

Whoever wants to become great among you must be your servant,
and whoever wants to be first among you must be your slave;
just as the Son of Man did not come to be served, but to serve,
and to give His life—a ransom for many.

MATTHEW 20:26–28 HCSB

Jesus came to earth as a servant of man and the Savior of mankind. One way that we can demonstrate our love for the Savior is by obeying His commandment to serve one another.

Whom will you choose to serve today? Will you be a woman who cheerfully meets the needs of family and friends? And will you meet those needs with love in your heart and encouragement on your lips? As you plan for the day ahead, remember that the needs are great and the workers are few. And remember that God is doing His very best to enlist able-bodied believers—like you.

God wants us to serve Him with a willing spirit,
one that would choose no other way.

BETH MOORE

Dear Lord, create in me a servant's heart. And let me be a person who follows in the footsteps of Your Son Jesus who taught us by example that to be great in Your eyes, Lord, is to serve others humbly, faithfully, and lovingly. Amen.

122

THE CURE FOR PANIC IS GOD

Anxiety in the heart of man causes depression,
but a good word makes it glad.

PROVERBS 12:25 NKJV

We are members of an anxious society, a society in which the changes we face threaten to outpace our abilities to make adjustments. No wonder we sometimes find ourselves beset by feelings of anxiety and panic.

At times, our anxieties may stem from physical causes. In such cases, modern medicine offers solutions for those who suffer. But oftentimes, our fears and anxieties have psychological or spiritual origins. In such cases, the cure can be found, not at the local pharmacy, but in the unerring promises found in God's holy Word.

If you're experiencing full-blown panic attacks, see your doctor. But if you're simply living under a cloud of pessimism and doubt, consult a higher authority: your heavenly Father. He is always available, and He wants to hear from you now.

He treats us as sons, and all he asks in return is that we shall
treat Him as a Father whom we can trust without anxiety.
We must take the son's place of dependence and trust, and we
must let Him keep the father's place of care and responsibility.

HANNAH WHITALL SMITH

Dear Lord, when I am tempted to lose faith in the future, touch my heart with Your enduring love. And keep me mindful, Lord, that nothing, absolutely nothing, will happen this day that You and I cannot handle together. Amen.

123

IF YOU ASK YOU WILL RECEIVE

Ask, and it will be given to you; seek, and you will find;
knock, and it will be opened to you. For everyone who asks receives,
and he who seeks finds, and to him who knocks it will be opened.

MATTHEW 7:7-8 NKJV

Are you a person who asks God for guidance and strength? If so, then you're continually inviting your Creator to reveal Himself in a variety of ways. As a follower of Christ, you must do no less.

Jesus made it clear to His disciples: they should petition God to meet their needs. So should we. Prayer produces powerful changes in us and in our world. When we lift our hearts to God, we open ourselves to a never-ending source of divine wisdom and infinite love.

Whatever your need, no matter how great or small, pray about it and never lose hope. God is not just near; He is here, and He's perfectly capable of answering your prayers. Now it's up to you to ask.

Timely Tip: If you want more from life, ask more from God. And if you're beset by troubling anxieties or irrational fears, talk to God about it. If you're seeking a worthy goal, ask for His help—and keep asking—until He answers your prayers.

Dear Lord, today I will ask You for the things I need. In every situation, I will come to you in prayer. You know what I want, Lord, and more importantly, You know what I need. Yet even though I know that You know, I still won't be too timid—or too busy—to ask. Amen.

124

FACE YOUR FEARS AND TRUST GOD

Don't be afraid, because I am your God. I will make you strong and will help you; I will support you with my right hand that saves you.

ISAIAH 41:10 NCV

Are you feeling anxious or fearful? If so, trust God to handle those problems that are simply too big for you to solve. Entrust the future—your future—to God. The two of you, working together, can accomplish great things for His kingdom.

The next time you find yourself in a fear-provoking situation, consider these words of wisdom as permission to trust God and face your fears.

God shields us from most of the things we fear, but when He chooses not to shield us, He unfailingly allots grace in the measure needed.

ELISABETH ELLIOT

A perfect faith would lift us absolutely above fear.

GEORGE MACDONALD

It is good to remind ourselves that the will of God comes from the heart of God and that we need not be afraid.

WARREN WIERSBE

Dear Lord, I ask for the courage to face my fears and the wisdom to trust You in every situation. I will trust You, Father, to guide me and protect me, now and forever. And today, I pray for the strength to rise above my irrational fears and to do what needs to be done. Amen.

125

PRACTICE WHAT YOU PREACH

*If the way you live isn't consistent
with what you believe, then it's wrong.*

ROMANS 14:23 MSG

In describing our beliefs, our actions are far better descriptors than our words. Yet far too many of us spend more energy talking about our beliefs than living by them—with predictably poor results.

As believers, we must beware: our actions should always give credence to the changes that Christ can make in the lives of those who walk with Him.

Your beliefs shape your values, and your values shape your life. Is your life a clearly crafted picture book of your creed? Are your actions always consistent with your beliefs? Are you willing to practice the philosophies that you preach? Hopefully so; otherwise, you'll be tormented by inconsistencies between your beliefs and your behaviors.

Timely Tip: When you stand up for your beliefs—and when you follow your conscience no matter the consequences—you'll feel better about yourself, you'll feel better about your life, and you'll feel better about your current circumstances.

Dear Lord, it is so much easier to speak of the righteous life than it is to live it. Let me live righteously, and let my actions be consistent with my beliefs. Let every step that I take reflect Your truth, and let me live a life that is worthy of Your Son. Amen.

126

BE NOURISHED BY THE WORD

*You will be a good servant of Christ Jesus, nourished by the words
of the faith and of the good teaching that you have followed.*

1 Timothy 4:6 HCSB

Do you read your Bible a lot . . . or not? The answer to this simple question
will determine, to a surprising extent, the quality of your life and the direction
of your faith.

As you establish priorities for life, you must decide whether God's Word
will be bright spotlight that guides your path every day or a tiny nightlight that
occasionally flickers in the dark. The decision to study the Bible—or not—is
yours and yours alone. But make no mistake: how you choose to use your Bible
will have a profound impact on you and your loved ones.

The Bible is the ultimate guide for life; make it your guidebook as well.
When you do, you can be comforted in the knowledge that your steps are guided
by a source of wisdom and truth that never fails.

*Gather the riches of God's promises. Nobody can take away from
you those texts from the Bible which you have learned by heart.*

Corrie ten Boom

Heavenly Father, You have given me instructions for life here on earth and for
life eternal. I will use the Bible as my guide. I will study it and meditate upon it
as I trust You, Lord, to speak to me through Your holy Word. Amen.

127

RID YOURSELF OF BITTERNESS

Don't insist on getting even; that's not for you to do.
"I'll do the judging," says God. "I'll take care of it."
ROMANS 12:19 MSG

Bitterness is a spiritual sickness. It will consume your soul; it is dangerous to your emotional health. It can destroy you if you let it . . . so don't let it! If you are caught up in intense feelings of anger or resentment, you know all too well the destructive power of these emotions. How can you rid yourself of these feelings? First, you must prayerfully ask God to cleanse your heart. Then, you must learn to catch yourself whenever thoughts of bitterness or hatred begin to attack you. Your challenge is this: you must learn to resist negative thoughts before they hijack your emotions.

Matthew 7:1 teaches us that if we judge our brothers and sisters, we, too, will be subject to judgment. Let us refrain, then, from judging our neighbors. Instead, let us forgive them and love them, while leaving their judgment to a far more capable authority: the One who sits on His throne in heaven.

Bitterness sentences you to relive the hurt over and over.
LEE STROBEL

Dear Lord, free me from the poison of bitterness and the futility of blame. Let me turn away from destructive emotions so that I may know the perfect peace and spiritual abundance that can be mine through Your Son, and when I discover His peace, let me share it with praise on my lips and love in my heart. Amen.

128

ARE YOU TOO BUSY?

Careful planning puts you ahead in the long run;
hurry and scurry puts you further behind.

Proverbs 21:5 MSG

Are you one of those people who is simply too busy for your own good? Has the hectic pace of life robbed you of the peace that might otherwise be yours through Jesus Christ? If so, you're doing a disservice to yourself and your family.

Through His Son Jesus, God offers you a peace that passes human understanding, but He won't force His peace upon you. In order to experience it, you must slow down long enough to sense His presence and His love.

Today, as a gift to yourself, to your family, and to the world, be still and claim the inner peace that is your spiritual birthright—the peace of Jesus Christ. It is offered freely; it has been paid for in full; it is yours for the asking. So ask. And then share.

Timely Tip: Do first things first, focus on high-priority tasks, and don't beat yourself up if you leave low-priority tasks undone. And remember this: your highest priority should be your relationship with God and His Son.

Dear Lord, when the quickening pace of life leaves me with little time for worship or for praise, help me to reorder my priorities, and let me turn to Jesus for the peace that only He can give. Amen.

129

DON'T BEND THE TRUTH

*And put on the new self, which in the likeness of God
has been created in righteousness and holiness of the truth.
Therefore, laying aside falsehood, speak truth each one of you,
with his neighbor, for we are members of one another.*

EPHESIANS 4:24–25 NASB

We live in a world that presents us with countless temptations to wander far from God's path. These temptations have the potential to destroy us, in part, because they cause us to be dishonest with ourselves and with others. Dishonesty is a habit. Once we start bending the truth, we're likely to keep bending it. A far better strategy, of course, is to acquire the habit of being completely forthright with God, with other people, and with ourselves.

Honesty is also a habit—a habit that pays powerful dividends for those who place character above convenience. So the next time you're tempted to bend the truth—or to break it—ask yourself this simple question: What does God want me to do? Then listen carefully to your conscience. When you do, your actions will be honorable, your choices will be pleasing to the Lord, and your character will take care of itself.

*The commandment of absolute truthfulness is
only another name for the fullness of discipleship.*

DIETRICH BONHOEFFER

Dear Lord, help me see the truth, help me speak the truth, and help me live the truth—today and every day of my life. Amen.

130

BLAMING OTHERS IS FUTILE

Walking down the street, Jesus saw a man blind from birth.
His disciples asked, "Rabbi, who sinned: this man or his parents,
causing him to be born blind?" Jesus said, "You're asking the wrong
question. You're looking for someone to blame. There is no
such cause-effect here. Look instead for what God can do."

JOHN 9:1–3 MSG

To blame others for our own problems is the height of futility. Yet blaming others is a favorite human pastime. Why? Because blaming is much easier than fixing, and criticizing *others* is so much easier than improving *ourselves*. So instead of solving our problems legitimately (by doing the work required to solve them) we are inclined to fret, to blame, and to criticize, while doing precious little else. When we do, our problems, quite predictably, remain unsolved.

Have you acquired the bad habit of blaming others for problems that you could or should solve yourself? If so, you are not only disobeying God's Word, you are also wasting your own precious time. So instead of looking for someone to blame, look for something to fix, and then get busy fixing it. And as you consider your own situation, remember this: God has a way of helping those who help themselves, but He doesn't spend much time helping those who don't.

Timely Tip: Blame focuses your mind on the negative aspects of your life. So learn to count your blessings, not your misfortunes. And while you're at it, remember that you can't ever win the blame game, so don't play.

Dear Lord, when I make a mistake, I want to admit it. Help me not blame others for the mistakes that I make. And when I make a mistake, help me to learn from it. Amen.

131

WHAT IS YOUR RELATIONSHIP WITH THE CREATOR?

I am always praising you; all day long I honor you.
PSALM 71:8 NCV

As you think about the nature of your relationship with God, remember this: you will *always* have some type of relationship with Him—it is inevitable that your life *must* be lived in relationship to God. The question is not if you will have a relationship with Him; the burning question is whether or not that relationship will be one that seeks to honor Him.

Are you willing to place God first in your life? And are you willing to welcome God's Son into your heart? Unless you can honestly answer these questions with a resounding yes, then your relationship with God isn't what it could be or should be. Thankfully, God is always available, He's always ready to forgive, and He's waiting to hear from you now. The rest, of course, is up to you.

Christianity is not a religion. It is a relationship.
EDWIN LOUIS COLE

Dear Lord. I praise You from the depths of my heart, and I give thanks for Your goodness, for Your mercy, and for Your Son. Let me honor You every day of my life through my words and my deeds. Let me honor You, Father, with all that I have and all that I am. Amen.

132

WHEN YOUR FAITH IS TESTED, TRUST GOD

God is our protection and our strength. He always helps in times of trouble.
PSALM 46:1 NCV

All of us must endure difficult circumstances, those tough times when our faith is tested and our strength is stretched to the limit. We find ourselves in situations that we didn't ask for and probably don't deserve. During these difficult days, we try our best to "hold up under the circumstances." But God promises that He has a better plan. He intends for us to rise above our circumstances, and He's promised to help us do it.

Are you dealing with a difficult situation or a tough problem? Do you struggle with occasional periods of discouragement and doubt? Are you worried, weary, or downcast? If so, don't face tough times alone. Face them with God as your partner, your protector, and your guide. Talk to Him often, ask for His guidance, and listen carefully for His response. When you do, He will give you the strength meet any challenge, the courage to face any problem, and the patience to endure—and to eventually rise above—any circumstance.

When we choose the pathway of worship and giving thanks, especially in the midst of difficult circumstances, there is a fragrance, a radiance, that issues forth out of our lives to bless the Lord and others.
NANCY LEIGH DEMOSS

Heavenly Father, whatever my circumstances, I will trust You. In good times and in difficult times, I will trust You and praise You, knowing that You understand the wisdom of Your perfect plan. Today is the day that You have made. I will rejoice and be glad in it. Amen.

133

MIRACLES HAPPEN
EVERY DAY

You are the God who works wonders;
You revealed Your strength among the peoples.

PSALM 77:14 HCSB

God's miracles are not limited to special occasions, nor are they witnessed by a select few. God is crafting His wonders all around us: the miracle of the birth of a new baby; the miracle of a world renewing itself with every sunrise; the miracle of lives transformed by God's love and grace. Each day, God's handiwork is evident for all to see and experience.

Today, seize the opportunity to inspect God's hand at work. His miracles come in a variety of shapes and sizes, so keep your eyes and your heart open. Be watchful, and you'll soon be amazed.

Beware in your prayers, above everything else, of limiting God,
not only by unbelief, but by fancying that you know
what He can do. Expect unexpected things.

ANDREW MURRAY

God's specialty is raising dead things to life and making impossible
things possible. You don't have the need that exceeds His power.

BETH MOORE

Heavenly Father, nothing is impossible for You. Today and every day, keep me always mindful of Your strength and Your love. And when I encounter a situation that is too big for me, let me never be afraid to pray for a miracle. Amen.

134

WHEN YOU WALK WITH JESUS, YOU WILL NEVER WALK IN DARKNESS

Then Jesus spoke to them again: "I am the light of the world. Anyone who follows Me will never walk in the darkness, but will have the light of life."

JOHN 8:12 HCSB

Jesus made a promise to His disciples and to you. He promised that if you follow Him, you will never walk in darkness. But following in the footsteps of God's only begotten Son is not always easy. When Christ instructed His disciples to take up their cross and follow Him. His disciples knew that prisoners were often forced to carry their own crosses to the location where they would be put to death. So the message was clear: in order to follow Him, the disciples must deny themselves and, instead, trust Him completely. Nothing has changed since then.

If we are to be disciples of Christ, we must put Him first in our thoughts and our lives. Jesus never comes "next." He is always first. The paradox, of course, is that only by sacrificing ourselves to Him do we gain salvation for ourselves.

Do you sincerely want to follow in Christ's footsteps as His disciples did? Then pick up your cross today, tomorrow, and every day that you live. When you do, He will bless you today, tomorrow, and forever.

A disciple is a follower of Christ. That means you take on His priorities as your own. His agenda becomes your agenda. His mission becomes your mission.

CHARLES STANLEY

Heavenly Father, today, I will strive to follow in the footsteps of Your Son. I offer my life to You, Lord, so that I might live according to Your commandments and live accordance with Your plan for me. Amen.

135

FIND CONTENTMENT THROUGH CHRIST

The LORD will give strength to His people;
the LORD will bless His people with peace.

PSALM 29:11 NKJV

Everywhere we turn, or so it seems, the world promises us contentment and happiness. But the contentment that the world offers is fleeting and incomplete. Thankfully, the contentment that God offers is all encompassing and everlasting. Happiness, of course, depends less upon our circumstances than upon our thoughts. When we turn our thoughts to God, to His gifts, and to His glorious creation, we experience the joy that God intends for His children. But when we focus on the negative aspects of life—or when we disobey God's commandments—we cause ourselves needless suffering.

Do you sincerely want to be a contented Christian? Then set your mind and your heart upon God's love and His grace. Seek first the salvation that is available through a personal relationship with Jesus Christ, and then claim the joy, the contentment, and the spiritual abundance that the shepherd offers His sheep.

Those who are God's without reserve are, in every sense, content.

HANNAH WHITALL SMITH

Dear Lord, You offer me contentment and peace; let me accept Your peace. Help me to trust Your Word, to follow Your commandments, and to welcome the peace of Jesus into my heart, today and forever. Amen.

136

ARE YOU RUNNING ON EMPTY?

Come to Me, all of you who are weary and burdened, and I will give you rest. All of you, take up My yoke and learn from Me, because I am gentle and humble in heart, and you will find rest for yourselves. For My yoke is easy and My burden is light.

MATTHEW 11:28–30 HCSB

Even the most inspired Christians can, from time to time, find themselves running on empty. Why? Because the inevitable demands of daily life can drain us of our strength and rob us of the joy that is rightfully ours in Christ. Thankfully, God stands ready to renew our spirits, even on the darkest of days. God's Word is clear: when we genuinely lift our hearts and prayers to Him, He renews our strength.

Are you seeking a renewed sense of purpose? Turn your heart toward God in prayer. Are you weak or worried? Take the time to delve deeply into God's holy Word. Are you spiritually depleted? Call upon fellow believers to support you, and call upon Christ to renew your spirit and your life. When you do, you'll discover that the Creator of the universe stands always ready and always able to create a new sense of wonderment and joy in you.

The moment you wake up each morning, all your wishes and hopes for the day rush at you like wild animals. And the first job each morning consists in shoving it all back; in listening to that other voice, taking that other point of view, letting that other, larger, stronger, quieter life coming flowing in.

C. S. LEWIS

Dear Lord, every day of my life is a journey with You. Today is another day on that journey. Guide my steps today, Father, and keep me mindful that today offers yet another opportunity to celebrate Your blessings, Your love, and Your Son. Amen.

137

LET GOD DECIDE

We can make our plans,
but the LORD determines our steps.

PROVERBS 16:9 NLT

Are you facing a difficult decision, a troubling circumstance, or a powerful temptation? If so, it's time to step back, to stop focusing on the world, and to focus, instead, on the will of your Father in heaven. The world will often lead you astray, but God will not. His counsel leads you to Himself, which, of course, is the path He has always intended for you to take.

Everyday living is an exercise in decision-making. Today and every day you must make choices—choices about what you will do, what you will worship, and how you will think. When in doubt, make choices that you sincerely believe will bring you to a closer relationship with God. And if you're uncertain of your next step, pray about it. When you do, answers will come—the right answers for you.

Timely Tip: Never take on a major obligation of any kind without first taking sufficient time to carefully consider whether or not you should commit to it. The bigger the obligation, the more days you should take to decide. If someone presses you for an answer before you are ready, your automatic answer should always be no.

Dear Lord, help me to make decisions that are pleasing to You. Help me to be honest, patient, thoughtful, and obedient. And above all, help me to follow the teachings of Jesus, not just today, but every day. Amen.

138

DREAM BIG

*With God's power working in us, God can do much,
much more than anything we can ask or imagine.*

EPHESIANS 3:20 NCV

Are you willing to entertain the possibility that God has big plans in store for you? Hopefully so. Yet sometimes, especially if you've recently experienced a life-altering disappointment, you may find it difficult to envision a brighter future for yourself and your family. If so, it's time to reconsider your own capabilities . . . and God's.

Your heavenly Father created you with unique gifts and untapped talents; your job is to tap them. When you do, you'll begin to feel an increasing sense of confidence in yourself and in your future. So even if you're experiencing difficult days, don't abandon your dreams. Instead, trust that God is preparing you for greater things.

*The future lies all before us. Shall it only be a slight advance
upon what we usually do? Ought it not to be a bound, a leap forward
to altitudes of endeavor and success undreamed of before?*

ANNIE ARMSTRONG

*Always stay connected to people and seek out things that bring you joy.
Dream with abandon. Pray confidently.*

BARBARA JOHNSON

Dear Lord, give me the courage to dream and the faithfulness to trust in Your perfect plan. When I am worried or weary, give me strength for today and hope for tomorrow. Keep me mindful of Your healing power, Your infinite love, and Your eternal salvation. Amen.

139

LOOK FOR OPPORTUNITIES TO ENCOURAGE OTHERS

But encourage each other daily, while it is still called today,
so that none of you is hardened by sin's deception.

HEBREWS 3:13 HCSB

The 118th Psalm reminds us, "This is the day which the LORD hath made; we will rejoice and be glad in it" (v. 24 KJV). As we rejoice in this day that the Lord has given us, let us remember that an important part of today's celebration is the time we spend celebrating others. Each day provides countless opportunities to encourage others and to praise their good works. When we do, we not only spread seeds of joy and happiness, we also follow the commandments of God's holy Word.

How can we build others up? By celebrating their victories and their accomplishments. So look for the good in others and celebrate the good that you find. When you do, you'll be a powerful force of encouragement in the world . . . and a worthy servant to your God.

Encouragement starts at home, but it should never end there.

MARIE T. FREEMAN

We can never untangle all the woes in other people's lives.
We can't produce miracles overnight. But we can bring a cup of cool
water to a thirsty soul, or a scoop of laughter to a lonely heart.

BARBARA JOHNSON

Dear Lord, You have blessed all of Your children with special gifts and talents. Today, help me to use the talents You have given me, and in turn, let me help others find the strength and courage to use their gifts according to Your master plan. Amen.

140

GUARD AGAINST ENVY

Therefore, laying aside all malice, all deceit, hypocrisy,
envy, and all evil speaking, as newborn babes,
desire the pure milk of the word, that you may grow thereby.

1 PETER 2:1–2 NKJV

Because we are frail, imperfect human beings, we are sometimes envious of others. But God's Word warns us that envy is sin. Thus we must guard ourselves against the natural tendency to feel resentment and jealousy when other people experience good fortune. As believers, we have absolutely no reason to be envious of any people on earth. After all, as Christians we are already recipients of the greatest gift in all creation: God's grace. We have been promised the gift of eternal life through God's only begotten Son, and we must count that gift as our most precious possession.

So here's a simple suggestion that is guaranteed to bring you happiness: fill your heart with God's love, God's promises, and God's Son . . . and when you do so, leave no room for envy, hatred, bitterness, or regret.

Contentment comes when we develop an attitude
of gratitude for the important things we do have
in our lives that we tend to take for granted if we
have our eyes staring longingly at our neighbor's stuff.

DAVE RAMSEY

Dear Lord, when I am envious of others, redirect my thoughts to the blessings I have received from You. Make me a thankful Christian, Father, and deliver me from envy. Amen.

141

YOU CAN HAVE LIFE ETERNAL

In a little while the world will see Me no longer,
but you will see Me. Because I live, you will live too.

JOHN 14:19 HCSB

How marvelous it is that God became a man and walked among us. Had He not chosen to do so, we might feel removed from a distant Creator. But ours is not a distant God. Ours is a God who understands—far better than we ever could—the essence of what it means to be human.

God understands our hopes, our fears, and our temptations. He understands what it means to be angry and what it costs to forgive. He knows the heart, the conscience, and the soul of every person who has ever lived, including you. And God has a plan of salvation that is intended for you. Accept it. Accept God's gift through the person of His Son Christ Jesus, and then rest assured: God walked among us so that you might have eternal life; amazing though it may seem, He did it for you.

Once a man is united to God, how could he not live forever?

C. S. LEWIS

You need to think more about eternity and not less.

RICK WARREN

I know, dear Lord, that this world is not my home; I am only here for a brief while. And You have given me the priceless gift of eternal life through Your Son Jesus. Keep the hope of heaven fresh in my heart, and while I am in this world, help me to pass through it with faith in my heart and praise on my lips . . . for You. Amen.

142

MAKE NO EXCUSES

*And now, children, stay with Christ. Live deeply in Christ. Then we'll
be ready for him when he appears, ready to receive him with open arms,
with no cause for red-faced guilt or lame excuses when he arrives.*

1 JOHN 2:28 MSG

We live in a world where excuses are everywhere. And it's precisely because excuses are so numerous that they are also so ineffective. When we hear the words, "I'm sorry but . . . ", most of us know exactly what is to follow: the excuse. The dog ate the homework. Traffic was terrible. It's the company's fault. The boss is to blame. The equipment is broken. We're out of that. And so forth, and so on.

Because we humans are such creative excuse-makers, all of the really good excuses have already been taken. In fact, the high-quality excuses have been used, re-used, over-used, and ab-used. That's why excuses don't work—we've heard them all before.

So if you're wasting your time trying to concoct a new and improved excuse, don't bother. It's impossible. A far better strategy is this: do the work. Now. And let your excellent work speak loudly and convincingly for itself.

Making up a string of excuses is usually harder than doing the work.

MARIE T. FREEMAN

Heavenly Father, how easy it is to make excuses. But I want to be a person who accomplishes important work for You. Help me, Father, to strive for excellence, not excuses. Amen.

143

SO LAUGH!

A joyful heart makes a face cheerful.

PROVERBS 15:13 HCSB

Laughter is God's gift, and He intends that we enjoy it. Yet sometimes, because of the inevitable stresses of everyday life, laughter seems only a distant memory. As Christians we have every reason to be cheerful and to be thankful. Our blessings from God are beyond measure, starting, of course, with a gift that is ours for the asking, God's gift of salvation through Christ Jesus.

Few things in life are more absurd than the sight of a grumpy Christian. So today, as you go about your daily activities, approach life with a grin and a chuckle. After all, God created laughter for a reason . . . to use it. So laugh!

Laughter dulls the sharpest pain and flattens out the greatest stress. To share it is to give a gift of health.

BARBARA JOHNSON

Dear Lord, when I begin to take myself or my life too seriously, let me laugh. When I rush from place to place, slow me down, Lord, and let me laugh. Put a smile on my face, dear Lord, and let me share that smile with all who cross my path . . . and let me laugh. Amen.

144

EXCHANGE PATS ON THE BACK

*So then, we must pursue what promotes peace
and what builds up one another.*

ROMANS 14:19 HCSB

Life is a team sport, and all of us need occasional pats on the back from our teammates. In the book of Ephesians, Paul wrote, "Do not let any unwholesome talk come out of your mouths, but only what is helpful for building others up according to their needs, that it may benefit those who listen" (4:29 NIV). Paul reminds us that when we choose our words carefully, we can have a powerful impact on those around us.

Since we don't always know who needs our help, the best strategy is to encourage all the people who cross our paths. So today, be a world-class source of encouragement to everyone you meet. Never has the need been greater.

*Make it a rule, and pray to God to help you to keep it, never to lie down
at night without being able to say: "I have made at least one human
being a little wiser, a little happier, or a little better this day."*

CHARLES KINGSLEY

Dear heavenly Father, just as You have lifted me up, let me lift up others in a spirit of encouragement and hope. And if I can help a fellow traveler, even in a small way, dear Lord, may the glory be Yours. Amen.

145

YOUR POSITIVE EXAMPLE MAKES A DIFFERENCE

Be an example to the believers in word,
in conduct, in love, in spirit, in faith, in purity.

1 TIMOTHY 4:12 NKJV

As followers of Christ, we must each ask ourselves an important question: What kind of example am I? The answer to that question determines, in large part, whether or not we are positive influences on our own little corners of the world.

Are you a person whose life serves as a powerful example to family and friends? Are you a person whose behavior serves as a positive role model for young people? Are you the kind of Christian whose actions, day in and day out, are based upon integrity, fidelity, and a love for the Lord? If so, you are not only blessed by God, you are also a powerful force for good in a world that desperately needs positive influences such as yours.

There is nothing anybody else can do that can stop God
from using us. We can turn everything into a testimony.

CORRIE TEN BOOM

Dear Lord, I am aware that my behavior will influence others. Let my influence be positive. Let me follow in the footsteps of Your Son, and let others see Him through me. Amen.

146

MAKE GOD THE CORNERSTONE

[Fix] our eyes on Jesus, the pioneer and perfecter of faith.
For the joy set before him he endured the cross, scorning its shame,
and sat down at the right hand of the throne of God.

HEBREWS 12:2 NIV

Is Christ the focus of your life? Are you fired with enthusiasm for Him? Are you an energized Christian who allows God's Son to reign over every aspect of your day? Make no mistake: that's exactly what God intends for you to do.

The Lord has given you the gift of eternal life through His Son. In response to God's priceless gift, you are instructed to focus your thoughts, your prayers, and your energies upon God and His only begotten Son. To do so, you must resist the subtle yet powerful temptation to become a "spiritual dabbler." A person who dabbles in the Christian faith is unwilling to place God above all other things. Resist that temptation; make God the cornerstone and the touchstone of your life. When you do, He will give you all the strength and wisdom you need to live victoriously for Him.

When Jesus is in our midst, he brings His limitless power along as well.
But, Jesus must be in the middle, all eyes and hearts focused on Him.

SHIRLEY DOBSON

Heavenly Father, You have told me to give thanks always and to rejoice in Your marvelous creation. Let me be a joyful Christian, Lord, and let me focus my thoughts upon Your blessings and Your Love. Amen.

147

ESTABLISH FRIENDSHIPS
THAT HONOR GOD

If your life honors the name of Jesus, he will honor you.

2 THESSALONIANS 1:12 MSG

Some friendships help us honor God; those friendships should be nurtured. Other friendships place us in situations where we are tempted to dishonor God by disobeying His commandments; friendships such as these have the potential to do us great harm.

Because we tend to become like our friends, we must choose our friends carefully. Because our friends influence us in ways that are both subtle and powerful, we must ensure that our friendships are pleasing to God. When we spend our days in the presence of godly believers, we are blessed, not only by those friends, but also by our Creator.

The best times in life are made a thousand times better when shared with a dear friend.

LUCI SWINDOLL

Inasmuch as anyone pushes you nearer to God, he or she is your friend.

BARBARA JOHNSON

Dear Lord, let my friendships honor You. Keep me mindful that I am Your servant in every aspect of my life. Let me be a worthy servant, Lord, and a worthy friend. And may the love of Jesus shine in me and through me today and forever. Amen.

148

WHEN YOU TRUST GOD COMPLETELY, YOUR FUTURE IS BRIGHT

There is surely a future hope for you, and your hope will not be cut off.
PROVERBS 23:18 NIV

If you've entrusted your heart to Christ, your eternal fate is secure and your future is eternally bright. No matter how troublesome your present circumstances may seem, you need not fear because the Lord has promised that you are His now and forever.

Of course, you won't be exempt from the normal challenges of life here on earth. While you're here, you'll probably experience your share of anxiety-creating setbacks, disappointments, and failures. But these are only temporary defeats.

Are you willing to place your future in the hands of a loving and all-knowing God? Do you trust in the ultimate goodness of His plan for you? Will you face today's challenges with hope and optimism? You should. After all, the Lord created you for a very important purpose: His purpose. And you still have important work to do: His work. So today, as you live in the present and look to the future, remember that God has a marvelous plan for you. Act—and believe—accordingly.

Our future may look fearfully intimidating, yet we can look up to the Engineer of the Universe, confident that nothing escapes His attention or slips out of the control of those strong hands.
ELISABETH ELLIOT

Dear Lord, at times I am anxious about my future. Today, I will strive to do a better job of trusting You. If I am afraid, I will seek strength in You. If I become discouraged, I will turn to You. You are my Father, and I will place my hope, my trust, and my faith in You. Amen.

149

GIVE GENEROUSLY AND CHEERFULLY

Freely you have received, freely give.

MATTHEW 10:8 NKJV

Paul reminds us that when we sow the seeds of generosity, we reap bountiful rewards in accordance with God's plan for our lives. Thus we are instructed to give cheerfully and without reservation: "But this I say, He which soweth sparingly shall reap also sparingly; and he which soweth bountifully shall reap also bountifully. Every man according as he purposeth in his heart, so let him give; not grudgingly, or of necessity: for God loveth a cheerful giver" (2 Corinthians 9:6–7 KJV).

Today, make this pledge and keep it: be a cheerful, generous, courageous giver. The world needs your help, and you need the spiritual rewards that will be yours when you give it.

In Jesus the service of God and the service of the least of the brethren were one.

DIETRICH BONHOEFFER

We are never more like God than when we give.

CHARLES SWINDOLL

Dear Lord, You have given me so much. Let me share my blessings with those in need. Make me a generous, humble Christian, Lord, and let the glory be Yours and Yours alone. Amen.

150

HEAR THE CALL

One thing I do, forgetting those things which are behind
and reaching forward to those things which are ahead,
I press toward the goal for the prize of
the upward call of God in Christ Jesus.

PHILIPPIANS 3:13–14 NKJV

It is vitally important that you heed God's call. In John 15:16, Jesus said, "You did not choose me, but I chose you and appointed you so that you might go and bear fruit—fruit that will last" (NIV). In other words, you have been called by Christ, and now, it is up to you to decide precisely how you will answer.

Have you already found your calling? If so, you're a very lucky person. If not, keep searching and keep praying until you discover it. And remember this: God has important work for you to do—work that no one else on earth can accomplish but you.

Timely Tip: God has a plan for your life, a divine calling that you can either answer or ignore. How you choose to respond to God's calling will determine the direction you take and the contributions you make.

Heavenly Father, You have called me, and I acknowledge that calling. In these quiet moments before this busy day unfolds, I come to You. I will study Your Word and seek Your guidance. Give me the wisdom to know Your will for my life and the courage to follow wherever You may lead me, today and forever. Amen.

151

YOU ARE
NEVER ALONE

I am not alone, because the Father is with Me.

JOHN 16:32 HCSB

Do you set aside quiet moments each day to offer praise to your Creator? You should. During these moments of stillness, you will often sense the infinite love and power of our Lord.

The familiar words of Psalm 46:10 remind us to "Be still, and know that I am God" (NIV). When we do so, we encounter the awesome presence of our loving heavenly Father, and we are comforted in the knowledge that the Lord is always with us.

It is God to whom and with whom we travel, while He is the End of our journey, He is also at every stopping place.

ELISABETH ELLIOT

Do not limit the limitless God! With Him, face the future unafraid because you are never alone.

LETTIE COWMAN

God is an infinite circle whose center is everywhere.

ST. AUGUSTINE

Heavenly Father, You have promised that You are always with me, and I trust that promise. And You have promised that when I feel anxious or afraid, I can turn to You. Thank You, Lord, for Your love, for Your protection, and for Your blessings. Amen.

152

TRUST GOD'S TIMETABLE

Humble yourselves, therefore, under the mighty hand of God,
so that He may exalt you at the proper time, casting all
your care on Him, because He cares about you.

1 PETER 5:6–7 HCSB

Sometimes the hardest thing to do is to wait. This is especially true when we're in a hurry and when we want things to happen now, if not sooner! But God's plan does not always happen in the way that we would like or at the time of our own choosing. Our task—as believing Christians who trust in a benevolent, all knowing Father—is to wait patiently for God to reveal Himself.

We human beings are, by nature, impatient. And because we are impatient, we become dissatisfied and anxious about the direction of our lives. We know what we want, and we know exactly when we want it: RIGHT NOW! But God knows better. He has created a world that unfolds according to His own timetable, not ours . . . thank goodness!

Timely Tip: Perhaps you're in a hurry to understand God's unfolding plan for your life. If so, remember that He operates according to a perfect timetable. That timetable is His, not yours. So be patient.

Dear Lord, Your timing is always right for me. You have a plan for my life that is grander than I can imagine. When I am impatient, remind me that You are never early or late. You are always on time, Father, so let me trust in You . . . always. Amen.

153

GOD IS AT WORK IN YOUR LIFE

*For it is God who is working in you, enabling you both
to desire and to work out His good purpose.*

PHILIPPIANS 2:13 HCSB

As human beings with limited understanding, we can never fully comprehend the will of God. But as believers in a benevolent God, we must always *trust* the will of our heavenly Father.

Before His crucifixion, Jesus went to the Mount of Olives and poured out His heart to God. Jesus knew of the agony that He was destined to endure, but He also knew that God's will must be done. We, like our Savior, face trials that bring fear and trembling to the very depths of our souls, but like Christ, we, too, must ultimately seek God's will, not our own. When we entrust our lives to Him completely and without reservation, He gives us the strength to meet any challenge, the courage to face any trial, and the wisdom to live in His righteousness.

*It is good to remind ourselves that the will of God comes from
the heart of God and that we need not be afraid.*

WARREN WIERSBE

*In the center of a hurricane there is absolute quiet and peace.
There is no safer place than in the center of the will of God.*

CORRIE TEN BOOM

Dear Lord, You are the Creator of the universe, and I know that Your plan for my life is grander than I can imagine. Let Your purposes be my purposes, and let me trust in the assurance of Your promises. Amen.

154

HOW DO YOU TREAT OTHERS?

Therefore, whatever you want others to do for you,
do also the same for them—this is the Law and the Prophets.
MATTHEW 7:12 HCSB

Would you like to make the world a better place? If so, you can start by practicing the Golden Rule.

Is the Golden Rule your rule, or is it just another Bible verse that goes in one ear and out the other? Jesus made Himself perfectly clear: He instructed you to treat other people in the same way that you want to be treated. But sometimes, especially when you're feeling pressures of everyday living, obeying the Golden Rule can seem like an impossible task—but it's not. So if you want to know how to treat other people, ask the person you see every time you look into the mirror. The answer you receive will tell you exactly what to do.

Here lies the tremendous mystery—that God should be all-powerful,
yet refuse to coerce. He summons us to cooperation. We are honored
in being given the opportunity to participate in his good deeds.
Remember how He asked for help in performing his miracles:
Fill the water pots, stretch out your hand, distribute the loaves.
ELISABETH ELLIOT

Dear Lord, I thank You for friends and family members who practice the Golden Rule. Because I expect to be treated with kindness, let me be kind. Because I wish to be loved, let me be loving. In all things, Lord, let me live by the Golden Rule, and let me express my gratitude to those who offer kindness to me. Amen.

155

MAKE GOOD HABITS; BREAK BAD HABITS

Do not be deceived:
"Evil company corrupts good habits."
1 CORINTHIANS 15:33 NKJV

It's an old saying and a true one: First, you make your habits, and then your habits make you. Some habits will inevitably bring you closer to God; other habits will lead you away from the path He has chosen for you. If you sincerely desire to improve your spiritual health, you must honestly examine the habits that make up the fabric of your day. And you must abandon those habits that are displeasing to God.

If you trust God, and if you keep asking for His help, He can transform your life. If you sincerely ask Him to help you, the same God who created the universe will help you defeat the harmful habits that have heretofore defeated you. So if at first you don't succeed, keep praying. God is listening, and He's ready to help you become a better person if you ask Him . . . so ask today.

Since behaviors become habits,
make them work with you and not against you.
E. STANLEY JONES

Dear Lord, help me break bad habits and form good ones. And let my actions be pleasing to You, today and every day. Amen.

156

TRUST GOD'S HEALING TOUCH

I am the LORD that healeth thee.
EXODUS 15:26 KJV

Are you concerned about your spiritual, physical, or emotional health? If so, there is a timeless source of comfort and assurance that is as near your bookshelf. That source is the Holy Bible.

God's Word has much to say about every aspect of your life, including your health. And when you face concerns of any sort—including health-related challenges—God is with You. So trust your medical doctor to do his or her part, but place your ultimate trust in your benevolent heavenly Father. His healing touch, like His love, endures forever.

> *Ultimate healing and the glorification*
> *of the body are certainly among the blessings*
> *of Calvary for the believing Christian.*
> *Immediate healing is not guaranteed.*
>
> WARREN WIERSBE

Dear Lord, place your healing hand upon me. Heal my body and my soul. Let me trust Your promises, Father, and let me turn to You for hope, for restoration, for renewal, and for salvation. Amen.

157

LOOK BEFORE YOU LEAP

An impulsive vow is a trap;
later you'll wish you could get out of it.

PROVERBS 20:25 MSG

Are you, at times, just a little bit impulsive? Are you in the habit of looking before you leap or thinking before you speak? If so, God wants to have a little chat with you.

God's Word is clear: as believers, we are called to lead lives of discipline, diligence, moderation, and maturity. But the world often tempts us to behave otherwise. Everywhere we turn, or so it seems, we are faced with powerful temptations to behave in undisciplined, ungodly ways. Yet God's Word instructs us to be disciplined in our thoughts and our actions; God's Word warns us against the dangers of impulsive behavior. As believers in a just God, we should act and react accordingly.

Timely Tip: If you can't seem to put the brakes on impulsive behavior, you're not praying hard enough. Ask God to help you slow down, to think before you act and look before you leap.

Dear Lord, sometimes I can be an impulsive person. Slow me down, calm me down, and help me make wise decisions . . . today and every day of my life. Amen.

158

IF YOU DO NOT JUDGE OTHERS, YOU WILL NOT BE JUDGED

Judge not, and you shall not be judged. Condemn not,
and you shall not be condemned. Forgive, and you will be forgiven.

LUKE 6:37 NKJV

The need to judge others seems woven into the very fabric of human consciousness. We mortals feel compelled to serve as informal judges and juries, pronouncing our own verdicts on the actions and perceived motivations of others, all the while excusing—or oftentimes hiding—our own shortcomings. But God's Word instructs us to let Him be the judge. He knows that we, with our limited knowledge and personal biases, are simply ill-equipped to assess the actions of others. The act of judging, then, becomes not only an act of futility, but also an affront to our Creator.

When Jesus came upon a woman who had been condemned by the Pharisees, He spoke not only to the people who had gathered there, but also to all generations. Christ warned, "He that is without sin among you, let him first cast a stone at her" (John 8:7 KJV). The message is clear: because we are all sinners, we must refrain from the temptation to judge others.

So the next time you're tempted to cast judgment on another human being, resist that temptation. God hasn't called you to be a judge; He's called you to be a witness. And He wants you to be a worthy witness, not an unqualified judge.

Heavenly Father, sometimes I am too quick to judge others. Today, I ask for the strength and the wisdom to refrain from judging. You know every human heart, and You love all Your children. So should I. Amen.

159

MISTAKES HAPPEN; DON'T OVERREACT

If you listen to correction to improve your life,
you will live among the wise.

PROVERBS 15:31 NCV

Everybody makes mistakes, and so will you. In fact, occasional mistakes are simply the price that all of us must pay as we meet the challenges and accept the risks of everyday life. Our responsibility, of course, is to learn from our mistakes and refrain from repeating them.

When you fall short of your expectations, don't overreact and don't be too hard on yourself. Instead, try to learn something, try to make amends, and try to move on as quickly as possible.

By the mercy of God, we may repent a wrong choice
and alter the consequences by making a right choice.

A. W. TOZIER

Mistakes offer the possibility for redemption and a new start in God's
kingdom. No matter what you're guilty of, God can restore your innocence.

BARBARA JOHNSON

It is human to err, but it is devilish to remain willfully in error.

ST. AUGUSTINE

Dear Lord, You already know that I am an imperfect being. I make mistakes, Father, and You still love me. Today, I ask for the wisdom to recognize my mistakes, to learn from them, the courage to correct them.

160

THE GREATEST
OF THESE IS LOVE

Now these three remain: faith, hope, and love.
But the greatest of these is love.
1 CORINTHIANS 13:13 HCSB

The beautiful words of First Corinthians 13 remind us that love is God's commandment: Faith is important, of course. So, too, is hope. But love is more important still. We are commanded (not advised, not encouraged . . . commanded!) to love one another just as Christ loved us (John 13:34). That's a tall order, but as Christians, we are obligated to follow it.

Christ showed His love for us on the cross, and we are called upon to return Christ's love by sharing it. Today, let us spread Christ's love to families, friends, and even strangers, so that through us, others might come to know Him.

Love is the seed of all hope. It is the enticement
to trust, to risk, to try, and to go on.
GLORIA GAITHER

Dear Lord, love is Your commandment. Help me always to remember that the gift of love is a precious gift indeed. Let me nurture love and treasure it, today and forever. Amen.

161

FOCUS BEYOND MATERIALISM

For what does it benefit a man to gain the whole world yet lose his life?
What can a man give in exchange for his life?

MARK 8:36–37 HCSB

In our modern society, we need money to live. But as Christians, we must never make the acquisition of money the central focus of our lives. Money is a tool, but it should never overwhelm our sensibilities. The focus of life must be squarely on things spiritual, not things material.

Whenever we place our love for material possessions above our love for God—or when we yield to the countless other temptations of everyday living—we find ourselves engaged in a struggle between good and evil. Let us respond to this struggle by freeing ourselves from that subtle yet powerful temptation: the temptation to love the world more than we love God.

Timely Tip: God's Word warns against the spiritual trap of materialism. Material possessions may seem appealing at first, but they pale in comparison to the spiritual gifts that God gives to those who put Him first. Count yourself among that number.

Dear Lord, my greatest possession is my relationship with You through Jesus Christ. You have promised that when I first seek Your kingdom and Your righteousness, You will give me whatever I need. Let me trust You completely, Lord, for my needs, both material and spiritual, this day and always. Amen.

162

GOD'S POWER AND LOVE ARE LIMITLESS

I pray that the perception of your mind may be enlightened so you may know what is the hope of His calling, what are the glorious riches of His inheritance among the saints, and what is the immeasurable greatness of His power to us who believe, according to the working of His vast strength.

EPHESIANS 1:18–19 HCSB

Because God's power is limitless, it is far beyond the comprehension of mortal minds. Yet even though we cannot fully understand the awesome power of God, we can praise it. When we worship the Lord with faith and assurance, when we place Him at the absolute center of our lives, we invite His love into our hearts. In turn, we grow to love Him more deeply as we sense His love for us. St. Augustine wrote, "I love you, Lord, not doubtingly, but with absolute certainty. Your Word beat upon my heart until I fell in love with you, and now the universe and everything in it tells me to love you."

Let us pray that we, too, will turn our hearts to the Creator, knowing with certainty that His heart has ample room for each of us, and that we, in turn, must make room in our hearts for Him.

The greatness of His power to create and design and form and mold and make and build and arrange defies the limits of our imagination. And since He created everything, there is nothing beyond His power to fix or mend or heal or restore.

ANNE GRAHAM LOTZ

Heavenly Father, You are all-knowing and all-powerful. Today, I praise You for Your love, and I marvel at the glory of Your Creation. With You as my protector, Lord, I am secure, today and forever. Amen.

NEVER LOSE HOPE

The LORD is good to those whose hope is in him, to the one who seeks him;
it is good to wait quietly for the salvation of the LORD.

LAMENTATIONS 3:25–26 NIV

Hope for the future is simply one aspect of trusting God. When you seek God's guidance in every aspect of your life, your future is secure. So don't worry too much about the distant future. Instead, remember that whatever tomorrow holds, God will be there, and you'll be protected.

These words of wisdom can serve as a reminder that the Lord is always available and that you should never lose hope.

Jesus gives us hope because He keeps us company,
has a vision and knows the way we should go.

MAX LUCADO

If your hopes are being disappointed just now,
it means that they are being purified.

OSWALD CHAMBERS

Seize this very minute. What you can do, or dream you can,
begin it. Boldness has genius, power, and magic in it.

GOETHE

Heavenly Father, I know that you are with me always. If I become discouraged, I will turn to You. If I grow weary, I will seek strength in You. You are my shepherd, Lord, and I place my hope and my faith in You. Amen.

164

GOD IS CONSTANTLY PROVIDING OPPORTUNITIES FOR RENEWAL AND GROWTH

Is anything too hard for the LORD?
GENESIS 18:14 NKJV

As you look at the landscape of your life, do you see opportunities, possibilities, and blessings, or do you focus, instead, upon the more negative scenery? Do you believe the Bible promise that God is making all things new—including you—or do you believe that's a promise that applies only to other people? If you've acquired the unfortunate habit of focusing too intently upon the negative aspects of your life, then your spiritual vision is in need of correction.

Whether you realize it or not, opportunities are whirling around you like stars crossing the night sky: beautiful to observe, but too numerous to count. Yet you may be too concerned with the challenges of everyday living to notice those opportunities. That's why you should slow down, catch your breath, and focus you thoughts on two things: the talents God has given you and the opportunities that He has placed before you. God is leading you in the direction of those opportunities. Your task is to watch carefully, to pray fervently, and to act accordingly.

If you're consistently looking for the silver linings instead of the clouds, you'll discover that opportunities have a way of turning up in the most unexpected places. But if you've acquired the unfortunate habit of looking for problems instead of possibilities, you'll find that troubles have a way of turning up in unexpected places too. Since you're likely to find what you're looking for, why not look for opportunities? They're out there. And the rest is up to you.

Dear Lord, whatever this day may hold for me, I will thank You for the gift of life. And I thank You, Father, for the opportunity to live joyfully and abundantly. Let me lean upon You, Lord—and trust You—now and forever. Amen.

165

BE DILIGENT NOW

Do not lack diligence; be fervent in spirit; serve the Lord.
ROMANS 12:11 HCSB

God's Word reminds us again and again that our Creator expects us to lead disciplined lives. God doesn't reward laziness, misbehavior, or apathy. To the contrary, He expects believers to behave with dignity and discipline.

We live in a world in which leisure is glorified and indifference is often glamorized. But God has other plans. He did not create us for lives of mediocrity; He created us for far greater things. Life's greatest rewards seldom fall into our laps; to the contrary, our greatest accomplishments usually require lots of work, which is perfectly fine with God. After all, He knows that we're up to the task, and He has big plans for us; may we, as disciplined believers, always be worthy of those plans.

True will power and courage are not only on the battlefield,
but also in everyday conquests over our inertia, laziness, and boredom.
D. L. MOODY

Dear Lord, You expect Your children to be diligent and disciplined. You have told us that the fields are ripe and the workers are few. Lead me to Your fields, Lord, and make me a disciplined worker in the service of Your Son. Amen.

166

REPLACE DOUBT WITH TRUST

Oh, taste and see that the Lord is good;
blessed is the man who trusts in Him!
PSALM 34:8 NKJV

The Bible promises that God's power is limitless, yet sometimes, we behave as if the Lord had taken a leave of absence. Instead of trusting Him and taking sensible risks in the service of His kingdom, we give in to emotional paralysis. Unwilling to entertain great hopes for the tomorrow, we focus on the unfairness of the today. Unwilling to trust God completely, we take timid half-steps when the Lord intends that we make giant leaps.

Today, ask God for the courage to step beyond the boundaries of your doubts. Ask Him to guide you to a place where you can realize your full potential—a place where you are freed from the fear of failure. Ask Him to do His part, and promise Him that you will do your part. Don't ask Him to lead you to a "safe" place; ask Him to lead you to the "right" place . . . and remember: those two places are seldom the same.

Timely Tip: If you're about to make a big decision or take a significant risk, always pray about it first. And the bigger the decision, the more you should pray about it.

Dear Lord, I don't want to be reckless, but I want to be totally committed to Your kingdom's work. Sometimes that will involve risk. Help me to know when I need to take sensible risks in service to my family and my service to You. Amen.

167

YOUR TESTIMONY MATTERS

You must worship Christ as Lord of your life. And if you are asked about your Christian hope, always be ready to explain it.

1 PETER 3:15 NLT

Those of us who are Christians should be willing to talk about the things Christ has done for us. Undeniably, our personal testimonies are vitally important, but sometimes, because of shyness or insecurities, we're afraid to share our experiences. And that's unfortunate.

In his second letter to Timothy, Paul encouraged his friend to share his testimony courageously and often. And the same message applies to us. We live in a world that desperately needs the healing message of Jesus Christ. Every believer, each in his or her own way, bears responsibility for sharing the good news. And it is important to remember that we bear testimony through both words and actions.

You know how Jesus has touched your heart; now it's time for you to help Him do the same for others.

The enemy's hope for Christians is that we will either be so ineffective we have no testimony, or we'll ruin the one we have.

BETH MOORE

When you talk, choose the very same words that you would use if Jesus were looking over your shoulder. Because He is.

MARIE T. FREEMAN

Dear Lord, You have offered me the gift of eternal life through the sacrifice of Your Son. Give me the courage to share the story of my salvation with others so that they, too, might dedicate their lives to Christ and receive His eternal gifts. Amen.

168

IT PAYS TO PRAISE

*Through Him then, let us continually offer up a sacrifice of praise
to God, that is, the fruit of lips that give thanks to His name.*

HEBREWS 13:15 NASB

The Bible makes it clear: it pays to praise God. But sometimes, we allow ourselves to become so preoccupied with the demands of daily life that we forget to say thank You to the Giver of all good gifts.

Worship and praise should be a part of everything we do. Otherwise, we quickly lose perspective as we fall prey to the demands of the moment.

Do you sincerely desire to be a worthy servant of the One who has given you eternal love and eternal life? Then praise Him for who He is and for what He has done for you. Praise Him every day, for as long as you live and then for all eternity.

*The more perfect sort of prayer is praise,
rather than petition.*

ST. STEPHEN OF MURET

*The time for universal praise is sure to come some day.
Let us begin to do our part now.*

HANNAH WHITALL SMITH

Heavenly Father, I come to You today with hope in my heart and praise on my lips. I place my trust in You, dear Lord, knowing that with You as my Protector, I have nothing to fear. I thank You, Lord, for Your grace, for Your Love, and for Your Son. Amen.

169

WE MUST HONOR AND OBEY

*This is how we are sure that we have come to know Him:
by keeping His commands.*

1 JOHN 2:3 HCSB

When we seek righteousness in our own lives—and when we seek the companionship of those who do likewise—we reap the spiritual rewards that God intends for us to enjoy. When we behave ourselves as godly men and women, we honor God. When we live righteously and according to God's commandments, He blesses us in ways that we cannot fully understand.

Today, as you fulfill your responsibilities, hold fast that which is good, and associate yourself with believers who behave themselves in like fashion. When you do, your good works will serve as a powerful example for others and as a worthy offering to your Creator.

*Study the Bible and observe how the persons behaved and how God
dealt with them. There is explicit teaching on every condition of life.*

CORRIE TEN BOOM

Dear Lord, this world has countless temptations, distractions, interruptions, and frustrations. When I allow my focus to drift away from You and Your Word, I suffer. But when I turn my thoughts and my prayers to You, heavenly Father, You guide my path. Let me discover the right thing to do—and let me do it—this day and every day that I live. Amen.

170

BE GENTLE WITH YOURSELF

You're blessed when you're content with just who you are—no more,
no less. That's the moment you find yourselves
proud owners of everything that can't be bought.

MATTHEW 5:5 MSG

Being patient with other people can be difficult. But sometimes, we find it even more difficult to be patient with ourselves. We have high expectations and lofty goals. We want to receive God's blessings now, not later. And, of course, we want our lives to unfold according to our own wishes and our own time-tables—not God's. Yet throughout the Bible, we are instructed that patience is the companion of wisdom. Proverbs 16:32 teaches us that "Patience is better than strength" (NCV). God's message, then, is clear: we must be patient with all people, beginning with that particular person who stares back at us each time we gaze into the mirror.

The Bible affirms the importance of self-acceptance by exhorting believers to love others as they love themselves (Matthew 22:39). Furthermore, the Bible teaches that when we genuinely open our hearts to Him, the Lord accepts us just as we are. And if He accepts us—faults and all—then who are we to believe otherwise?

I think that if God forgives us we might forgive ourselves. Otherwise it is
almost like setting up ourselves as a higher tribunal than Him.

C. S. LEWIS

Dear Lord, I have so much to learn and so many ways to improve myself, but You love me just as I am. Thank You for Your love and for Your Son. And help me to become the person that You want me to become. Amen.

171

GOD IS LOVE

God is love, and the one who remains in
love remains in God, and God remains in him.

1 John 4:16 HCSB

The Bible makes this promise: God is love. It's a sweeping statement, a profoundly important description of what God is and how God works. God's love is perfect. When we open our hearts to His perfect love, we are touched by the Creator's hand, and we are transformed.

Today, even if you can only carve out a few quiet moments, offer sincere prayers of thanksgiving to your Creator. He loves you now and throughout all eternity. Open your heart to His presence and His love.

There is no limit to God. There is no limit to His power.
There is no limit to His love. There is no limit to His mercy.

Billy Graham

There is no pit so deep that God's love is not deeper still.

Corrie ten Boom

Dear God, You are love. You love me, Father, and I love You. As I love You more, Lord, I am also able to love of my family and friends more. I will be Your loving servant, Lord, today and throughout eternity. Amen.

172

DEVELOP AN ATTITUDE OF GRATITUDE

*And let the peace of God rule
in your hearts . . . and be ye thankful.*

Colossians 3:15 KJV

For most of us, life is busy and complicated. We have countless responsibilities, some of which begin before sunrise and many of which end long after sunset. Amid the rush and crush of the daily grind, it is easy to worry, and it's easy to lose sight of God's blessings. But when we forget to slow down and say thank You to our Maker, we rob ourselves of His presence, His peace, and His joy.

Our task, as believers, is to praise God many times each day. Then, with gratitude in our hearts, we can face our daily duties with the perspective and power that only He can provide.

Timely Tip: To experience the full measure of God's blessings, you must give praise and thanks to the Giver. So make it a point to thank God for His blessings many times each day.

Dear Lord, make me a person with a grateful heart. You have given me much; when I think of Your grace and goodness, I am humbled and thankful. Today, I will praise You with my words my deeds . . . and may all the glory be Yours. Amen.

173

TO GOD BE THE GLORY

*Clothe yourselves with humility toward one another,
because God resists the proud but gives grace to the humble.*

1 PETER 5:5 HCSB

As Christians, we have a profound reason to be humble: we have been refashioned and saved by Jesus Christ, and that salvation came not because of our own good works but because of God's grace. Thus we are not "self-made," we are "God-made," and "Christ-saved." How, then, can we be boastful?

Dietrich Bonhoeffer observed, "It is very easy to overestimate the importance of our own achievements in comparison with what we owe others." In other words, reality breeds humility. So instead of puffing out your chest and saying, "Look at me!," give credit where credit is due, starting with God. And rest assured: there is no such thing as a self-made man. All of us are made by God, and He deserves the glory, not us.

*We can never have more of true faith
than we have of true humility.*

ANDREW MURRAY

Dear Lord, keep me mindful that all my gifts come from You. Let me grow beyond my need for earthly praise, God, and let me look only to You for approval. Amen.

POINT YOUR THOUGHTS IN THE RIGHT DIRECTION

Fix your thoughts on what is true, and honorable, and right, and pure, and lovely, and admirable. Think about things that are excellent and worthy of praise.

PHILIPPIANS 4:8 NLT

When you manage to direct your thoughts in a positive direction—when you focus on God's blessings, God's love, and the opportunities He has placed before you—those thoughts have a way of lifting your spirits and improving your day. Negative thoughts, on the other hand, have the opposite effect; they have a way of hijacking your emotions and sapping your energy.

So if you sense that your thoughts are turning negative and your emotions are beginning to spin out of control, slow down, take a few deep breaths, and try to reconnect with reality. Here are the facts: God's love is real; His peace is real; His support is real. Don't ever let your emotions obscure these truths.

*When you think on the powerful truths of Scripture,
God uses His Word to change your way of thinking.*

ELIZABETH GEORGE

*Change always starts in your mind. The way you think determines
the way you feel, and the way you feel influences the way you act.*

RICK WARREN

Heavenly Father, I will focus on Your love, Your power, Your Promises, and Your Son. When I am weak, I will turn to You for strength; when I am worried, I will turn to You for comfort; when I am troubled, I will turn to You for patience and perspective. Help me guard my thoughts, Lord, so that I may honor You this day and forever. Amen.

175

CHOOSE THE GOOD LIFE

And in that day you will ask Me nothing. Most assuredly, I say to you,
whatever you ask the Father in My name He will give you. Until now you have
asked nothing in My name. Ask, and you will receive, that your joy may be full.

JOHN 16:23–24 NKJV

God offers us abundance through His Son, Jesus. Whether or not we accept God's abundance is, of course, up to each of us. When we entrust our hearts and our days to the One who created us, we experience abundance through the grace and sacrifice of His Son, Jesus. But when we turn our thoughts and our energies away from God's commandments, we inevitably forfeit the spiritual abundance that might otherwise be ours.

What is your focus today? Are you focused on God's Word and His will for your life? Or are you focused on the distractions and temptations of a difficult world. The answer to this question will, to a surprising extent, determine the quality and the direction of your day.

If you sincerely seek the spiritual abundance that your Savior offers, then follow Him completely and without reservation. When you do, you will receive the love, the life, and the abundance that He has promised.

Yes, we were created for His holy pleasure, but we will ultimately—
if not immediately—find much pleasure in His pleasure.

BETH MOORE

Dear Lord, thank You for the abundant life that is mine through Christ Jesus. Give me courage to claim the spiritual riches that You have promised, and lead me according to Your plan for my life, today and always. Amen.

176

PASS IT ON

Do not neglect the gift that is in you.
1 Timothy 4:14 HCSB

God has given you an array of talents, and He has given you unique opportunities to share those talents with the world. Your Creator intends for you to use your talents for the glory of His kingdom in the service of His children. Will you honor Him by sharing His gifts? And will you share His gifts humbly and lovingly? Hopefully you will.

The old saying is both familiar and true: "What you are is God's gift to you; what you become is your gift to God." As a Christian who has been touched by the transforming love of Jesus Christ, your obligation is clear: you must strive to make the most of your own God-given talents, and you must encourage your family and friends to do likewise. So make this promise to yourself and to God: promise to use your talents to minister to your family, to your friends, and to the world. And remember: the best way to say thank you for God's gifts is to use them.

In the great orchestra we call life, you have an instrument and a song, and you owe it to God to play them both sublimely.

Max Lucado

Dear Lord, You have given all of us talents, and I am no exception. You have blessed me with a gift—let me discover it, nurture it, and use it for the glory of Your kingdom. I will share my gifts with the world, and I will praise You, the Giver of all things good. Amen.

177

GET BETTER ACQUAINTED
WITH YOURSELF

*A devout life does bring wealth, but it's the rich simplicity
of being yourself before God.*

1 TIMOTHY 6:6 MSG

As you journey through life, you should continue to become better aquatinted with yourself. How? One way is to examine the patterns in your own life and understand this: unless you make the conscious effort to change those patterns, you're likely to repeat them. So if you don't like some of the results you've earned, change your behaviors. The sooner you change, the sooner your results will change too. And while you're creating the new-and-improved you, pay careful attention to the following words of wisdom.

*The man who does not like self-examination
may be pretty certain that things need examining.*

C. H. SPURGEON

*A humble knowledge of oneself is a surer road
to God than a deep searching of the sciences.*

THOMAS À KEMPIS

Observe all men, thyself most.

BEN FRANKLIN

Heavenly Father, I have so much to learn about myself. And I have so many things to learn about Your world. Today and every day, help me learn what you want me to know, and help me become the person that You want me to become. Amen.

178

TRUST GOD'S PLAN

The LORD says, "I will guide you along the best pathway
for your life. I will advise you and watch over you."
PSALM 32:8 NLT

God has a plan for your life. He has things He wants you to do and places He wants you to go. The most important decision of your life is, of course, your commitment to accept Jesus Christ as your personal Lord and Savior. And once your eternal destiny is secured, you will undoubtedly ask yourself the question, What now, Lord?

As you continually seek God's purpose for your life, be patient: your heavenly Father may not always reveal himself as quickly as you would like. But rest assured: He intends to use you in wonderful, unexpected ways. He desires to lead you along a path of His choosing. Your challenge is to watch, to listen, and to follow.

Every experience God gives us, every person he brings into our lives,
is the perfect preparation for the future that only he can see.
CORRIE TEN BOOM

God has a course mapped out for your life, and all the inadequacies in the
world will not change His mind. He will be with you every step of the way.
CHARLES STANLEY

Dear Lord, I will seek Your plan for my life. Even when I don't understand why things happen, I will trust You. Even when I am uncertain of my next step, I will trust You. There are many things that I cannot do, Lord, and there are many things that I cannot understand. But one thing I can do is to trust You always. And I will. Amen.

179

LIVE BEYOND ANXIETY

In the multitude of my anxieties within me,
Your comforts delight my soul.

PSALM 94:19 NKJV

God calls us to live above and beyond anxiety. He calls us to live by faith, not by fear. He instructs us to trust Him completely, this day and forever. But sometimes trusting God is difficult, especially when we become caught up in the incessant demands of an anxious world.

When you feel anxious—and you will—return your thoughts to God's love. Then take your concerns to Him in prayer, and to the best of your ability, leave them there. Whatever "it" is, God is big enough to handle it. Let Him. Now.

Timely Tip: Make a brief inventory of the things you're most worried about. Then jot down a few simple steps that you can take to begin resolving those challenges. Finally, pray for guidance, courage, and the peace that comes from trusting God completely.

Dear Lord, sometimes this world is a difficult place, and as a frail human being, I am fearful. When I am worried, restore my faith. When I am anxious, turn my thoughts to You. Amen.

180

KEEPING UP APPEARANCES IS FUTILE

We justify our actions by appearances; God examines our motives.
PROVERBS 21:2 MSG

The world sees you as you appear to be; God sees you as you really are. He sees your heart, and He understands your intentions. The opinions of others should be relatively unimportant to you; however, God's view of you—His understanding of your actions, your thoughts, and your motivations—should be vitally important.

Few things in life are more futile than "keeping up appearances" for the sake of neighbors. What *is* important, of course, is pleasing your Father in heaven. You please Him when your intentions are pure and your actions are just.

If the narrative of the Scriptures teaches us anything, from the serpent in the Garden to the carpenter in Nazareth, it teaches us that things are rarely what they seem, that we shouldn't be fooled by appearances.
JOHN ELDREDGE

Outside appearances, things like the clothes you wear or the car you drive, are important to other people but totally unimportant to God. Trust God.
MARIE T. FREEMAN

Heavenly Father, examine my heart and show me ways that I can become a better person. Let my motives be pure, Lord, and let my actions please you, today and every day of my life. Amen.

181

GOD IS HERE

Draw near to God, and He will draw near to you.

JAMES 4:8 HCSB

God is constantly making Himself available to you; therefore, when you approach Him obediently and sincerely, You will most certainly find Him. God is always available to you. Whenever it seems to you that God is distant, disinterested, or altogether absent, you may rest assured that your feelings are a reflection of your own emotional state, not an indication of God's absence.

The next time you feel anxious, worried, or fearful, remind yourself that your heavenly Father is with you. He has a plan for your life, and He understands that plan perfectly, even if you are unsure of your next step. Turn your concerns over to Him. Whatever your problem, whatever your burden, whatever your fear, He can handle it.

Mark it down. You will never go where God is not.

MAX LUCADO

You need not cry very loudly; he is nearer to us than we think.

BROTHER LAWRENCE

Dear Lord, Thank You for You constant presence and Your constant love. I draw near to You this day with the confidence that You are ready to guide me. Help me walk closely with You, Father, and help me share Your good news with all who cross my path. Amen.

182

WHEN TIMES ARE TOUGH, BE COURAGEOUS AND TRUST GOD

They won't be afraid of bad news;
their hearts are steady because they trust the Lord.
PSALM 112:7 NCV

The Bible promises that God always hears our prayers. And it also promises that, in His own time and in His own way, He answers those prayers. God invites us to ask Him for the things we need, and He promises to respond in a way that fulfills His ultimate purpose for our lives here on earth and His plans for our eternal lives together with Him in heaven. The Lord is always available and He's always ready to help us. And He knows precisely what we need. But He still instructs us to ask.

Do you make a habit of asking God for the things you need? Hopefully so. After all, the Father most certainly has a plan for your life. And He can do great things through you if you have the courage to ask for His guidance and His help. So be fervent in prayer and don't hesitate to ask the Creator for the tools you need to accomplish His plan for your life. When you do your part, God will most certainly do His part. And great things are bound to happen.

On the darkest day of your life, God is still in charge. Take comfort in that.
MARIE T. FREEMAN

Dear Lord, give me courage in every circumstance and in every stage of life. Give me the wisdom, Father, to place my hope and my trust in Your perfect plan and Your boundless love. Amen.

183

LET YOUR ACTIONS BE GUIDED BY GOD'S WORD

You love Him, though you have not seen Him. And though not seeing Him now, you believe in Him and rejoice with inexpressible and glorious joy, because you are receiving the goal of your faith, the salvation of your souls.

1 PETER 1:8–9 HCSB

If you'd like to partake in the peace that only God can give, make certain that your actions are guided by His Word. And while you're at it, pay careful attention to the conscience that God, in His infinite wisdom, has placed in your heart. Don't treat your faith as if it were separate from your everyday life. Weave your beliefs into the very fabric of your day. When you do, God will honor your good works, and your good works will honor God.

If you seek to be a responsible believer, you must realize that it is never enough to hear the instructions of God; you must also live by them. And it is never enough to wait idly by while others to do God's work here on earth; you, too, must act. Doing God's work is a responsibility that every Christian (including you) should bear. And when you do, your loving heavenly Father will reward your efforts with a bountiful harvest

Our Lord is searching for people who will make a difference. Christians dare not dissolve into the background or blend into the neutral scenery of the world.

CHARLES SWINDOLL

Dear Lord, today I will worry less about pleasing other people and more about pleasing You. I will stand up for my beliefs, and I will honor You with my thoughts, my actions, and my prayers. And I will worship You, Father, with thanksgiving in my heart, this day and forever. Amen.

184

YOU DON'T HAVE TO BE PERFECT

*Even though good people may be bothered
by trouble seven times, they are never defeated.*

PROVERBS 24:16 NCV

In heaven, we will know perfection. Here on earth, we have a few short years to wrestle with the challenges of imperfection. God is perfect; we human beings are not. May we live—and forgive—accordingly.

So do your best to please God, and don't worry too much about what other people think. And when it comes to meeting the unrealistic expectations of a world gone haywire, forget about trying to be perfect—it's impossible.

*The happiest people in the world are not those who
have no problems, but the people who have learned
to live with those things that are less than perfect.*

JAMES DOBSON

What makes a Christian a Christian is not perfection but forgiveness.

MAX LUCADO

*How important it is that we give up our
expectations of perfection in any area of our lives.*

FRED ROGERS

Dear Lord, this world has so many expectations of me, but today I will not seek to meet the world's expectations; I will do my best to meet Your expectations. I will make You my ultimate priority, Lord, by serving You, by praising You, by loving You, and by obeying You. Amen.

185

SET THE RIGHT PRIORITIES

This is my prayer for you: that your love will grow more and more;
that you will have knowledge and understanding with your love.

PHILIPPIANS 1:9 NCV

If you fail to prioritize your day, life will automatically do the job for you. So your choice is simple: prioritize or be prioritized. It's a choice that will help determine the quality of your life. You don't have time to do everything, so it's perfectly okay to say no to the things that mean less so that you'll have time for the things that matter more.

If your to-do list is maxed out and your energy is on the wane, it's time to restore a sense of balance to your life. You can do so by turning the concerns and the priorities of this day over to God—prayerfully, earnestly, and often. Then you must listen for His answers and trust the answers that He gives.

A disciple is a follower of Christ. That means you take on
His priorities as your own. His agenda becomes your agenda.
His mission becomes your mission.

CHARLES STANLEY

Put first things first and we get second things thrown in;
put second things first and we lose both first and second things.

ELIZABETH GEORGE

Heavenly Father, give me the wisdom to set priorities that are pleasing to You. Guide me away from the distractions and temptations that surround me, so that I can honor You, Lord, with my thoughts, my actions, and my prayers. Amen.

186

FORGIVENESS, YES; BITTERNESS, NO

Let all bitterness, wrath, anger, clamor, and evil speaking be put away from you, with all malice. And be kind to one another, tenderhearted, forgiving one another, even as God in Christ forgave you.

EPHESIANS 4:31–32 NKJV

Are you mired in the quicksand of bitterness or regret? If so, you are not only disobeying God's Word, you are also wasting your time. The world holds few if any rewards for those who remain angrily focused upon the past. Still, the act of forgiveness is difficult for all but the most saintly men and women.

Perhaps granting forgiveness is hard for you. If so, you are not alone. Genuine, lasting forgiveness is often difficult to achieve—difficult but not impossible. Thankfully, with God's help, all things are possible, and that includes forgiveness. But even though God is willing to help, He expects you to do some of the work. And make no mistake: forgiveness is work, which is okay with God. He knows that the payoffs are worth the effort.

Timely Tip: The Bible warns that bitterness is both dangerous and self-destructive. So today, make a list of the people you need to forgive and the things you need to forget. Then ask God to give you the strength to forgive and move on.

Heavenly Father, free me from anger and bitterness. Keep me mindful that forgiveness is Your commandment. Let me turn away from bitterness and instead claim the spiritual abundance that You offer through the gift of Your Son. Amen.

187

LIFE IS A SERIES OF CHOICES

But seek first the kingdom of God and His righteousness,
and all these things will be provided for you.
MATTHEW 6:33 HCSB

Your life is a series of choices. From the instant you wake up in the morning until the moment you nod off to sleep at night, you make countless decisions—decisions about the things you do, decisions about the words you speak, and decisions about the way that you choose to direct your thoughts.

As a believer who has been transformed by the love of Jesus, you have every reason to make wise choices. But sometimes, when the daily grind threatens to grind you up and spit you out, you may make choices that are displeasing to God. When you do, you'll pay a price because you'll forfeit the happiness and the peace that might otherwise have been yours.

So as you pause to consider the kind of Christian you are—and the kind of Christian you want to become—ask yourself whether you're sitting on the fence or standing in the light. The choice is yours . . . and so are the consequences.

Every day, I find countless opportunities to decide whether
I will obey God and demonstrate my love for Him or try to please
myself or the world system. God is waiting for my choices.
BILL BRIGHT

Heavenly Father, I have many choices to make. Help me choose wisely as I follow in the footsteps of Your only begotten Son. Amen.

188

KEEP POSSESSIONS IN PERSPECTIVE

He then told them, "Watch out and be on guard against all greed because one's life is not in the abundance of his possessions."
LUKE 12:15 HCSB

All too often, we focus our thoughts and energies on the accumulation of earthly treasures, leaving precious little time to accumulate the only treasures that really matter: the spiritual kind. Our material possessions have the potential to do great good or terrible harm, depending upon how we choose to use them. As believers, our instructions are clear: we must use our possessions in accordance with God's commandments, and we must be faithful stewards of the gifts He has seen fit to bestow upon us. But if we focus too intently on the material aspects of life, we create needless stress for ourselves and our loved ones.

Today, let us honor God by placing no other gods before Him. God comes first; everything else comes next—and "everything else" most certainly includes all of our earthly possessions.

Timely Tip: Everything we have is on loan from God. Holocaust survivor Corrie ten Boom wrote, "I have held many things in my hands, and I have lost them all; but whatever I have placed in God's hands, that I still possess." Remember: your real riches are in heaven, so conduct yourself accordingly.

Dear Lord, Your Word teaches me to seek first Your kingdom and Your righteousness. Today, I will trust You completely for my needs, both spiritual and material. Thank You, Father, for Your protection, for Your Love, and for Your Son. Amen.

189

CHARACTER-BUILDING TAKES TIME

*For this very reason, make every effort to supplement
your faith with goodness, goodness with knowledge,
knowledge with self-control, self-control with endurance,
endurance with godliness.*

2 PETER 1:5–6 HCSB

Character is built slowly over a lifetime. It is the sum of every right decision, every honest word, every noble thought, and every heartfelt prayer. It is forged on the anvil of honorable work and polished by the twin virtues of generosity and humility. Character is a precious thing—difficult to build but easy to tear down.

As believers in Christ, we must seek to live each day with discipline, honesty, and faith. When we do, integrity becomes a habit, and God blesses us with unexpected riches: the spiritual kind.

*Every problem is a character-building opportunity,
and the more difficult it is, the greater the potential
for building spiritual muscle and moral fiber.*

RICK WARREN

Heavenly Father, Your Word instructs me to walk in righteousness and in truth. Make me Your worthy servant, Lord. Let my words be true, and let my actions lead others to You. Amen.

190

SHARE THE GIFT OF CHEERFULNESS

Worry is a heavy load, but a kind word cheers you up.
PROVERBS 12:25 NCV

Cheerfulness is a gift that we give to others and to ourselves. And as believers who have been saved by a risen Christ, why shouldn't we be cheerful? The answer, of course, is that we have every reason to honor our Savior with joy in our hearts, smiles on our faces, and words of celebration on our lips.

Christ promises us lives of abundance and joy if we accept His love and His grace. Yet sometimes even the most righteous among us are beset by fits of ill temper and frustration. During these moments, we may not feel like turning our thoughts and prayers to Christ, but that's precisely what we should do. When we do so, we simply can't stay grumpy for long.

> *Be assured, my dear friend, that it is no joy to God*
> *in seeing you with a dreary countenance.*
> C. H. SPURGEON

Dear Lord, You have given me so many reasons to celebrate. Today, let me choose an attitude of cheerfulness. Let me be a joyful Christian, Lord, quick to smile and slow to anger. And let me share Your goodness with all whom I meet so that Your love might shine in me and through me. Amen.

191

MAKE CHOICES THAT PLEASE GOD

I have set before you life and death, blessing and curse. Choose life so that you and your descendants may live, love the LORD your God, obey Him, and remain faithful to Him. For He is your life, and He will prolong your life in the land the LORD swore to give to your fathers Abraham, Isaac, and Jacob.

DEUTERONOMY 30:19–20 HCSB

Sometimes, because you're an imperfect human being, you may become so wrapped up in meeting society's expectations that you fail to focus on God's expectations. To do so is a mistake of major proportions—don't make it. Instead, seek God's guidance as you focus your energies on becoming the best "you" that you can possibly be. And when it comes to matters of conscience, seek approval not from your peers, but from your Creator.

Whom will you try to please today: God or man? Your primary obligation is not to please imperfect men and women. Your obligation is to strive diligently to meet the expectations of an all-knowing and perfect God. Trust Him always. Love Him always. Praise Him always. And make choices that please Him. Always.

Every day, I find countless opportunities to decide whether I will obey God and demonstrate my love for Him or try to please myself or the world system. God is waiting for my choices.

BILL BRIGHT

Dear Lord, Today, I will choose to please You and only You. I will obey Your commandments, and I will praise You for Your gifts, for Your Love, and for Your Son. Amen.

192

GROW YOUR RELATIONSHIP WITH GOD

But grow in the grace and knowledge of our Lord and Savior Jesus Christ.
To Him be the glory both now and to the day of eternity.

2 PETER 3:18 HCSB

Your relationship with God is ongoing; it unfolds day by day, and it offers countless opportunities to grow closer to Him, or not. As each new day unfolds, you are confronted with a wide range of decisions: how you will behave, where you will direct your thoughts, whom you will associate with, and what you will choose to worship. These choices, along with many others like them, are yours and yours alone. How you choose determines how your relationship with God will unfold.

Are you continuing to grow in your love and knowledge of the Lord, or are you "satisfied" with the current state of your spiritual health? Hopefully, you're determined make yourself a growing Christian. Your Savior deserves no less, and neither, by the way, do you.

Becoming a Christian takes only a single step;
being a Christian means walking with Christ the rest of your life.

BILLY GRAHAM

Dear Lord, Thank You for the opportunity to walk with Your Son. And thank You for the opportunity to grow closer to You each day. I thank You for the person I am, Heavenly Father, and, more importantly, for the person I can become. Amen.

193

COMFORT OTHERS

Carry one another's burdens;
in this way you will fulfill the law of Christ.

GALATIANS 6:2 HCSB

We live in a world that is, on occasion, a frightening place. Sometimes we sustain life-altering losses that are so profound and so tragic that it seems we could never recover. But with God's help and with the help of encouraging family members and friends, we can recover.

God's Word is clear: as believers, we must offer comfort to those in need by sharing not only our courage but also our faith. As the revivalist Vance Havner observed, "No journey is complete that does not lead through some dark valleys. We can properly comfort others only with the comfort wherewith we ourselves have been comforted of God." Enough said.

God's promises are medicine for the broken heart.
Let Him comfort you. And, after He has comforted you,
try to share that comfort with somebody else.
It will do both of you good.

WARREN WIERSBE

Dear Lord, this world can be a difficult place, a place full of suffering and tears. Let me give comfort to those in need, and let me share Your love with those who grieve. When I meet those who mourn, guide my speech. And when I, too, become discouraged, keep me mindful of Your infinite love. Amen.

194

PRAY ABOUT YOUR FEARS

I asked the LORD for help, and he answered me. He saved me from all that I feared.

PSALM 34:4 NCV

Would you like to overcome irrational fears and exaggerated worries? If the answer to that question is yes, then you should set aside ample time for prayer and praise. As Christians, we are instructed to pray often. But it is important to note that genuine prayer requires much more than bending our knees and closing our eyes. Heartfelt prayer is an attitude of the heart.

Too many of us, even well-intentioned believers, tend to compartmentalize our waking hours into a few familiar categories: work, rest, play, family time, and worship. To do so is a mistake. Worship and praise should be woven into the fabric of our lives; prayer should never be relegated to a weekly three-hour visit to church on Sunday morning. Theologian Wayne Oates once admitted, "Many of my prayers are made with my eyes open. You see, it seems I'm always praying about something, and it's not always convenient—or safe—to close my eyes." Dr. Oates understood that God always hears our prayers and that the relative position of our eyelids is of no concern to Him.

So today, instead of focusing on your fears, find a little more time to pray about them. And while you're at it, praise your heavenly Father for all that He has done. Whether your eyes are open or closed, He's listening.

Prayer wonderfully clears the vision; steadies the nerves; defines duty; stiffens the purpose; sweetens and strengthens the spirit.

S. D. GORDON

Dear Lord, when I am anxious or fearful, I will open my heart to You. I know that You are my loving Father, so I will accept Your will and trust Your promises today and every day. Amen.

195

DON'T COMPLAIN!

Do everything without grumbling and arguing,
so that you may be blameless and pure.

PHILIPPIANS 2:14–15 HCSB

Because we are imperfect human beings, we often lose sight of our blessings. Ironically, most of us have more blessings than we can count, but we may still find reasons to complain about the minor frustrations of everyday life. To do so, of course, is not only wrong; it is also the pinnacle of shortsightedness and a serious roadblock on the path to spiritual abundance.

Are you tempted to complain about the minor frustrations of everyday living? Don't do it! Today and every day, make it a practice to count your blessings, not your hardships. It's the truly decent way to live.

Timely Tip: Try to keep track of the times you complain, either to someone else or to yourself. Also make note of the times you express gratitude to the Lord. Then answer this question: Do you spend more time complaining or praising?

Dear Lord, I know that the choice is mine—I can either count my blessings or recount my disappointments. Today, help me to focus my thoughts upon my blessings, my gifts, and my opportunities. Amen.

196

LISTEN TO THE INNER VOICE

*Let us draw near with a true heart in full assurance
of faith, our hearts sprinkled clean from an
evil conscience and our bodies washed in pure water.*

HEBREWS 10:22 HCSB

When you act in accordance with your beliefs, you inevitably feel more comfortable with your decisions. Why? Because you know intuitively, as well as from experience, that your conscience seldom leads you astray.

Whenever you're about to make an important decision, you should listen carefully to the quiet voice inside. Sometimes, of course, it's tempting to do otherwise. From time to time you'll be tempted to abandon your better judgment by ignoring your conscience. But remember: a conscience is a terrible thing to waste. So instead of ignoring that quiet little voice, pay careful attention to it. If you do, your conscience will lead you in the right direction—in fact, it's trying to lead you right now. So listen . . . and learn.

*Most of us follow our conscience as we follow a wheelbarrow.
We push it in front of us in the direction we want to go.*

BILLY GRAHAM

*The inner voice of God does not argue; it does not try to convince you.
It just speaks, and it is self-authenticating.*

E. STANLEY JONES

Dear Lord, today, I will honor the quiet voice that You have placed in my heart. I will strive to obey Your Word as I follow in the footsteps of Your Son today, tomorrow, and every day of my life. Amen.

197

CONTENTMENT IS FROM GOD

But godliness with contentment is a great gain. For we brought nothing into the world, and we can take nothing out. But if we have food and clothing, we will be content with these. But those who want to be rich fall into temptation, a trap, and many foolish and harmful desires, which plunge people into ruin and destruction.

1 TIMOTHY 6:6–9 HCSB

The preoccupation with happiness and contentment is an ever-present theme in the modern world. We are bombarded with messages that tell us where to find peace and pleasure in a world that worships materialism and wealth. But lasting contentment is not found in material possessions; genuine contentment is a spiritual gift from God to those who trust in Him and follow His commandments.

When God dwells at the center of our lives, peace and contentment will belong to us just as surely as we belong to God.

Timely Tip: Contentment comes, not from your circumstances, but from your attitude and your faith. So today and every day, focus on God's love, stay positive, be patient, and remember that faith is the foundation of a contented life.

Heavenly Father, You are my contentment and my peace. I find protection when I seek Your healing hand; I discover joy when I welcome Your healing Spirit. Let me look to You, Lord, for the peace and contentment that You have offered me through the gift of Your Son. Amen.

198

CONSIDER HIS SACRIFICE

*But God proves His own love for us in that while
we were still sinners Christ died for us!*

ROMANS 5:8 HCSB

As we consider Christ's sacrifice on the cross, we should be profoundly humbled. And today, as we come to Christ in prayer, we should do so in a spirit of humble devotion.

Christ humbled Himself on a cross—for you. He shed His blood—for you. He has offered to walk with you through this life and throughout all eternity. As you approach Him today in prayer, think about His sacrifice and His grace. And be humble.

He came all the way from the comfort and beauty of heaven to the blood-stained cross of Palestine, not just for someone like me in the theoretical, but for precisely me in the personal and practical.

BILL BRIGHT

Live your lives in love, the same sort of love which Christ gives us, and which He perfectly expressed when He gave Himself as a sacrifice to God.

CORRIE TEN BOOM

Dear Lord, when I am called upon to make sacrifices for causes that are just, give me courage. Let my words and deeds be pleasing to You, and let my service to others be worthy of the One who sacrificed His life for mine. Help me to understand what cross I am to bear this day. Give me the strength and the courage to carry that cross along the path of Your choosing so that I may be a worthy disciple of Your Son. Amen.

199

LET GOD SOLVE LIFE'S RIDDLES

If you don't know what you're doing, pray to the Father. He loves to help.
You'll get his help, and won't be condescended to when you ask for it. Ask
boldly, believingly, without a second thought. People who "worry their prayers"
are like wind-whipped waves. Don't think you're going to get anything from
the Master that way, adrift at sea, keeping all your options open.

JAMES 1:5–8 MSG

Life presents each of us with countless questions, conundrums, doubts, and problems. Thankfully, the riddles of everyday living are not too difficult to solve if we look for answers in the right places. When we have questions, we should consult God's Word, we should seek the guidance of the Holy Spirit, and we should trust the counsel of God-fearing friends and family members.

Are you facing a difficult decision? Take your concerns to the Lord and avail yourself of the messages and mentors that He has placed along your path. When you do, God will speak to you in His own way and in His own time, and when He does, you can most certainly trust the answers that He gives.

> *Good and evil both increase at compound interest.*
> *That is why the little decisions you and I*
> *make every day are of such infinite importance.*

C. S. LEWIS

Dear Lord, today I come to You seeking guidance. I will trust You to show me the path that I should take, and I will strive, as best I can, to follow in the footsteps of Your Son. Amen.

200

SHARE WORDS OF HOPE

*And let us be concerned about one another
in order to promote love and good works.*
HEBREWS 10:24 HCSB

Hope, like other human emotions, is contagious. When we associate with hope-filled Christians, we are encouraged by their faith and optimism. But if we spend too much time in the company of naysayers and pessimists, our attitudes, like theirs, tend to be cynical and negative.

Are you trying to be a hopeful, optimistic, encouraging believer? And do you associate with like-minded people who are trying to count their blessings instead of their hardships? Hopefully so. As a faithful follower of the One from Galilee, you have every reason to be hopeful, and you have every reason to share your hopes with others. So today, look for reasons to celebrate God's endless blessings. And while you're at it, look for people who will join you in the celebration. You'll be better for their company, and they'll be better for yours.

Timely Tip: As a Christian, you have many reasons to be excited about your life and your future here on earth and in heaven. Share the excitement!

Dear Lord, make me a source of genuine, lasting encouragement to my family and friends. Today, I will celebrate Your blessings, and I will share Your good news with those who cross my path. Let my words and deeds be worthy of Your Son, the One who gives me strength and salvation. Amen.

201

MAKE THE CHOICE
TO FORGIVE

Then Peter came to Him and said, "Lord, how often shall my brother sin against me, and I forgive him? Up to seven times?" Jesus said to him, "I do not say to you, up to seven times, but up to seventy times seven."

MATTHEW 18:21–22 NKJV

Sometimes the act of forgiveness can be hard. Very hard. So if you're having trouble forgiving someone, you are not alone. The world is filled with people who carry grudges to the grave, never fully understanding that forgiveness is a choice that frees us from the bonds of bitterness, hatred, and regret.

When you make the choice to forgive, when you genuinely let go of all anger and resentment, you'll feel better about yourself and your world. Why? Because God grants peace to those who honor Him by obeying His commandments and following in the footsteps of His Son.

Today, as a gift to yourself and to your loved ones, forgive everyone who has ever harmed you. Then claim the inner peace that is your spiritual birthright: the peace of Jesus Christ. It is always available; it has been paid for in full; it is yours for the asking. So ask, receive, and share.

Forgiveness is an act of the will, and the will can function regardless of the temperature of the heart.

CORRIE TEN BOOM

Dear Lord, sometimes I find it difficult to forgive. Today, Father, I ask You to help me move beyond feelings of bitterness and anger. Jesus forgave those who hurt Him; let me walk in His footsteps by forgiving those who have injured me. Amen.

TAKE RESPONSIBILITY FOR YOUR ACTIONS

But each person should examine his own work, and then he will have a reason for boasting in himself alone, and not in respect to someone else. For each person will have to carry his own load.

GALATIANS 6:4-5 HCSB

God's Word encourages us to take responsibility for our actions, but the world tempts us to do otherwise. The media tries to convince us that we're "victims" of our upbringing, our government, our economic strata, or our circumstances, thus ignoring the countless blessings—and the gift of free will—that God has given each of us. We're also tempted to blame our problems on the people who make our lives difficult. It's an easy excuse, but a shortsighted one.

Your heavenly Father wants you to be a faithful steward of the gifts He has given you. But you live in a society that may encourage you to do otherwise. You face countless temptations to squander your time, your resources, and your talents. So you must be keenly aware of the inevitable distractions that can waste your time, your energy, and your opportunities.

Who's responsible for your behavior? And who's responsible for utilizing the talents that the Lord has given you? God's Word says that you are. It's your life, which means that the person you see in the mirror is the very same person who's responsible for the things you do, the things you say, and the way you utilize your talents. No exceptions.

Dear Lord, help me to see my responsibilities and fulfill them. And as I meet my responsibilities, let me follow in the footsteps of Your Son. Amen.

203

ACCEPT THE PAST AND LOOK TO THE FUTURE

People may make plans in their minds,
but the LORD decides what they will do.

PROVERBS 16:9 NCV

If you're like most people, you want things to happen according to your wishes and according to your timetable. But sometimes, God has other plans . . . and He always has the final word.

Are you embittered by a personal tragedy that you did not deserve and cannot understand? If so, it's time to make peace with life. It's time to forgive others, and, if necessary, to forgive yourself. It's time to accept the unchangeable past, to embrace the priceless present, and to have faith in the promise of tomorrow. It's time to trust God completely. And it's time to reclaim the peace—His peace—that can and should be yours.

So if you've encountered unfortunate circumstances that are beyond your power to control, accept those circumstances and trust God. When you do, you can be comforted in the knowledge that your Creator is both loving and wise, and that He understands His plans perfectly, even when you do not.

Turn the past over to God. He is strong enough to take it.
Give Him your future. He will make you strong enough to live it.

KAREN BERNARD

Dear Lord, when I am discouraged, give me hope. When I am anxious, give me peace. When I face circumstances that I cannot change, give me a spirit of acceptance. In all things great and small, let me trust Your plans and entrust my future to You. Amen.

204

FACE UP TO OLD MAN TROUBLE

When you pass through the waters, I will be with you. . . .
When you walk through fire, you will not be burned, . . .
This is because I, the LORD, am your God.

ISAIAH 43:2–3 NCV

As life here on earth unfolds, all of us encounter occasional setbacks. Those occasional visits from Old Man Trouble are simply a fact of life, and none of us are exempt. When tough times arrive, we may be forced to rearrange our plans and our priorities. But even on our darkest days, we must remember that God's love remains constant.

The fact that we encounter adversity is not nearly so important as the way we choose to deal with it. When tough times arrive, we have a clear choice: we can begin the difficult work of tackling our troubles . . . or not. When we summon the courage to look Old Man Trouble squarely in the eye, an amazing thing usually happens: he blinks.

We should not be upset when unexpected and upsetting things happen.
God, in His wisdom, means to make something of us which we
have not yet attained and is dealing with us accordingly.

J. I. PACKER

Heavenly Father, You are my refuge. As I journey through this day, I know that I may encounter disappointments and losses. When I am troubled, let me turn to You. Keep me steady, Lord, and renew a right spirit inside of me this day and forever. Amen.

205

YOU CAN LIVE AND THRIVE IN AN ANXIOUS WORLD

Cast all your anxiety on him because he cares for you.

1 PETER 5:7 NIV

We live in a world that often breeds anxiety and fear. When we come face-to-face with tough times, we may fall prey to discouragement, doubt, or depression. But our Father in heaven has other plans. God has promised that we may lead lives of abundance, not anxiety. In fact, His Word instructs us to "be anxious for nothing" (Philippians 4:6 NKJV). But how can we put our fears to rest? By taking those fears to God and leaving them there.

As you face the challenges of daily life, you may find yourself becoming anxious, troubled, discouraged, or fearful. If so, turn every one of your concerns over to your heavenly Father. The same God who created the universe will comfort you *if* you ask Him . . . so ask Him and trust Him. And then watch in amazement as your anxieties melt into the warmth of His loving hands.

*Anxiety is not only a pain which we must ask God to assuage
but also a weakness we must ask him to pardon,
for he's told us to take no care for the morrow.*

C. S. LEWIS

Heavenly Father, sometimes troubles and distractions preoccupy my thoughts and trouble my soul. When I am anxious, Lord, let me turn my prayers to You. When I am worried, give me faith in You. Let me live courageously, dear God, knowing that You love me and that You will protect me, today and forever. Amen.

206

IF YOU HAVE QUESTIONS OR CONCERNS, GOD HAS ANSWERS

Now if any of you lacks wisdom, he should ask God, who gives to all generously and without criticizing, and it will be given to him.

JAMES 1:5 HCSB

Jesus taught His disciples to ask God for the things they needed. We should do likewise. Prayer produces powerful changes in us *and* in our world. When we lift our prayers to God, we open ourselves to a never-ending source of divine wisdom and infinite love.

Do you have questions about your future that you simply can't answer? Do you have needs that you simply can't meet by yourself? Do you sincerely seek to know God's unfolding plans for your life? If so, ask Him for direction, for protection, and for strength—and then keep asking Him every day that you live. Whatever your need, no matter how great or small, pray about it and never lose hope. God is not just near; He is here, and He's perfectly capable of answering your prayers. Now it's up to you to ask.

We honor God by asking for great things when they are a part of His promise. We dishonor Him and cheat ourselves when we ask for molehills where He has promised mountains.

VANCE HAVNER

Dear Lord, when I have questions about my purpose in life, I will turn to You. When I am weak, I will seek Your strength. When I am discouraged, Father, I will be mindful of Your love and Your grace. I will ask You for the things I need, Father, and I will trust Your answers, today and forever. Amen.

207

GOD'S WORD IS
A PRICELESS GIFT

Man shall not live by bread alone,
but by every word that proceeds from the mouth of God.

MATTHEW 4:4 NKJV

The Bible is a priceless gift, a tool for Christians to use as they share the good news and follow in the footsteps of God's only begotten Son. Yet far too many Christians keep their spiritual tool kits tightly closed and out of sight.

Jonathan Edwards advised, "Be assiduous in reading the holy Scriptures. This is the fountain whence all knowledge in divinity must be derived. Therefore let not this treasure lie by you neglected."

God's holy Word is, indeed, a priceless, one-of-a-kind treasure. Handle it with care, but more importantly, handle it every day . . . no exceptions.

Meditating upon His Word will inevitably
bring peace of mind, strength of purpose,
and power for living.

BILL BRIGHT

Heavenly Father, Your holy Word is a treasure to me; I will study it, trust it, and share it. In all that I do, help me be a worthy witnesses for You as I share the good news of Your perfect Son and Your perfect Word. Amen.

208

ASK GOD TO HELP YOU FOCUS ON THE THINGS THAT REALLY MATTER

You can't go wrong when you love others. When you add up everything in the law code, the sum total is love. But make sure that you don't get so absorbed and exhausted in taking care of all your day-by-day obligations that you lose track of the time and doze off, oblivious to God.

ROMANS 13:10–11 MSG

Each waking moment holds the potential to think a creative thought or offer a heartfelt prayer. So even if you're a person with too many demands and too few hours in which to meet them, don't panic. Instead, be comforted in the knowledge that when you sincerely seek to discover God's priorities for your life, He will provide answers in marvelous and surprising ways.

Remember: this is the day that God has made and that He has filled it with countless opportunities to love, to serve, and to seek His guidance. Seize those opportunities. And as a gift to yourself, to your family, and to the world, slow down and claim the inner peace that is your spiritual birthright: the peace of Jesus Christ. It is yours for the asking. So ask . . . and be thankful.

We are not called to be burden-bearers, but cross-bearers and light-bearers. We must cast our burdens on the Lord.

CORRIE TEN BOOM

Dear Lord, when the demands of the day leave me distracted and discouraged, help me establish priorities that are pleasing to You. Let me accept the spiritual abundance that is mine through Christ, let me share His message with the world, and let me share His love with all who cross my path. Amen.

209

PRAY ABOUT YOUR CHALLENGES AND TRUST YOUR HEAVENLY FATHER

Trust the LORD with all your heart, and don't depend on your own understanding. Remember the LORD in all you do, and he will give you success.

PROVERBS 3:5–6 NCV

Prayer is a powerful antidote to anxiety; so, too, is a regular time of devotional reading and meditation. When we spend quiet moments in the divine presence of our heavenly Father, we are reminded once again that our troubles are temporary, but His love is not.

As you face the inevitable challenges of everyday living, do you find yourself becoming anxious, troubled, discouraged, or fearful? If so, turn every one of your concerns over to your heavenly Father. The same God who created the universe will comfort you if you ask Him. Your job, simply put, is to ask Him.

Worry and anxiety are sand in the machinery of life; faith is the oil.

E. STANLEY JONES

So often we pray and then fret anxiously, waiting for God to hurry up and do something. All the while God is waiting for us to calm down, so He can do something through us.

CORRIE TEN BOOM

Dear Lord, when I am anxious, I will turn to You for strength and comfort. And when I need help from friends or mentors, give me the wisdom to listen and learn. Amen.

210

ARE YOU A CHEERFUL CHRISTIAN?

Be cheerful. Keep things in good repair. Keep your spirits up.
Think in harmony. Be agreeable. Do all that,
and the God of love and peace will be with you for sure.

2 Corinthians 13:11 MSG

Lettie Cowman, the author of the classic devotional text *Streams in the Desert*, wrote, "Two wings are necessary to lift our souls toward God: prayer and praise. Prayer asks. Praise accepts the answer." That's why we should find the time to lift our concerns to God in prayer, and to praise Him for all that He has done.

John Wesley correctly observed, "Sour godliness is the devil's religion." His words remind us that pessimism and doubt are some of the most important tools that Satan uses to achieve his objectives. Our challenge, of course, is to ensure that Satan cannot use these tools *on us*.

Are you a cheerful Christian? You should be! And what is the best way to attain the joy that is rightfully yours? By giving Christ what is rightfully His: your heart, your soul, and your life.

The practical effect of Christianity is happiness,
therefore let it be spread abroad everywhere!

C. H. Spurgeon

Dear Lord, Your Word reminds me that this is the day that You have created; let me rejoice in it. Today, let me choose an attitude of cheerfulness and celebration. Let me be a joyful Christian, Lord, quick to smile and slow to anger. And let me share Your goodness with all whom I meet so that Your love might shine in me and through me. Amen.

211

MAKE CHOICES THAT PLEASE GOD

Therefore, whether we are at home or away,
we make it our aim to be pleasing to Him.

2 Corinthians 5:9 HCSB

Every day of your life you are confronted with choices. Lots of them. We have so many decisions to make, and with so little information. Yet decide we must. The stories of our lives are, quite literally, human dramas woven together by the habits we form and the choices we make.

Are you willing to invest the time, the effort, and the prayers that are required to make wise decisions? Are you willing to take your concerns to the Lord? And are you willing to avail yourself of the messages and mentors He has placed along your path? If you answered yes to these questions, you'll most certainly make better decisions—decisions that, by the way, will lead directly and inexorably to a better life.

There's no way around it: if you want to lead a life that is pleasing to God, you must make choices that are pleasing to Him. He deserves no less. And neither, for that matter, do you.

Good and evil both increase at compound interest. That is why the little
decisions you and I make every day are of such infinite importance.

C. S. Lewis

Dear Lord, help me to make choices that are pleasing to You. Help me to be honest, patient, and kind. And above all, help me to follow the teachings of Jesus, not just today, but every day. Amen.

WHAT IS YOUR FOCUS?

Look straight ahead, and fix your eyes on what lies before you.
Mark out a straight path for your feet; stay on the safe path.
Don't get sidetracked; keep your feet from following evil.

PROVERBS 4:25–27 NLT

What is your focus today? Are you willing to focus your thoughts and energies on God's blessings and upon His will for your life? Or will you turn your thoughts to other things? This day—and every day hereafter—is a chance to celebrate the life that God has given you. It's also a chance to give thanks to the One who has offered you more blessings than you can possibly count.

Today, why not focus your thoughts on the joy that is rightfully yours in Christ? Why not take time to celebrate God's glorious creation? Why not trust your hopes instead of your fears? When you do, you will think optimistically about yourself and your world . . . and you can then share your optimism with others. They'll be better for it, and so will you. But not necessarily in that order.

Whatever we focus on determines what we become.

E. STANLEY JONES

Dear Lord, help me to face this day with a spirit of optimism and thanksgiving. And let me focus my thoughts on You and Your incomparable gifts. Amen.

213

A CLEAR CONSCIENCE IS A REWARD

If then you were raised with Christ, seek those things which are above,
where Christ is, sitting at the right hand of God.
Set your mind on things above, not on things on the earth.

COLOSSIANS 3:1–2 NKJV

A clear conscience is one of the rewards we earn when we obey God's Word and follow His will. When we follow God's will and follow in the footsteps of His Son, our earthly rewards are never-ceasing, and our heavenly rewards are everlasting.

The following words of wisdom remind us to pay careful attention to the quiet voice that God has placed within our hearts.

God considers a pure conscience a very valuable thing—
one that keeps our faith on a steady course.

CHARLES STANLEY

One of the ways God has revealed Himself to us is in the conscience.
Conscience is God's lamp within the human breast.

BILLY GRAHAM

It is neither safe nor prudent to do anything against one's conscience.

MARTIN LUTHER

Dear Lord, You have given me a conscience that tells me right from wrong. Let me listen to that quiet voice so that I might do Your will and follow Your Word today and every day. Amen.

214

FIND CONTENTMENT

*Come unto me, all ye that labor and are
heavy laden, and I will give you rest.*

MATTHEW 11:28 KJV

Where can we find contentment? Is it a result of wealth or power or beauty or fame? Hardly. Genuine contentment is a gift from God to those who trust Him and follow His commandments.

Our modern world seems preoccupied with the search for happiness. We are bombarded with messages telling us that happiness depends upon the acquisition of material possessions. These messages are false. Enduring peace is not the result of our acquisitions; it is a spiritual gift from God to those who obey Him and accept His will.

If we don't find contentment in God, we will never find it anywhere else. But if we seek Him and obey Him, we will be blessed with an inner peace that is beyond human understanding.

*Contentment is something we learn by adhering to the basics—
cultivating a growing relationship with Jesus Christ, living daily,
and knowing that Christ strengthens us for every challenge.*

CHARLES STANLEY

Contentment is possible when we stop striving for more.

CHARLES SWINDOLL

Dear Lord, let me find contentment and balance. Let Your priorities be my priorities. And when I have done my best, give me the wisdom to place my faith and my trust in You. Amen.

215

MAKE YOUR GENEROSITY
LIKE CHRIST'S

*But God proves His own love for us in that
while we were still sinners Christ died for us!*

ROMANS 5:8 HCSB

Christ showed His love for us by willingly sacrificing His own life so that we might have eternal life. We, as Christ's followers, are challenged to share His love. And when we walk each day with Jesus—and obey the commandments found in God's holy Word—we are worthy ambassadors for Him.

Just as Christ has been—and will always be—the ultimate friend to His flock, so should we be Christlike in the love and generosity we extend to those in need. When we share the love of Christ, we share a priceless gift. As His servants, we must do no less.

*Find out how much God has given you and from it
take what you need; the remainder is needed by others.*

ST. AUGUSTINE

*Charity—giving to the poor—is an essential part of Christian morality.
I do not believe one can settle how much we ought to give.
I am afraid the only safe rule is to give more than we can spare.*

C. S. LEWIS

Father, Your gifts are priceless. You gave Your Son Jesus to save us, and Your motivation was love. I pray that the gifts I give to others will come from an overflow of my heart, and that they will echo the great love You have for all of Your children. Amen.

216

AN INTENSELY BRIGHT FUTURE IS YOURS

I came to give life—life in all its fullness.

John 10:10 NCV

Are you excited about the opportunities of today and thrilled by the possibilities of tomorrow? Do you confidently expect God to lead you to a place of abundance, peace, and joy? And when your days on earth are over, do you expect to receive the priceless gift of eternal life? If you trust God's promises, and if you have welcomed God's Son into your heart, then you believe that your future is intensely and eternally bright.

It takes courage to dream big dreams. You will discover that courage when you do three things: accept the past, trust God to handle the future, and make the most of the time He has given you today. No dreams are too big for God—not even yours. So start living—and dreaming—accordingly.

You're never too old to set a new goal or dream a new dream.

C. S. Lewis

Every noble work is at first impossible.

Thomas Carlyle

Dear Lord, my hope is in You. Give me the courage to face the future with certainty, and give me the wisdom to follow in the footsteps of Your Son, today and forever. Amen.

217

OUR WORDS HAVE POWER

No foul language is to come from your mouth, but only what is good for building up someone in need, so that it gives grace to those who hear.

EPHESIANS 4:29 HCSB

The words that we speak have the power to do great good or great harm. If we speak words of encouragement and hope, we can lift others up. And that's exactly what God commands us to do!

Sometimes, when we feel uplifted and secure, it easy to speak kind words. Other times, when we are discouraged or tired, we can scarcely summon the energy to uplift ourselves, much less anyone else. God intends that we speak words of kindness, wisdom, and truth, no matter our circumstances, no matter our emotions. When we do, we share a priceless gift with the world, and we give glory to the One who gave His life for us. As believers, we must do no less.

Timely Tip: You can't lift other people up without lifting yourself up too. The more encouragement you give, the more you'll receive in return.

Lord, make me mindful of my words. Make me a powerful source of encouragement to those in need, and let my words and deeds be worthy of Your Son, the One who gives me courage and strength for this day and for all eternity. Amen.

218

TAKE TIME TO ASK

He granted their request because they trusted in Him.

1 Chronicles 5:20 HCSB

Sometimes amid the demands and the frustrations of everyday life, we forget to slow ourselves down long enough to talk with God. Instead of turning our thoughts and prayers to Him, we rely upon our own resources. Instead of praying for strength and courage, we seek to manufacture it within ourselves. Instead of asking God for guidance, we depend only upon our own limited wisdom. The results of such behaviors are unfortunate and, on occasion, tragic.

Are you in need? Ask God to sustain you. Are you anxious? Take your worries to Him in prayer. Are you weary? Seek God's strength. In all things great and small, seek God's wisdom and His grace. He hears your prayers, and He will answer. All you must do is ask.

Timely Tip: Today, think of a specific need that is weighing heavily on your heart. Then spend a few quiet moments asking God for His guidance and for His help.

Lord, when I have questions or fears, let me turn to You. When I am weak, let me seek Your strength. When I am discouraged, Father, keep me mindful of Your love and Your grace. In all things, let me seek Your will and Your way, dear Lord, today and forever. Amen.

219

BE A POWERFUL EXAMPLE

*Make yourself an example of good works
with integrity and dignity in your teaching..*
TITUS 2:7 HCSB

What kind of example are you? Are you a person whose life serves as a powerful example of decency and morality? Does your behavior serve as a positive role model for others? Are you the kind of person whose actions, day in and day out, are based upon integrity, fidelity, and a love for the Lord? If so, you are not only blessed by God, you are also a powerful force for good in a world that desperately needs positive influences such as yours. And that's good because your family and friends are watching . . . and so, for that matter, is God.

*When our lives are filled with peace, faith and joy,
people will want to know what we have.*
DAVID JEREMIAH

*It is a great deal better to live a holy life than to talk about it.
Lighthouses do not ring bells and fire cannons
to call attention to their shining—they just shine.*
D. L. MOODY

*In our faith we leave footprints to guide others. A child, a friend,
a recent convert. None should be left to walk the trail alone.*
MAX LUCADO

Lord, make me a worthy example to my family and friends. And let my words and my actions show people how my life has been changed by You. I will praise You, Father, by following in the footsteps of Your Son. Let others see Him through me. Amen.

220

SAY YES TO GOD

Fear thou not; for I am with thee.

ISAIAH 41:10 KJV

Your decision to seek a deeper relationship with God will not remove all problems from your life; to the contrary, it will bring about a series of personal crises as you constantly seek to say yes to God although the world encourages you to do otherwise. Each time you are tempted to distance yourself from the Creator, you will face a spiritual crisis. A few of these crises may be monumental in scope, but most will be the small, everyday decisions of life. In fact, life here on earth can be seen as one test after another—and with each crisis comes yet another opportunity to grow closer to God . . . or to distance yourself from His plan for your life.

Today, you will face many opportunities to say yes to your Creator—and you will also encounter many opportunities to say no to Him. Your answers will determine the quality of your day and the direction of your life, so answer carefully . . . *very* carefully.

Christianity is the total plan for the human machine.

C. S. LEWIS

Dear Lord, when life seems chaotic, remind me of Your love and protection. Difficult times provide opportunities for me to grow closer to You. Thank You for all that this day has to offer. Amen.

221

FIND FULFILLMENT

For You, O God, have tested us; You have refined us
as silver is refined. . . . we went through fire and through water;
but You brought us out to rich fulfillment.

PSALM 66:10–12 NKJV

At almost every turn, we are confronted with messages that happiness and fulfillment are commodities that are available to the highest bidder. The world promises its own brand of contentment, a sense of satisfaction that is based on material possessions or earthly power. But the contentment that the world offers is fleeting and incomplete. The world makes promises that it cannot keep. So amid the inevitable hustle and bustle of life here on earth, we can forfeit—albeit temporarily—the joy of Christ as we wrestle with the challenges of daily living. Yet God's Word is clear: fulfillment through Christ is available to all who seek it and claim it. Count yourself among that number. Seek first a personal, transforming relationship with Jesus, and then claim the joy, the fulfillment, and the spiritual abundance that the shepherd offers His sheep.

By trying to grab fulfillment everywhere, we find it nowhere.
ELISABETH ELLIOT

Jesus wants Life for us; Life with a capital L.
JOHN ELDREDGE

Dear Lord, when I turn my thoughts and prayers to You, I feel peace and fulfillment. But sometimes, when I am distracted by the busyness of the day, fulfillment seems far away. Today, let me trust Your will, let me follow Your commands, and let me accept Your peace. Amen.

222

HIS HAND DIRECTS THE FUTURE

Don't brashly announce what you're going to do tomorrow;
you don't know the first thing about tomorrow.

PROVERBS 27:1 MSG

The old saying is both familiar and true: "Man proposes and God disposes." Our world unfolds according to God's plans, not our wishes. Thus boasting about future events is to be avoided by those who acknowledge God's sovereignty over all things.

Are you planning for a better tomorrow for yourself and your family? If so, you are to be congratulated: God rewards forethought in the same way that He often punishes impulsiveness. But as you make your plans, do so with humility, with gratitude, and with trust in your heavenly Father. His hand directs the future; to think otherwise is both arrogant and naïve.

No situation is beyond God's control. Over my wife's desk are
these words: "Fear not for the future. God is already there."

BILLY GRAHAM

Whether our fear is absolutely realistic or out of proportion
in our minds, our greatest refuge is Jesus Christ.

LUCI SWINDOLL

Dear Lord, as I look to the future, I will place my trust in You. If I become discouraged, I will turn to You. If I am weak, I will seek strength in You. You are my Father, and I will place my hope, my trust, and my faith in You. Amen.

223

WHEN YOU ASK GOD FOR WISDOM, HE WILL GIVE IT

But if any of you needs wisdom, you should ask God for it. He is generous to everyone and will give you wisdom without criticizing you.

JAMES 1:5 NCV

The quality of the decisions you make today will determine, to a surprising extent, the quality of this particular day *and* the direction of all the ones that follow it. And as you're making those decisions, it's important to remember that if you ask God for wisdom, He has promised to provide it.

If you're feeling anxious, worried, or sad, it's time to take a deeper dive into God's Word. When you study the Bible every day, you'll inevitably feel better about your day, your future, and your eternal destiny. And, by the way, you'll make better decisions. The following words of wisdom are powerful reminders that important decisions are best made in consultation with the Lord.

We have ample evidence that the Lord is able to guide.
The promises cover every imaginable situation.
All we need to do is to take the hand he stretches out.

ELISABETH ELLIOT

We must always invite Jesus to be the navigator of our plans,
desires, wills, and emotions, for He is the way, the truth, and the life.

BILL BRIGHT

Dear Lord, as I experience another day of life, guide me along a path of Your choosing. Help me make choices that are pleasing to You. Help me to be honest, patient, and obedient. And above all, help me to follow in the footsteps of Your Son, today and every day. Amen.

224

LET GOD HANDLE "IT"

Your righteousness reaches heaven,
God, You who have done great things; God, who is like You?

PSALM 71:19 HCSB

It's a promise that is made over and over again in the Bible: Whatever "it" is, God can handle it. So when you're feeling worried or fearful, it's helpful to remember that the Lord will guide you and protect you, today, tomorrow, and forever.

Life isn't always easy. Far from it. Sometimes life can be very, very difficult. But even then, even during our darkest moments, we're protected by a loving heavenly Father. When we're worried, God can reassure us; when we're sad, God can comfort us. When our hearts are broken, God is not just near, He is here. So we must lift our thoughts and prayers to Him. When we do, He will answer our prayers. Why? Because He is our shepherd, and He has promised to protect us now and forever.

As you walk through the valley of the unknown, you will find
the footprints of Jesus both in front of you and beside you.

CHARLES STANLEY

As sure as God puts his children in the furnace,
he will be in the furnace with them.

C. H. SPURGEON

Dear Lord, when I obey Your commandments, I am blessed. Today, I invite You to reign over my heart. I will sense Your presence, Father; I will accept Your love; and I will praise You for the Savior of my life: Your Son Jesus. Amen.

225

HONOR GOD

Honor GOD with everything you own; give him the first and the best.
Your barns will burst, your wine vats will brim over.

PROVERBS 3:9–10 MSG

Whom will you choose to honor today? If you honor God and place Him at the center of your life, every day is a cause for celebration. But if you fail to honor your heavenly Father, you're asking for trouble, and lots of it.

At times your life is probably hectic, demanding, and complicated. And if the complications begin to spin out of control, you may experience anxious moments or feelings of sadness. When the demands of life leave you rushing from place to place with scarcely a moment to spare, you may fail to pause and thank your Creator for the blessings He has bestowed upon you. But that's a big mistake. So honor God for who He is and for what He has done for you. And don't just honor Him on Sunday morning. Praise Him all day long, every day, for as long as you live . . . and then for all eternity.

Praise opens the window of our hearts, preparing us to walk
more closely with God. Prayer raises the window of our spirit,
enabling us to listen more clearly to the Father.

MAX LUCADO

I praise You, Lord, from the depths of my heart, and I give thanks for Your goodness, for Your mercy, and for Your Son. Let me honor You every day of my life through my words and my deeds. Let me honor You, Father, with all that I am. Amen.

226

SOMETIMES IT'S HARD
TO BE KIND

Don't be obsessed with getting your own advantage.
Forget yourselves long enough to lend a helping hand.
PHILIPPIANS 2:4 MSG

Sometimes, when we feel happy or generous, we find it easy to be kind. Other times, when we are discouraged or tired, we can scarcely summon the energy to utter a single kind word. But God's commandment is clear: He intends that we make the conscious choice to treat others with kindness and respect, no matter our circumstances, no matter our emotions.

Today, as you consider all the things that Christ has done in your life, honor Him by following His commandment and obeying the Golden Rule. He expects no less, and He deserves no less.

Timely Tip: When dealing with other people, try, as best you can, to "walk in their shoes." And remember this: when you treat others with respect, you won't just feel better about them; you'll also feel better about yourself.

Dear Lord, because I expect to be treated with kindness, let me be kind. Because I wish to be loved, let me love others. Because I need forgiveness, let me be merciful. In all things, Lord, let me live by the Golden Rule, today and every day. Amen.

227

LEARN THE LESSONS OF TOUGH TIMES

I waited patiently for the LORD, and He turned to me and heard my
cry for help. He brought me up from a desolate pit, out of the muddy clay,
and set my feet on a rock, making my steps secure.
He put a new song in my mouth, a hymn of praise to our God.

PSALM 40:1–3 HCSB

Have you experienced a recent setback? If so, look for the lesson that God is trying to teach you. Instead of complaining about life's sad state of affairs, learn what needs to be learned, change what needs to be changed, and move on. View failure as an opportunity to reassess God's will for your life. View life's inevitable disappointments as opportunities to learn more about yourself and your world. And then, when you've learned those lessons, focus on your future, not your past.

Life can be difficult at times. And everybody makes mistakes. Your job is to make them only once.

God is able to take mistakes, when they are committed to Him,
and make of them something for our good and for His glory.

RUTH BELL GRAHAM

Mistakes offer the possibility for redemption and a new start in God's
kingdom. No matter what you're guilty of, God can restore your innocence.

BARBARA JOHNSON

Lord, I know that I am imperfect and that I fail You in many ways. Thank You for Your forgiveness and for Your unconditional love. Show me the error of my ways, Lord, that I might confess my wrongdoing and correct my mistakes. And let me grow each day in wisdom, in faith, and in my love for You. Amen.

228

LOVE YOUR NEIGHBOR

Each one of us needs to look after the good of the people around us,
asking ourselves, "How can I help?" That's exactly what Jesus did.
ROMANS 15:2–3 MSG

Neighbors. We know that we are instructed to love them, and yet there's so little time . . . and we're so busy. No matter. As Christians, we are commanded by our Lord and Savior Jesus Christ to love our neighbors just as we love ourselves. Period.

This very day you will encounter someone who needs a word of encouragement or a pat on the back or a helping hand or a heartfelt prayer. And if you don't reach out to your friend, who will? If you don't take the time to understand the needs of your neighbors, who will? If you don't love your brothers and sisters, who will? So today, look for a neighbor in need . . . and then do something to help. Father's orders.

> *Do all the good you can, by all the means you can,*
> *in all the places you can, at all the times you can,*
> *to all the people you can, as long as ever you can.*
> JOHN WESLEY

> *When you add value to others,*
> *you do not take anything away from yourself.*
> JOHN MAXWELL

Heavenly Father, help me be a good Samaritan to the people You place along my path. Help me to be a grateful, generous follower of Your Son, today, tomorrow, and every day of my life. Amen.

229

BE A CONFIDENT CHRISTIAN

You are my hope; O Lord GOD, You are my confidence.

PSALM 71:5 NASB

We Christians have many reasons to be confident. God is in His heaven; Christ has risen, and we are the sheep of His flock. Yet sometimes even the most devout Christians can become anxious or discouraged. Discouragement, however, is not God's way; He is a God of possibility not negativity.

Are you a confident Christian? You should be. God's grace is eternal and His promises are unambiguous. So count your blessings, not your hardships. And live courageously. God is the Giver of all things good, and He watches over you today and forever.

The truth of Christ brings assurance and so removes the former problem of fear and uncertainty.

A. W. TOZER

Down through the centuries, in times of trouble and trial, God has brought courage to the hearts of those who love Him. The Bible is filled with assurances of God's help and comfort in every kind of trouble which might cause fears to arise in the human heart. You can look ahead with promise, hope, and joy.

BILLY GRAHAM

Lord, when I place my confidence in the things of this earth, I will be disappointed. But when I put my confidence in You, I am secure. In every aspect of my life, Father, let me place my hope and my trust in Your infinite wisdom and Your boundless grace. Amen.

230

JESUS IS THE WORLD'S BEST FRIEND

No one has greater love than this, that someone
would lay down his life for his friends.

JOHN 15:13 HCSB

Who's the best friend this world has ever had? The answer, of course, is Jesus. When you invite Him into your heart, He will be your friend, too . . . your friend forever. Jesus has offered to share the gifts of everlasting life and everlasting love with the world . . . and with you. If you make mistakes, He will still love you. If you behave badly, He will forgive you. If you feel sorry or sad, He will help you feel better about your world and yourself.

Jesus wants you to have a joyful, meaningful, abundant life. He wants you to be generous and kind, and He wants you to follow Him. The rest, of course, is up to you. You can do it! And with a friend like Jesus, you most certainly will.

Timely Tip: An old hymn begins, "What a friend we have in Jesus, . . ." How true. Jesus is, indeed, the sovereign friend and ultimate Savior of mankind. May we all follow Him, praise Him, and share His message of salvation with our neighbors and with the world.

Dear Jesus, You are my Savior and my protector. Give me the courage to trust You completely. Today, I will praise You, I will honor You, and I will live according to Your commandments. Amen.

231

DO YOU HAVE TOO MANY POSSESSIONS?

Do not love the world or the things that belong to the world.
If anyone loves the world, love for the Father is not in him.

1 JOHN 2:15 HCSB

On the grand stage of a well-lived life, material possessions should play a rather small role. Of course, we all need the basic necessities of life, but once we meet those needs for ourselves and for our families, the piling up of possessions creates more problems than it solves. Our real riches, of course, are not of this world. We are never really rich until we are rich in spirit.

How much stuff is too much stuff? Well, if your desire for stuff is getting in the way of your desire to know God, then you've got too much stuff—it's as simple as that. So if you find yourself wrapped up in the concerns of the material world, it's time to reorder your priorities. And it's time to begin storing up riches that will endure throughout eternity—the spiritual kind.

We own too many things that aren't worth owning.

MARIE T. FREEMAN

As faithful stewards of what we have, ought we not
to give earnest thought to our staggering surplus?

ELISABETH ELLIOT

Dear Lord, keep me mindful that material possession cannot bring me joy—my joy comes from You. I will share that joy with family, with friends, and with neighbors, this day and every day. Amen.

232

ESTABLISH COMMON-SENSE BOUNDARIES

Stay away from a fool, for you will not find knowledge on their lips.

Proverbs 14:7 NIV

When you become involved in relationships that require you to compromise your values, you'll make yourself miserable. Why? Because when you find yourself in situations where other people are encouraging you to do things you know to be wrong, your guilty conscience simply won't allow you to be happy. And if you find yourself surrounded by people who are unstable, impulsive, or addicted, you'll soon discover that emotional distress is contagious, as are its consequences.

In a perfect world populated by perfect people, our relationships would be trouble-free. But the world isn't perfect, and neither are the people who inhabit it. As a consequence, we occasionally find ourselves struggling in less-than-perfect relationships that make us anxious or fearful or both. As we work to make those imperfect relationships a little happier and healthier, we must first try to establish sensible boundaries. And if we find ourselves in relationships that are debilitating or dangerous, we should accept the fact that complete separation may be necessary.

To fully experience God's gifts, you need to establish sensible boundaries with people whose emotional challenges present threats to your emotional or physical health. After all, you deserve relationships that will bring abundance to you, to your family, and to God's world.

Dear Lord, let Your will be my will, and let Your boundaries be my boundaries, today and every day. Amen.

233

GOD REWARDS OBEDIENCE

Jesus answered, "If people love me, they will obey my teaching. My Father will love them, and we will come to them and make our home with them."

JOHN 14:23 NCV

God's instructions to mankind are contained in a book like no other: the Holy Bible. When we obey God's commandments and listen carefully to the conscience He has placed in our hearts, He has promised that we are secure. But if we disobey our Creator, if we choose to ignore the teachings and the warnings of His Word, we do so at great peril.

Susanna Wesley said, "There are two things to do about the Gospel: believe it and behave it." Her words serve as a powerful reminder that, as Christians, we are called to take God's promises seriously and to live in accordance with His teachings.

God gave us His commandments for a reason: so that we might obey them and be blessed. Yet we live in a world that presents us with countless temptations to stray far from His path. It is our responsibility to resist those temptations with vigor. Obedience isn't just the best way to experience the full measure of God's blessings; it's the only way.

To yield to God means to belong to God, and to belong to God means to have all His infinite power. To belong to God means to have all.

HANNAH WHITALL SMITH

Heavenly Father, I ask that You guide me so that I can live in accordance with Your plan for my life. Deliver me, Lord, from the painful mistakes that I make when I stray from Your commandments. Let me trust Your promises and follow in the footsteps of Your Son this day and every day. Amen.

234

BE EXCITED ABOUT GLORIOUS OPPORTUNITIES

Make the most of every opportunity.

COLOSSIANS 4:5 NIV

Are you excited about the opportunities of today and thrilled by the possibilities of tomorrow? Do you confidently expect God to lead you to a place of abundance, peace, and joy? And when your days on earth are over, do you expect to receive the priceless gift of eternal life? If you trust God's promises, and if you have welcomed God's Son into your heart, then you believe that your future is intensely and eternally bright.

Today, as you prepare to meet the duties of everyday life, pause and consider God's promises. And then think for a moment about the wonderful future that awaits all believers, including you. God has promised that your future is secure. Trust that promise, and celebrate the life of abundance and eternal joy that is now yours through Christ.

The past is our teacher;
the present is our opportunity;
the future is our friend.

EDWIN LOUIS COLE

Lord, as I take the next steps on my life's journey, let me take them with You. Whatever this day may bring, I thank You for the opportunity to live abundantly. Let me lean upon You, Father—and trust You—this day and forever. Amen.

235

WHEN YOU'RE ANXIOUS OR STRESSED, TRUST GOD

But the salvation of the righteous is from the LORD;
He is their strength in the time of trouble.

PSALM 37:39 NKJV

Every life, including yours, is a series of successes and failures, celebrations and disappointments, joys and sorrows, hopes and doubts. But even when you feel very distant from God, remember that He is never distant from you. When you sincerely seek His presence, He will touch your heart, calm your fears, and restore your confidence. No challenge is too big for Him. Not even yours. So if you're dealing with a stressful situation—or if you're juggling several of them—keep praying, trust God, and pay careful attention to these words of wisdom:

When frustrations develop into problems that stress you out,
the best way to cope is to stop, catch your breath,
and do something for yourself, not out of selfishness, but out of wisdom.

BARBARA JOHNSON

Stress is as necessary to fine-tuning in life as it is to fine-tuning a guitar string.

EDWIN LOUIS COLE

The creation of a new heart, the renewing of a right spirit
is an omnipotent work of God. Leave it to the Creator.

HENRY DRUMMOND

Dear Lord, when I am troubled, help me to trust You more. And when I encounter difficult situations, keep me mindful that no problems are too big for You . . . not even mine. Amen.

236

WE MUST BE PATIENT WITH OURSELVES

To your knowledge, add self-control;
and to your self-control, add patience;
and to your patience, add service for God.

2 PETER 1:6 NCV

Being patient with other people can be difficult. But sometimes, we find it even more difficult to be patient with ourselves. We have high expectations and lofty goals. We want to accomplish things now, not later. And, of course, we want our lives to unfold according to our own timetables, not God's.

Throughout the Bible, we are instructed that patience is the companion of wisdom. God's message, then, is clear: we must be patient with all people, beginning with that particular person who stares back at us each time we gaze into the mirror.

I think that if God forgives us we might
forgive ourselves. Otherwise it is almost like setting up
ourselves as a higher tribunal than Him.

C. S. LEWIS

Dear Lord, You have been so patient with me, and I praise You for Your forgiveness. Let me be patient with myself, Father, even when I fall short of my own expectations. You have forgiven me, Lord—now I must forgive myself. Amen.

AVOID FOOLISH PRIDE

*Do nothing out of rivalry or conceit,
but in humility consider others
as more important than yourselves.*

PHILIPPIANS 2:3 HCSB

Sometimes our faith is tested more by prosperity than by adversity. Why? Because in times of plenty, we are tempted to stick out our chests and say, "I did that." But nothing could be farther from the truth. All of our blessings start and end with God, and whatever "it" is, He did it. And He deserves the credit.

Who are the greatest among us? Are they the proud and the powerful? Hardly. The greatest among us are the humble servants who care less for their own glory and more for God's glory. If we seek greatness in God's eyes, we must forever praise God's good works, not our own.

*All kindness and good deeds, we must keep silent.
The result will be an inner reservoir of personality power.*

CATHERINE MARSHALL

*Jesus had a humble heart. If He abides in us,
pride will never dominate our lives.*

BILLY GRAHAM

Lord, give me a humble heart. Keep me mindful, dear God, that all my gifts come from You. Let me grow beyond my need for earthly praise, Lord, and when I seek approval, let me look only to You. Amen.

238

ULTIMATE ACCOUNTABILITY WILL COME

*We encouraged, comforted, and implored
each one of you to walk worthy of God,
who calls you into His own kingdom and glory.*

1 THESSALONIANS 2:12 HCSB

For most of us, it is a daunting thought: one day, perhaps soon, we'll come face-to-face with our heavenly Father, and we'll be called to account for our actions here on earth. Our personal histories will certainly not be surprising to God; He already knows everything about us. But the full scope of our activities may be surprising to us: some of us will be pleasantly surprised; others will not be.

Today, do whatever you can to ensure that your thoughts and your deeds are pleasing to your Creator. Because you will, at some point in the future, be called to account for your actions. And the future may be sooner than you think.

Our walk counts far more than our talk, always!

GEORGE MUELLER

Dear Lord, let my words and actions show the world the changes that You have made in my life. You sent Your Son so that I might have abundant life and eternal life. Thank You, Father, for my Savior, Christ Jesus. I will follow Him, honor Him, and share His good news, this day and every day. Amen.

239

BE A WORTHY DISCIPLE

He has told you men what is good
and what it is the LORD requires of you:
to act justly, to love faithfulness,
and to walk humbly with your God.

MICAH 6:8 HCSB

When Jesus addressed His disciples, He warned that each one must, "take up his cross, and follow me" Mark 8:34. The disciples must have known exactly what the Master meant. In Jesus' day, prisoners were forced to carry their own crosses to the location where they would be put to death. Thus Christ's message was clear: in order to follow Him, Christ's disciples must deny themselves and, instead, trust Him completely. Nothing has changed since then.

If we are to be disciples of Christ, we must trust Him and place Him at the very center of our beings. Jesus never comes "next." He is always first.

Do you seek to be a worthy disciple of Christ? Then pick up your cross today and every day that you live. When you do, He will bless you now and forever.

Our Lord's conception of discipleship
is not that we work for God,
but that God works through us.

OSWALD CHAMBERS

Dear Lord, thank You for the gift of Your Son Jesus, my personal Savior. Let me be a worthy disciple of Christ, and let me be ever grateful for His love. I will praise You always, Father, as I give thanks for Your Son and for Your everlasting love. Amen.

240

IF YOU ENTRUST YOUR FUTURE TO GOD, YOU NEED NOT FOCUS ON YOUR PAST

"I say this because I know what I am planning for you," says the LORD. "I have good plans for you, not plans to hurt you. I will give you hope and a good future."

JEREMIAH 29:11 NCV

Since we can't change the pains and disappointments of the past, why do so many of us insist upon replaying them over and over again in our minds? Perhaps it's because we can't find it in our hearts to forgive the people who have hurt us. Being mere mortals, we seek revenge, not reconciliation, and we harbor hatred in our hearts, sometimes for decades.

Some of life's greatest roadblocks are not the ones we see through the windshield; they are, instead, the roadblocks that seem to fill the rearview mirror. Because we are imperfect human beings who lack perfect control over our thoughts, we may allow ourselves to become "stuck" in the past. Instead of focusing our thoughts and energies on the opportunities of today, we may allow painful memories to fill our minds and sap our strength. We simply can't seem to let go of our pain, so we relive it again and again. Thankfully, God has other plans.

Today is filled with opportunities to live, to love, to work, to play, and to celebrate life. If we wish to build a better tomorrow, we can start building it today. So if you've endured a difficult past, accept it, learn from it, and forgive everybody, including yourself. Once you've made peace with your past, live in the precious present, where opportunities abound and change is still possible.

Dear Lord, sometimes I focus too intently on past disappointments. Keep me mindful, Father, that I must forgive others, just as you have forgiven me. Today, help me accept the past, treasure the present, and entrust my future to You. Amen.

241

SAY YES TO COMPETENCE; NO TO EXCUSES

Do you see people skilled in their work?
They will work for kings, not for ordinary people.
Proverbs 22:29 NCV

Excuses are everywhere . . . excellence is not. If you seek excellence (and the rewards that accompany it), you must avoid the bad habit of making excuses.

Whatever your job description, it's up to you, and no one else, to become a master of your craft. It's up to you to do your job right—and to do it right now. When you do, you'll discover that excellence is its own reward . . . but not its only reward.

Rationalization: It's what we do when we substitute false explanations for true reasons. It's when we cloud our actual motives with nice-sounding excuses.
Charles Swindoll

Few things fire up a person's commitment like dedication to excellence.
John Maxwell

There is a canyon of difference between doing your best to glorify God and doing whatever it takes to glorify yourself. The quest for excellence is a mark of maturity. The quest for power is childish.
Max Lucado

Dear Lord, I will strive to become a person of dedication and skill. Today, I will do my best, and I will expect the best. Amen.

242

TRUE GREATNESS IS ACHIEVED THROUGH SERVICE

The greatest among you will be your servant. For those who exalt themselves will be humbled, and those who humble themselves will be exalted.

MATTHEW 23:11–12 NIV

The Bible teaches us that the most esteemed men and women are not necessarily rich *or* famous. To the contrary, Jesus made it clear that the greatest among us are those who choose to minister and to serve.

If you genuinely seek to discover God's unfolding purpose for your life, you must ask yourself this question: How does God want me to serve?

Whatever your path, whatever your calling, you may be certain of this: service to others is an integral part of God's plan for you. Christ was the ultimate servant, the Savior who gave His life for mankind. If we are to follow Him, we, too, must become humble servants.

Every single day of your life, including this one, God will give you opportunities to serve Him by serving His children. Welcome those opportunities with open arms. They are God's gift to you, His way of allowing you to achieve greatness in His kingdom.

Through our service to others, God wants to influence our world for Him.

VONETTE BRIGHT

Heavenly Father, give me a servant's heart. Give me a passion for my daily responsibilities, and when I have completed my work, let all the honor and glory be Yours. Amen.

243

JOURNEY WITH GOD

*For it is God who is working in you, enabling you both
to desire and to work out His good purpose.*

PHILIPPIANS 2:13 HCSB

Your life is a journey, and every step of the way, God is with you. If you seek to live in accordance with God's will for your life—and you should—then you will live in accordance with His commandments. You will study God's Word, and you will be watchful for His signs. You will associate with fellow Christians who will encourage your spiritual growth, and you will listen to that inner voice that speaks to you in the quiet moments of your daily devotions.

Sometimes God's plans seem unmistakably clear to you. But other times, He may lead you through the wilderness before He directs you to the promised land. So be patient and keep seeking His will for your life. When you do, you'll be amazed at the marvelous things that an all-powerful, all-knowing God can do.

God intends to use you in wonderful, unexpected ways if you let Him. The decision to seek God's plan and to follow it is yours and yours alone. The consequences of that decision have implications that are both profound and eternal, so choose carefully.

*With God, it's never "Plan B" or "second best." It's always "Plan A."
And, if we let Him, He'll make something beautiful of our lives.*

GLORIA GAITHER

Dear Lord, You created me for a reason. Give me the wisdom to follow Your direction for my life's journey. Let me do Your work here on earth by seeking Your will and living it, knowing that when I trust in You, Father, I am eternally blessed. Amen.

244

GOD CAN HEAL YOUR HEART

Believe in the Lord your God, and you will be able to stand firm.
Believe in his prophets, and you will succeed.

2 Chronicles 20:20 NLT

All of us must, from time to time, endure unfortunate circumstances that test our faith. No man or woman, no matter how righteous, is exempt. Christians, however, face their suffering and grief with the ultimate armor: God's promises. God will help heal us if we welcome Him into our hearts.

You don't have to be alone in your hurt! Comfort is yours.
Joy is an option. And it's all been made possible by your Savior.

Joni Eareckson Tada

Suffering is never for nothing. It is that you and I
might be conformed to the image of Christ.

Elisabeth Elliot

God whispers to us in our pleasures, speaks in our conscience,
but shouts in our pains: it is His megaphone to rouse a deaf world.

C. S. Lewis

Dear Lord, I know that You are my shepherd. You care for me; You comfort me; and You watch over me. Today, I will praise You, Father, for Your glorious works, for Your protection, for Your love, and for Your Son. Amen.

245

BE A SHINING LIGHT

*While ye have light, believe in the light,
that ye may be the children of light.*

JOHN 12:36 KJV

The Bible says that you are "the light that gives light to the world" (Matthew 5:14 NCV). What kind of light have you been giving off? Hopefully, you've been a worthy example for all to see. Why? Because this troubled world needs all the light it can get, and that includes your light too.

The old familiar hymn begins, "What a friend we have in Jesus, . . ." No truer words were ever penned. Jesus is the sovereign friend and ultimate Savior of mankind. As a response to His sacrifice, you must let your light shine today and every day. When you do, He will bless you now and forever.

*Light is stronger than darkness—
darkness cannot "comprehend" or "overcome" it.*

ANNE GRAHAM LOTZ

*When we are in a situation where Jesus
is all we have, we soon discover he is all we really need.*

GIGI GRAHAM TCHIVIDJIAN

Dear Lord, You are the way and the truth and the light. Today—as I follow Your way and share Your good news—let me be a worthy example to others and a worthy servant to You. Amen.

246

WHEN YOU ARE CONSISTENTLY KIND, YOU'LL REAP A BOUNTIFUL HARVEST

Kind people do themselves a favor, but cruel people bring trouble on themselves.

PROVERBS 11:17 NCV

The Bible promises that good deeds and kind words are rewarded. And on those days when the sun is shining and all is well, we find it easier to be kind and generous. When we feel happy or prosperous, it seems natural to share our gifts and our blessings. But the sun doesn't shine every day. On difficult days, when we feel discouraged or tired, we can scarcely summon the energy to say a single kind word or share a single pat on the back. But God's commandment is clear: if we want to reap a bountiful harvest, we must not grow weary of doing good.

God intends that we make the conscious choice to treat others with kindness and respect, no matter our circumstances, no matter our emotions. Kindness, therefore, is a choice that we, as Christians must make many times each day. When we weave the thread of kindness into the very fabric of our lives, we give a priceless gift to others, and we give glory to the One who gave His life for us. As believers, we must do no less.

It is one of the most beautiful compensations of life that no one can sincerely try to help another without helping himself.

BARBARA JOHNSON

Heavenly Father, help me see the needs of those around me. Let me spread kind words of encouragement and hope. Let forgiveness rule my heart. And let my willingness to follow Christ be demonstrated through deeds of kindness and service, today and every day. Amen.

247

RELY UPON HIM

*Be humble under God's powerful hand so he will
lift you up when the right time comes.
Give all your worries to him, because he cares about you.*

1 PETER 5:6–7 NCV

God is a never-ending source of support and courage for those of us who call upon Him. When we are weary, He gives us strength. When we see no hope, God reminds us of His promises. When we grieve, God wipes away our tears.

Do the demands of this day threaten to overwhelm you? Are you anxious, fearful, or grief-stricken? If so, you must rely not only upon your own resources but also upon the promises of your Father in heaven. The Lord is, indeed, your shepherd, and He will never abandon you. So even if your circumstances are difficult, trust the Father. His love is eternal and His goodness endures forever.

*We shouldn't think about ourselves and how weak we are.
We should think about God and how strong He is.*

BILLY GRAHAM

*We are all faced with a series of great opportunities
brilliantly disguised as impossible situations.*

CHARLES SWINDOLL

Heavenly Father, You never leave or forsake me. You are always with me, protecting me and encouraging me. Whatever this day may bring, I thank You for Your love and Your strength. Amen.

PRACTICE / LEARN DECISION-MAKING 101

An indecisive man is unstable in all his ways.

JAMES 1:8 HCSB

From the instant you wake in the morning until the moment you nod off to sleep at night, you have the opportunity to make countless decisions—decisions about the things you do, decisions about the words you speak, and decisions about the thoughts you choose to think.

If you're facing one of life's major decisions, here are some things you can do:

1. Gather as much information as you can.
2. Rely on the advice of trusted friends and mentors.
3. Pray for guidance.
4. Trust the quiet inner voice of your conscience.
5. When the time for action arrives, act. Procrastination is the enemy of progress; don't let it defeat you.

People who can never quite seem to make up their minds usually make themselves miserable. So when in doubt, be decisive. It's the decent way to live.

*A man who honors God privately will
show it by making good decisions publicly.*

EDWIN LOUIS COLE

Dear Lord, give me the insight to make wise decisions and the courage to act upon the decisions that I make. Amen.

249

SHARE WITH OTHERS

The greatest among you will be your servant.
Whoever exalts himself will be humbled,
and whoever humbles himself will be exalted.

MATTHEW 23:11–12 HCSB

Jesus has much to teach us about generosity. He teaches that the most esteemed men and women are not the self-congratulatory leaders of society but are, instead, the humblest of servants. If you were being graded on generosity, how would you score? Would you earn high marks in philanthropy and humility? Hopefully so. But if your grades could stand a little improvement, this is the perfect day to begin.

Today, you may feel the urge to hoard your blessings. Don't do it. Instead, give generously to your neighbors, and do so without fanfare. Find a need and fill it . . . humbly. Lend a helping hand and share a word of kindness . . . anonymously. This is God's way.

The measure of a life, after all,
is not its duration but its donation.

CORRIE TEN BOOM

Dear Lord, make me a sacrificial giver. Let me give of my possessions, my talents, my time, and my testimony. Let me give cheerfully, faithfully, and prayerfully. And make me a humble steward of my talents, Lord, so that the praise might be Yours, not mine. Amen.

250

TO REDUCE ANXIETY AND STRESS, SIMPLIFY YOUR LIFE

Better a little with the fear of the LORD than great wealth with turmoil.

PROVERBS 15:16 NIV

Perhaps you think that the more things you acquire, the happier you'll be. If that's what you're thinking, think again.

Simplicity and peace are two concepts that are closely related. Complexity and peace are not. When in doubt, take the simpler route. And while you're taking steps to simplify your life, consider the following words of wisdom and take them to heart.

The more complicated life becomes,
the more we need to quiet our souls before God.

ELISABETH ELLIOT

The simplicity which is in Christ is rarely found among us.
In its stead are programs, methods, organizations,
and a world of nervous activities which occupy time and attention.

A. W. TOZER

Simplifying your life means focusing on who you are physically, emotionally,
and spiritually. If you want to choose joy daily, that's the place to start.

KAY WARREN

Dear Lord, help me understand the joys of simplicity. Life is complicated enough without my adding to the confusion. Wherever I happen to be, help me to keep it simple—very simple. Amen.

251

THE LORD IS OUR ROCK

And he said: "The Lord is my rock and my fortress and my deliverer;
the God of my strength, in whom I will trust."

2 Samuel 22:2–3 NKJV

When we are feeling anxious or afraid, the Lord will give us comfort and hope if we turn to Him. He is, indeed, our fortress in every season of life.

Psalm 145 promises, "The Lord is near to all who call on him, to all who call on him in truth. He fulfills the desires of those who fear him; he hears their cry and saves them." (v. 18–20 NIV). And the words of Jesus offer us comfort: "These things I have spoken to you, that in Me you may have peace. In the world you will have tribulation; but be of good cheer, I have overcome the world" (John 16:33 NKJV).

As believers, we know that God loves us and that He will protect us. In times of hardship, He will strengthen us; in times of sorrow, He will dry our tears. When we are troubled or weak or sorrowful, God is always with us. So we must build our lives on the rock that cannot be shaken: we must trust God. And then we must get on with the hard work of facing our fears and tackling our problems because if we don't, who will? Or should?

Timely Tip: When tough times arrive and you're tempted to give in or give up, don't. Instead, work hard and pray harder. Better days may be just around the corner.

Heavenly Father, You are my strength. I can face the difficulties of this day because You are my rock. As I stand with You, Father, I can overcome adversity just as Jesus overcame this world. Amen.

252

DON'T UNDERESTIMATE THE VALUE OF A GOOD NIGHT'S SLEEP

Rest in God alone, my soul, for my hope comes from Him.
PSALM 62:5 HCSB

If you're chronically anxious, fearful, or tired, perhaps you need a little more sleep. Try this experiment: turn off all your devices and go to bed at a reasonable hour. You'll be amazed at how good you feel when you get eight hours sleep.

And the next time you're tempted to stay up late and consume attention-hijacking, anxiety-producing, time-gobbling media, consider the following words of wisdom:

Take rest. A field that has rested gives a beautiful crop.
OVID

It is a common experience that a problem difficult at night is resolved in the morning after the committee of sleep has worked on it.
JOHN STEINBECK

Life is strenuous. See that your clock does not run down.
LETTIE COWMAN

Go to bed. Whatever you're staying up for isn't worth it.
ANDY ROONEY

Dear Lord, when I'm tired, give me the wisdom to do the wise thing: to turn out the lights, put my head on my pillow, and go to sleep. Amen.

253

PURSUE GOD'S TRUTH

But grow in the grace and knowledge of our Lord
and Savior Jesus Christ. To Him be the glory
both now and forever. Amen.

2 PETER 3:18 NKJV

Have you established a passionate relationship with God's holy Word? Hopefully so. After all, the Bible is a roadmap for life here on earth and for life eternal. And as a believer who has been touched by God's grace, you are called upon to study God's holy Word, to trust His Word, to follow its commandments, and to share its good news with the world.

The words of Matthew 4:4 remind us that, "Man shall not live by bread alone, but by every word that proceedeth out of the mouth of God." (KJV). As believers, we must study the Bible and meditate upon its meaning for our lives. Otherwise we deprive ourselves of a priceless gift from our Creator. God's Holy Word is, indeed, a transforming gift from the Father in heaven. That's why passionate believers must never live by bread alone . . .

Reading the Bible has a purifying effect upon your life.
Let nothing take the place of this daily exercise.

BILLY GRAHAM

Dear Lord, the Bible is Your gift to me; let me use it. When I place Your Word at the very center of my life, I am blessed. Make me a faithful student of Your Word so that I might be a faithful servant in Your world this day and every day. Amen.

254

CLAIM THE JOY

A cheerful heart has a continual feast.
PROVERBS 15:15 HCSB

On some days, as everyone knows, it's hard to be cheerful. Sometimes, as the demands of the world increase and our energy sags, we feel less like "cheering up" and more like "tearing up." But even in our darkest hours, we can turn to God, and He will give us comfort.

Few things in life are more sad, or, for that matter, more absurd, than a grumpy Christian. Christ promises us lives of abundance and joy, but He does not force His joy upon us. We must claim His joy for ourselves, and when we do, Jesus, in turn, fills our spirits with His power and His love.

When we place Jesus at the center of our lives and trust Him as our personal Savior, He will transform us, not just for today, but for all eternity. Then we, as God's children, can share Christ's joy and His message with a world that needs both.

*There are many more flies caught with honey
than with vinegar and there are many more sinners
brought to Christ by happy Christians than by doleful Christians.*
C. H. SPURGEON

Dear Lord, You have given me so many reasons to celebrate life. Today, let me be a joyful Christian—quick to smile and quick to laugh. And let Your love shine in me and through me, this day and forever. Amen.

255

MAKE WISE CHOICES

But the wisdom that is from above is first pure,
then peaceable, gentle, willing to yield, full of mercy and good fruits,
without partiality and without hypocrisy.

JAMES 3:17 NKJV

Because we are creatures of free will, we make choices—lots of them. When we make choices that are pleasing to our heavenly Father, we are blessed. When we make choices that cause us to walk in the footsteps of God's Son, we enjoy the abundance that Christ has promised to those who follow Him. But when make choices that are displeasing to God, we sow seeds that have the potential to bring forth a bitter harvest.

Today, as you encounter the challenges of everyday living, you will make hundreds of choices. Choose wisely. Make your thoughts and your actions pleasing to God. And remember: every choice that is displeasing to Him is the wrong choice—no exceptions.

Every time you make a choice, you are turning the central part of you,
the part that chooses, into something a little different from what it was before.

C. S. LEWIS

No matter how many books you read, no matter how many schools you
attend, you're never really wise until you start making wise choices.

MARIE T. FREEMAN

Dear Lord, today I will focus my thoughts on Your will for my life. I will strive to make decisions that are pleasing to You, and I will strive to follow in the footsteps of Your Son. Amen.

256

YOU'RE NOT STUCK

Therefore, with your minds ready for action, be serious and set your hope completely on the grace to be brought to you at the revelation of Jesus Christ.
1 PETER 1:13 HCSB

Are you in the habit of doing what needs to be done when it needs to be done, or are you more likely to put off the harder tasks until some vaguely defined date in the future? If you've acquired the habit of doing your most important work first (even if you'd rather be doing something else), congratulations! You're not only doing the right thing; you're also reducing anxiety and stress. But if you find yourself putting off all those unpleasant tasks until later (or never), it's time to think about the consequences of your behavior.

Chronic procrastinators unintentionally squeeze the joy out of their own lives and the lives of their loved ones. So your job is to summon the determination, the courage, and the wisdom to defeat Old Man Procrastination whenever he arrives at your doorstep.

You can free yourself from the emotional quicksand by paying less attention to your fears and more attention to your responsibilities. So when you're faced with a difficult choice or an unpleasant responsibility, don't spend endless hours fretting over your fate. Simply seek God's counsel and get busy. And while you're at it, remember that you're not stuck *unless* you allow yourself to be stuck.

*The fear of attempting something big immobilizes people.
To begin a task is usually the toughest step.*

JOHN MAXWELL

Dear Lord, You have many things You want me to do. When there are actions I need to take or things that I need to do, give me the courage and the wisdom to do them sooner rather than later. Amen.

257

REMEMBER THE SOURCE
OF OUR COMFORT

When I am filled with cares, Your comfort brings me joy.
PSALM 94:19 HCSB

In times of adversity, we are wise to remember the words of Jesus, who, when He walked on the waters, reassured His disciples, saying, "Take courage! It is I. Don't be afraid" (Matthew 14:27 NIV). Then, with Christ on His throne—and with trusted friends and loving family members at our sides—we can face our fears with courage and with faith.

Are you facing a difficult challenge? If so, remember that no problem is too big for God . . . not even yours.

*The knowledge that we are never alone calms
the troubled sea of our lives and speaks peace to our souls.*
A.W. TOZER

God is the light in my darkness, the voice in my silence.
HELEN KELLER

*God doesn't comfort us to make us comfortable,
but to make us comforters.*
BILLY GRAHAM

Dear Lord, when I am troubled, You comfort me. When I am discouraged, You lift me up. Whatever my circumstances, Lord, I will trust Your plan for my life. And when my family and friends are troubled, I will remind them of Your love, Your wisdom, and Your grace. Amen.

258

PLAN FOR ALL ETERNITY

*I assure you: Anyone who hears My word
and believes Him who sent Me has eternal life
and will not come under judgment,
but has passed from death to life.*

JOHN 5:24–25 HCSB

As mere mortals, our vision for the future, like our lives here on earth, is limited. God's vision is not burdened by such limitations: His plans extend throughout all eternity. Thus God's plans for you are not limited to the ups and downs of everyday life. Your heavenly Father has bigger things in mind . . . much bigger things.

Let us praise the Creator for His priceless gift, and let us share the good news with all who cross our paths. We return our Father's love by accepting His grace and by sharing His message and His love. When we do, we are blessed here on earth and throughout all eternity.

*Your choice to either receive or reject
the Lord Jesus Christ will determine
where you spend eternity.*

ANNE GRAHAM LOTZ

Dear Lord, I am only here on this earth for a brief while. But You have offered me the gift of eternal life through Your Son Jesus. I accept Your gift, Lord, with thanksgiving and praise. Let me share the good news of my salvation with those who need Your healing touch. Amen.

259

SOME RELATIONSHIPS ARE DANGEROUS TO YOUR EMOTIONAL HEALTH

It is safer to meet a bear robbed of her cubs
than to confront a fool caught in foolishness.

PROVERBS 17:12 NLT

Emotional health is contagious, and so is emotional distress. If you're fortunate enough to be surrounded by family members and friends who celebrate life and praise God, consider yourself blessed. But if you find yourself caught in an unhealthy relationship, it's time to look realistically at your situation.

In your dealings with difficult people, don't concern yourself too much with changing them; you can't do it. What you can do is to conduct yourself in a responsible fashion and insist that other people treat you with the dignity and consideration that you deserve.

God has grand plans for your life. But to fully experience God's gifts, you need happy, emotionally healthy people to share them with. It's up to you to make sure that you build the kinds of relationships that will bring abundance to you, to your family, and to God's world.

Timely Tip: If you're having trouble dealing with a difficult person, don't give up hope. There's always something you can do to build a better life, even if it means breaking off the relationship. But before you decide to end an important relationship, be sure to ask God for guidance, and be sure to forgive the other person, even if it's hard.

Dear Lord, sometimes people can be difficult to live with. Just as I want forgiveness from others, help me forgive those who have caused me inconvenience or pain. And let the love of Your Son fill my heart so that there is no room for bitterness, anger, or regret. Amen.

260

EXPECT A
TERRIFIC TOMORROW

*"For I know the plans I have for you"—this is the Lord's declaration—
"plans for your welfare, not for disaster, to give you a future and a hope."*
JEREMIAH 29:11 HCSB

How bright do you believe your future to be? Well, if you're a faithful believer, God has plans for you that are so bright that you'd better pack several pairs of sunglasses and a lifetime supply of sunblock!

The way that you think about your future will play a powerful role in determining how things turn out (it's called the self-fulfilling prophecy, and it applies to everybody, including you). So here's another question: Are you expecting a terrific tomorrow, or are you dreading a terrible one? The answer to that question will have a powerful impact on the way tomorrow unfolds.

Today, as you live in the present and look to the future, remember that God has an amazing plan for you. Act—and believe—accordingly. And one more thing: don't forget the sunblock.

*Trust the past to God's mercy, the present to God's love
and the future to God's providence.*
ST. AUGUSTINE

Dear Lord, sometimes when I think about the future, I worry. Today, I will do a better job of trusting You. You are my Father, and I will place my hope and my faith in You. Amen.

261

ACCEPT HIS COMFORTING HAND

But God, who comforts the humble, comforted us.
2 Corinthians 7:6 HCSB

If you have been touched by the transforming power of Christ's love—and if you're sincerely trying to follow in His footsteps—then you have every reason to live courageously. Still, even if you are a dedicated Christian, you may find yourself discouraged by the inevitable disappointments and tragedies that occur in the lives of believers and nonbelievers alike.

The next time you find your courage tested to the limit, lean upon God's promises. Trust His Son. Remember that the Lord is always near and that He is your protector and your deliverer. When you are worried, anxious, or afraid, call upon Him and accept the touch of His comforting hand. Remember that God rules both mountaintops and valleys—with limitless wisdom and love—now and forever.

When God allows extraordinary trials for His people,
He prepares extraordinary comforts for them.
Corrie ten Boom

Dear Lord, thank You for Your comfort. You lift me up when I am disappointed. You protect me in times of trouble. Today, I will be mindful of Your love, Your wisdom, and Your grace. Amen.

262

SEEK HIS WILL

Teach me to do Your will, for You are my God;
Your Spirit is good. Lead me in the land of uprightness.

Psalm 143:10 NKJV

God has a plan for our world and our lives. The Lord does not do things by accident; He is willful and intentional. Of course, we cannot always understand the will of God. Why? Because we are mortal beings with limited understanding. Although we cannot fully *comprehend* the will of God, we can always *trust* the will of God. And we should.

As this day unfolds, seek God's will and obey His Word. When you entrust your life to Him without reservation, He will give you the courage meet any challenge, the strength to endure any trial, and the wisdom to live in His righteousness and in His peace.

There's some task which the God of all the universe,
the great Creator, your redeemer in Jesus Christ
has for you to do, and which will remain
undone and incomplete, until by faith
and obedience, you step into the will of God.

Alan Redpath

Heavenly Father, I will study Your Word and seek Your guidance. Give me the wisdom to know Your will for my life and the courage to follow wherever You may lead me, today, tomorrow, and forever. Amen.

263

LOVE IS A CHOICE

Dear friends, if God loved us in this way, we also must love one another.
1 JOHN 4:11 HCSB

Love is always a choice. Sometimes, of course, we may "fall in love," but it takes work to stay there. Sometimes we may be "swept off our feet," but the sweeping is only temporary; sooner or later, if love is to endure, one must plant one's feet firmly on the ground. The decision to love another person for a lifetime is much more than the simple process of "falling in" or "being swept up." It requires "reaching out," "holding firm," and "lifting up." Love, then, becomes a decision to honor and care for the other person, come what may, as the following observations clearly attest:

It is important to know that you have to work to keep love alive;
you have to protect it and maintain it, just like you would a delicate flower.
JAMES DOBSON

God calls upon the loved not just to love but to be loving.
God calls upon the forgiven not just to forgive but to be forgiving.
BETH MOORE

Let us preach You without preaching, not by words but by example,
by the catching force, the sympathetic influence of what we do,
the evident fullness of the love our hearts bear for you..
MOTHER TERESA

Dear Lord, You have given me the gift of love; let me share that gift with others. And keep me mindful that the essence of love is not to receive it, but to give it, today and forever. Amen.

264

THERE ARE REWARDS FOR OBEDIENCE

And the world with its lust is passing away,
but the one who does God's will remains forever.

1 JOHN 2:17 HCSB

Since God created Adam and Eve, we human beings have been rebelling against our Creator. Why? Because we are unwilling to trust God's Word, and we are unwilling to follow His commandments. God has given us a guidebook for righteous living called the Holy Bible. It contains thorough instructions which, if followed, lead to fulfillment, to righteousness, and to contentment. But if we choose to ignore God's commandments, the results are as predictable as they are tragic.

Talking about God is easy; living by His commandments is considerably harder. But unless we are willing to abide by God's laws, all of our righteous proclamations ring hollow. So how can we best proclaim our love for the Lord? By obeying Him. And for further instructions, read the manual.

You may not always see immediate results,
but all God wants is your obedience and faithfulness.

VONETTE BRIGHT

Dear heavenly Father, You have blessed me with a love that is infinite and eternal. I will demonstrate my love for You by obeying Your commandments. Amen.

265

LET GOD GUIDE YOUR PATH

Trust in the LORD with all your heart; do not depend
on your own understanding. Seek his will in all you do,
and he will show you which path to take.

PROVERBS 3:5–6 NLT

Proverbs 3:5–6 makes this promise: if you acknowledge God's sovereignty over every aspect of your life, He will guide your path. And as you prayerfully consider the path that God intends for you to take, here are things you should do: You should study His Word and be ever watchful for His signs. You should associate with fellow believers who will encourage your spiritual growth. You should listen carefully to that inner voice that speaks to you in the quiet moments of your daily devotionals. And you should be patient. Your heavenly Father may not always reveal Himself as quickly as you would like, but rest assured that God intends to use you in wonderful, unexpected ways. Your challenge is to watch, to listen, to learn, and to follow.

Before God created the universe,
He already had you in mind.

ERWIN LUTZER

God will help us become the people
we are meant to be, if only we will ask Him.

HANNAH WHITALL SMITH

Dear Lord, let my plans and hopes be pleasing to You. Let me live according to Your commandments. Direct my path far from the temptations and distractions of this world. And let me discover Your will and follow it, Father, this day and always. Amen.

WHEN YOU PRAISE THE LORD WITH A GRATEFUL HEART, YOU WILL BE BLESSED

From the rising of the sun to its going down the LORD's name is to be praised.
PSALM 113:3 NKJV

As creatures of habit, we may find ourselves praising God only at particular times of the day or week. But praise for our Creator should never be reserved for mealtimes or bedtimes or church services. Instead, we should praise God all day, every day, to the greatest extent we can, with thanksgiving in our hearts, and with a song on our lips.

Worship and praise should be woven into the fabric of everything we do; they should not be relegated to a weekly three-hour visit to church on Sunday morning. So today and every day, find time to lift your prayers to God, and thank Him for all that He has done. Every time you notice a gift from the giver of all things good, praise Him. His works are marvelous, His gifts are beyond understanding, and His love endures forever.

Two wings are necessary to lift our souls toward God:
prayer and praise. Prayer asks. Praise accepts the answer.
LETTIE COWMAN

Nothing we do is more powerful or more life-changing than praising God.
STORMIE OMARTIAN

Heavenly Father, Your gifts are greater than I can imagine, and Your love for me is greater than I can fathom. I thank You, Lord, for Your grace, for Your Love, and for Your Son. Let me follow in Christ's footsteps today and every day. And then, when my work here is done, let me live with You forever. Amen.

267

LET GOD'S POWER TRANSFORM YOU

Your old sinful self has died,
and your new life is kept with Christ in God.

COLOSSIANS 3:3 NCV

God has the power to transform your day and your life. What He asks of you is this: He asks that you follow in the footsteps of His only begotten Son. When you do, you'll be transformed. So your task, simply put, is to accept Christ's grace with a humble, thankful heart as you receive the "new life" that can be yours through Him.

Believers who fashion their days around Jesus see the world differently; they act differently, and they feel differently about themselves and their neighbors. Hopefully, you, too, will be such a believer.

Do you desire to improve some aspect of your life? If so, don't expect changing circumstances to miraculously transform you into the person you want to become. Transformation starts with God, and it starts in the quiet corners of a willing human heart—like yours.

God's work is not in buildings, but in transformed lives.

RUTH BELL GRAHAM

Dear Lord, let my thoughts and my actions demonstrate the difference that Your Son has made in my life. Let me live righteously, and let my actions be consistent with my beliefs. Let every step that I take reflect Your truth, and let me live a life that is worthy of Your Son. Amen.

268

DON'T COPY THE WORLD'S BEHAVIORS AND CUSTOMS

Don't copy the behavior and customs of this world, but let God transform you into a new person by changing the way you think.

ROMANS 12:2 NLT

We live in the world, but we must not worship it. Our duty is to place God first and everything else second. But because we are fallible beings with imperfect faith, placing God in His rightful place is often difficult. In fact, at every turn, or so it seems, we are tempted to do otherwise.

The twenty-first-century world is a noisy, distracting place filled with countless opportunities to stray from God's will. The world seems to cry, "Worship me with your time, your money, your energy, and your thoughts!" But God commands otherwise: He commands us to worship Him and Him alone; everything else must be secondary.

As we have by faith said no to sin, so we should by faith say yes to God and set our minds on things above, where Christ is seated in the heavenlies.

VONETTE BRIGHT

The Lord Jesus Christ wants us to be in the world but not of it.

CHARLES STANLEY

Dear Lord, I am an imperfect human being living in an imperfect world. Direct my path far from the temptations and distractions of this world, and let me follow in the footsteps of Your Son today and forever. Amen.

269

EXERCISE SELF-DISCIPLINE

Do you not know that the runners in a stadium all race,
but only one receives the prize? Run in such a way to win the prize.
Now everyone who competes exercises self-control in everything.
However, they do it to receive a crown that will fade away,
but we a crown that will never fade away.

1 CORINTHIANS 9:24–25 HCSB

God is clear: we must exercise self-discipline in all matters. Self-discipline is not simply a proven way to get ahead, it's also an integral part of God's plan for our lives. If we genuinely seek to be faithful stewards of our time, our talents, and our resources, we must adopt a disciplined approach to life. Otherwise, our talents are wasted and our resources are squandered.

Our greatest rewards result from hard work and perseverance. May we, as disciplined believers, be willing to work for the rewards we so earnestly desire.

Think of something you ought to do and go do it.
Heed not your feelings. Do your work.

GEORGE MACDONALD

Success is not an event. It is an ongoing
process we engage in, time and again.

JOHN MAXWELL

Heavenly Father, make me a person who understands the need to live a disciplined life. Let me teach others by the faithfulness by my conduct, and let me follow Your will and Your Word, today and every day. Amen.

270

GOD LOVES YOUR FAMILY

Let the Word of Christ—the Message—have the run of the house.
Give it plenty of room in your lives.

COLOSSIANS 3:16 MSG

These are difficult days and anxious times for our nation and for our families. But thankfully, God is bigger than all of our challenges. God loves us and protects us. In times of trouble, he comforts us; in times of sorrow, He dries our tears. When we are troubled or weak or sorrowful, God is as near as our next breath.

Are you concerned for the well-being of your family? You are not alone. We live in a world where temptation and danger seem to lurk on every street corner and behind almost every video screen. Parents and children alike have good reason to be watchful. But despite the evils of our time, God remains steadfast. Even in these difficult days—even if you're feeling anxious or fearful or concerned—no problem is too big for God.

The only true source of meaning in life is found in love for God and his son
Jesus Christ, and love for mankind, beginning with our own families.

JAMES DOBSON

Apart from religious influence,
the family is the most important unit in society.

BILLY GRAHAM

Dear Lord, I am blessed to be part of the family of God where I find love and acceptance. You have also blessed me with my earthly family. Let me show love and acceptance for my own family so that through me, they might come to know You. Amen.

271

WORDS ARE POWERFUL

The wise store up knowledge, but the mouth of the fool hastens destruction.
PROVERBS 10:14 HCSB

All too often, in the rush to have ourselves heard, we speak first and think next . . . with unfortunate results. God's Word reminds us that, "The words of the reckless pierce like swords, but the tongue of the wise brings healing" (Proverbs 12:18 NIV). If we seek to be a source of encouragement to friends and family, then we must measure our words carefully. Words are important: they can hurt or heal. Words can uplift us or discourage us, and reckless words, spoken in haste, cannot be erased.

Today, measure your words carefully. Use words of kindness and praise, not words of anger or derision. Remember that you have the power to heal others or to injure them, to lift others up or to hold them back. When you lift them up, your wisdom will bring healing and comfort to a world that needs both.

Before you speak, it is necessary for you to listen,
for God speaks in the silence of the heart.
MOTHER TERESA

When you talk, choose the very same words that you would
use if Jesus were looking over your shoulder. Because He is.
MARIE T. FREEMAN

Dear Lord, You have commanded me to choose my words carefully so that I might be a source of encouragement and hope to all whom I meet. Keep me mindful, Lord, that I have influence on many people. Let the words that I speak today be worthy of the One who has saved me forever. Amen.

272

TRUST THE SHEPHERD

The LORD is my shepherd; I shall not want. He makes me to lie down in green pastures; He leads me beside the still waters. He restores my soul.

PSALM 23:1–3 NKJV

In the twenty-third Psalm, David teaches us that God is like a watchful shepherd caring for His flock. No wonder these verses have provided comfort and hope for generations of believers.

As a busy citizen of the twenty-first century, you know from firsthand experience that life is not always easy. But as a recipient of God's grace, you also know that you are protected by a loving heavenly Father. On occasion, you will confront circumstances that trouble you to the very core of your soul. When you are afraid, trust in God. When you are worried, turn your concerns over to Him. When you are anxious, be still and listen for the quiet assurance of God's promises. And then place your life in His hands. He is your shepherd today and throughout eternity. Trust the shepherd.

The Lord is my shepherd, is on Sunday, is on Monday,
and is through every day of the week; is in January,
is in December, and every month of the year; is at home,
and is in China; is in peace, and, is in war; in abundance, and in want.

HUDSON TAYLOR

Lord, You are my shepherd. You care for me; You comfort me; You watch over me; and You have saved me. I will praise you, Father, for Your glorious works, for Your protection, for Your love, and for Your Son. Amen.

273

HIS SON IS THE SAVIOR

And we have seen and testify that the Father
has sent the Son as Savior of the world.

1 JOHN 4:14 NKJV

Hannah Whitall Smith spoke to believers of every generation when she advised, "Keep your face upturned to Christ as the flowers do to the sun. Look, and your soul shall live and grow." How true. When we turn our hearts to Jesus, we receive His blessings, His peace, and His grace.

Christ is the ultimate Savior of mankind and the personal Savior of those who believe in Him. As his servants, we should place Him at the very center of our lives. And every day that God gives us breath, we should share Christ's love and His message with a world that needs both.

Don't let a storm keep you from counting on what Jesus has told you.
SHELIA WALSH

Jesus departed from our sight that he might
return to our hearts. He departed, and behold, he is here.
ST. AUGUSTINE

Dear Lord, keep me mindful of Your priceless gift: my personal Savior, Christ Jesus. I will praise You always, Lord, as I give thanks for Your Son Jesus and for Your everlasting love. Amen.

274

ANSWER GOD'S CALL

But as God has distributed to each one,
as the Lord has called each one, so let him walk.

1 CORINTHIANS 7:17 NKJV

It is terribly important that you heed God's calling by discovering and developing your talents and your spiritual gifts. If you seek to make a difference—and if you seek to bear eternal fruit—you must discover God's gifts and begin using them for the glory of His kingdom.

Every believer has at least one gift. In John 15:16, Jesus says, "You did not choose Me, but I chose you and appointed you that you should go and bear fruit, and that your fruit should remain, that whatever you ask the Father in My name He may give you."

Have you found your special calling? If not, keep searching and keep praying until you find it. God has important work for you to do, and the time to begin that work is now.

God has given you special talents—
now it's your turn to give them back to God.

MARIE T. FREEMAN

Dear Lord, You created me, and You have called me to do Your work here on earth. Today, I choose to seek Your will and to live it, knowing that when I trust in You, I am eternally blessed. Amen.

275

CATEGORIZE YOUR WORRIES

And I pray this: that your love will keep on growing in knowledge and every kind of discernment, so that you can approve the things that are superior and can be pure and blameless in the day of Christ.

PHILIPPIANS 1:9 HCSB

If you're being victimized by vague anxieties or irrational fears, it's inevitable: you worry. You worry about matters great and small and in between. And if you worry too much, those concerns can result in emotional paralysis.

Today, as a way of managing your emotions, divide your areas of concern into two categories: the things you *can* control and the things you *can't*. Then focus on the former and refuse to waste time on the latter. Instead of fretting about every problem under the sun, devote your full attention to things much closer to home: the things you can do something about.

And while you're doing the hard work of improving your little corner of the world one day at a time, remember that, although you may have legitimate concerns, God has divine solutions. Your challenge is to trust Him to solve the problems that are simply too big for you to resolve on your own.

The more you give your mental burdens to the Lord, the more exciting it becomes to see how God will handle things that are impossible for you to do anything about.

CHARLES SWINDOLL

Dear Lord, when I am anxious or fearful, help me trust You more. Then with praise on my lips and with the assurance of Your promises written upon my heart, let me live courageously, faithfully, prayerfully, and thankfully today and every day. Amen.

276

TRUST GOD'S PERFECT WISDOM

Therefore, everyone who hears these words of Mine and acts on them will be like a sensible man who built his house on the rock. The rain fell, the rivers rose, and the winds blew and pounded that house. Yet it didn't collapse, because its foundation was on the rock.

MATTHEW 7:24–25 HCSB

Where will you place your trust today? Will you trust in the wisdom of fallible men and women, or will you place your faith God's perfect wisdom? Where you choose to place your trust will determine the direction and quality of your life.

Are you tired? Discouraged? Fearful? Be comforted and trust God. Are you worried or anxious? Be confident in God's power and trust His holy Word. Are you confused? Listen to the quiet voice of your heavenly Father. He is not a God of confusion. Talk with Him; listen to Him; trust Him. He is steadfast, and He is your protector . . . forever.

If we neglect the Bible, we cannot expect to benefit from the wisdom and direction that result from knowing God's Word.

VONETTE BRIGHT

Knowledge is not wisdom. Wisdom is the proper use of knowledge.

VANCE HAVNER

Dear Lord, You are my wise teacher. Help me to learn from You. And then let me show others what it means to be a kind, generous, loving Christian. Amen.

277

LEND A HELPING HAND

*Then a Samaritan traveling down the road came to where
the hurt man was. When he saw the man, he felt
very sorry for him. The Samaritan went to him, poured olive oil
and wine on his wounds, and bandaged them.
Then he put the hurt man on his own donkey
and took him to an inn where he cared for him.*

LUKE 10:33–34 NCV

Sometimes we would like to help make the world a better place, but we're not sure how to do it. Jesus told the story of the "Good Samaritan," a man who helped a fellow traveler when no one else would. We, too, should be good Samaritans when we find people who need our help.

When bad things happen in our world, there's always something we can do. So what can *you* do to make God's world a better place? You can start by making your own corner of the world a little nicer place to live (by sharing kind words and good deeds). And then you can take your concerns to God in prayer. Whether you've offered a helping hand or a heartfelt prayer, you've done a lot.

We hurt people by being too busy, too busy to notice their needs.

BILLY GRAHAM

Dear Lord, let me help others in every way that I can. Jesus served others; I can too. I will serve other people with my good deeds and with my prayers, today and every day. Amen.

278

WHO'S RESPONSIBLE? YOU ARE.

*Now he who plants and he who waters are one, and each one
will receive his own reward according to his own labor.*

1 Corinthians 3:8 NKJV

It's time to state a rather obvious fact: you're responsible for your own behavior, and other people are responsible for theirs. But if you're not careful, you may find yourself spending too much time worrying about the myriad ways that other people are misbehaving and not enough time focusing on your own responsibilities. So instead of trying to improve other people, a better strategy is simply this: get busy trying to improve yourself.

God has blessed you with unique opportunities to serve Him, and He has given you every tool that you need to do so. Today, accept this challenge: value the talent that God has given you, nourish it, make it grow, and share it with the world. After all, the best way to say thank you for God's gifts is to use them.

It's easy to hold other people accountable, but real accountability begins with the person you see when you look in the mirror. So don't look for someone you can blame; look for something constructive you can do. When you accept responsibility and take the necessary steps to resolve your problems, you'll feel better about yourself *and* you'll get more done. Lots more.

Action springs not from thought, but from a readiness for responsibility.

Dietrich Bonhoeffer

Dear Lord, guide me away from the temptations and distractions of this world, and make me a champion of the faith. Today I will honor You, Father, with good thoughts, sincere prayers, and responsible behavior. And I will worship You, Lord, with gratitude in my heart and praise on my lips, this day and forever. Amen.

279

WHEN IT'S TIME TO FACE A CHALLENGE, FACE IT

Therefore, with your minds ready for action, be serious and set your hope completely on the grace to be brought to you at the revelation of Jesus Christ. As obedient children, do not be conformed to the desires of your former ignorance. But as the One who called you is holy, you also are to be holy in all your conduct.

1 PETER 1:13–15 HCSB

If you've been avoiding a necessary task—perhaps you've been avoiding an emotionally charged situation or a difficult person—it's time to pray for God's wisdom and His strength. Ask Him to help you deal with the problem in the best way possible, which usually means responding sooner rather than later. And if you need any extra motivation to do the right thing at the right time, take the following big ideas to heart:

The one word in the spiritual vocabulary is now.

OSWALD CHAMBERS

There's some task which the God of all the universe, the great Creator has for you to do, and which will remain undone and incomplete, until by faith and obedience, you step into the will of God.

ALAN REDPATH

Dear Lord, I have heard Your Word, and I have felt Your presence in my heart; let me act accordingly. Let my words and actions show people the changes You have made in my life. Let me praise You, Father, by following in the footsteps of Your Son, and let others see Him through me. Amen.

280

SHARE THE GOOD NEWS

As you go, announce this:
"The kingdom of heaven has come near."

MATTHEW 10:7 HCSB

The good news of Jesus Christ should be shouted from the rooftops by believers the world over. But all too often, it is not. For a variety of reasons, many Christians keep their beliefs to themselves, and when they do, the world suffers because of their failure to speak up.

As believers, we are called to share the transforming message of Jesus with our families, with our neighbors, and with the world. Jesus commands us to become fishers of men. And the time to go fishing is now. We must share the good news of Jesus Christ today—tomorrow may indeed be too late.

Ministry is not something we do for God;
it is something God does in and through us.

WARREN WIERSBE

Lord, even if I never leave home, make me a missionary for You. Let me share the good news of Your Son, and let me tell of Your love and of Your grace. Make me a faithful servant for You, Father, now and forever. Amen.

281

WHEN YOU'RE ANXIOUS OR WORRIED, TRUST GOD

In his kindness God called you to share in his eternal glory by means of Christ Jesus. So after you have suffered a little while, he will restore, support, and strengthen you, and he will place you on a firm foundation.

1 PETER 5:10 NLT

The Lord has a plan for your life, and He wants to bless you abundantly and eternally. Your job, simply put, is to trust Him completely in good times and trying times. So when you're feeling anxious or afraid, pay more attention to God and less attention to your fears. Just do your best, and trust Him to do the rest.

So the next time you find yourself tormented by irrational fears or unspoken anxieties, open your heart to God. And then, when you're finished, pay careful attention to the words of wisdom below:

What you trust to Him you must not worry over nor feel anxious about. Trust and worry cannot go together.

HANNAH WHITALL SMITH

Trust God's Word and His power more than you trust your own feelings and experiences. Remember, your Rock is Christ, and it is the sea that ebbs and flows with the tides, not Him.

LETTIE COWMAN

Dear Lord, give me courage in every circumstance and in every stage of life. Give me the wisdom, Father, to place my hope and my trust in Your perfect plan and Your boundless love. Amen.

282

KEEP MONEY
IN PERSPECTIVE

*For the love of money is a root of all kinds of evil,
and by craving it, some have wandered away from
the faith and pierced themselves with many pains.*

1 TIMOTHY 6:10 HCSB

Our society is in love with money and the things that money can buy. God is not. God cares about people, not possessions, and so must we. We must, to the best of our abilities, love our neighbors as ourselves, and we must, to the best of our abilities, resist the mighty temptation to place possessions ahead of people.

Money, in and of itself, is not evil; worshipping money is. So today, as you prioritize matters of importance for you and yours, remember that God is almighty, but the dollar is not. If we worship God, we are blessed. But if we worship "the almighty dollar," we are inevitably punished because of our misplaced priorities—and our punishment inevitably comes sooner rather than later.

*There is nothing wrong with people possessing riches.
The wrong comes when riches possess people.*

BILLY GRAHAM

Dear Lord, I will not worship money. Give me the wisdom and the discipline to be a responsible steward of my financial resources, and let me use those resources for glory of Your kingdom. Amen.

283

SHARE GOD'S LOVE

And we have this command from Him:
The one who loves God must also love his brother.

1 John 4:21 HCSB

God is love, and He intends that we share His love with the world. But He won't force us to be loving and kind. He places that responsibility squarely on our shoulders.

Love, like everything else in this world, begins and ends with God, but the middle part belongs to us. The Creator gives each of us the opportunity to be kind, to be courteous, and to be loving. He gives each of us the chance to obey the Golden Rule, or to make up our own rules as we go. If we obey God's instructions, we're secure, but if we do otherwise, we suffer.

Christ's words are clear: "'Love the Lord your God with all your heart and with all your soul and with all your mind.' This is the first and greatest commandment. And the second is like it: 'Love your neighbor as yourself.' All the Law and the Prophets hang on these two commandments" (Matthew 22:37–40 NIV). We are commanded to love the One who first loved us and then to share His love with the world. And the next move is always ours.

Scripture makes it clear that our first love is always to be for our Lord.

Billy Graham

Dear heavenly Father, You have blessed me with a love that is infinite and eternal. Let me love You, Lord, more and more each day. Make me a loving servant, Father, today and throughout eternity. And let me show my love for You by sharing Your message and Your love with others. Amen.

284

NO TEMPTATION IS TOO GREAT

*No temptation has overtaken you except what is common to humanity.
God is faithful and He will not allow you to be tempted
beyond what you are able, but with the temptation He will also
provide a way of escape so that you are able to bear it.*

1 CORINTHIANS 10:13 HCSB

This world is filled to the brim with temptations. Some of these temptations are small; eating a second scoop of ice cream, for example, is tempting, but not very dangerous. Other temptations, however, are not nearly so harmless. The devil is working 24/7, and he's causing pain and heartache in more ways than ever before. Thankfully, in the battle against Satan, we are never alone. God is always with us, and He gives us the power to resist temptation whenever we ask Him for the strength to do so.

In a letter to believers, Peter offered a stern warning: "Your adversary, the devil, prowls around like a roaring lion, seeking someone to devour" (1 Peter 5:8 NASB). As Christians, we must take that warning seriously, and we must behave accordingly.

*Temptation is not a sin. Even Jesus was tempted. The Lord Jesus
gives you the strength needed to resist temptation.*

CORRIE TEN BOOM

Dear Lord, this world is filled with temptations, distractions, and frustrations. When I turn my thoughts away from You and Your Word, Lord, I suffer bitter consequences. But when I trust in Your commandments, I am safe. Direct my path far from the temptations of the world, Father, this day and always. Amen.

285

EXPECT THE MIRACULOUS

Is anything too hard for the LORD?
GENESIS 18:14 KJV

Ours is a God of infinite possibilities. But sometimes, because of limited faith and limited understanding, we wrongly assume that God cannot or will not intervene in the affairs of mankind. Such assumptions are simply wrong.

Are you afraid to ask God to do big things in your life? Is your faith threadbare and worn? If so, it's time to abandon your doubts and reclaim your faith in God's promises. God's holy Word makes it clear: absolutely nothing is impossible for the Lord. And since the Bible means what it says, you can be comforted in the knowledge that the Creator of the universe can do miraculous things in your own life and in the lives of your loved ones. Your challenge, as a believer, is to take God at His word, and to expect the miraculous.

*We will see more and more that we are chosen
not because of our ability, but because of the Lord's power,
which will be demonstrated in our not being able.*

CORRIE TEN BOOM

Dear God, nothing is impossible for You—keep me always mindful of Your strength. When I lose hope, give me faith; when others lose hope, let me tell them of Your glory and Your works. Today, Lord, let me expect the miraculous, and let me trust in You. Amen.

286

EVERY DAY IS PRECIOUS

Teach us to realize the brevity of life, so that we may grow in wisdom.
PSALM 90:12 NLT

There's an old saying—trite but true—that goes something like this: "Today is the first day of the rest of your life." Perhaps that old adage states the obvious, but its message is so profound and so timely that it's worth repeating *and* worth thinking about.

Whatever your situation—whether you're experience a great day or a tough one—remember that each day, including this one, is a gift. Today holds boundless possibilities if you are wise enough and observant enough to claim them. And one of the best ways to thank God for another day of life is to use it wisely.

Each day is God's gift of a fresh unspoiled
opportunity to live according to His priorities.
ELIZABETH GEORGE

Faith does not concern itself with the entire journey. One step is enough.
LETTIE COWMAN

Life is short; none of us know how long we have.
Live each day as if it were your last—for someday it will be.
BILLY GRAHAM

Dear Lord, today and every day, give me the wisdom to appreciate the priceless gift of life. You have a plan for my life, Father. Give me the insight and the courage to use the talents and opportunities You have given me, so that I can honor You with my service. Amen.

287

DON'T JUST LISTEN TO GOD'S WORD; ACT UPON IT

But be doers of the word and not hearers only.

JAMES 1:22 HCSB

The Bible teaches us that it is not enough to merely hear God's instructions, nor is it enough to talk about them. We must act upon them. If we are to be responsible believers, we must realize that it is never enough to read the instructions of God; we must also live by them. And it is never enough to wait idly by while others do God's work here on earth; we, too, must act. Doing God's work is a responsibility that each of us must bear, and when we do, our loving heavenly Father rewards our efforts with a bountiful harvest.

So if you if you'd like to jumpstart your life, your relationships, your career, or anything else for that matter, ask God to give you the strength and the wisdom to do first things first, even if the first thing is hard. And while you're at it, use this time-tested formula for success: employ less talk and more action. Why? Because actions indeed speak louder than words—always have, always will. And a thousand good intentions pale in comparison to a single good deed.

Timely Tip: The Bible teaches us to be "doers of the word, not merely hearers." The best time to obey God's Word—and the appropriate time do His work—is now.

Dear Lord, I have heard Your Word, and I have felt Your presence in my heart; let me act accordingly. Let my words and deeds serve as a testimony to the changes You have made in my life. Let me praise You, Father, by following in the footsteps of Your Son, and let others see Him through me. Amen.

288

GOD GIVES US STRENGTH

And He said to me, "My grace is sufficient for you,
for My strength is made perfect in weakness."

2 CORINTHIANS 12:9 NKJV

The Christian faith, as communicated through the words of the Holy Bible, is a healing faith. Through the healing words of God's promises, Christians understand that the Lord continues to manifest His plan in good times and bad.

Do you need strength? Slow down, get more rest, engage in regular, sensible exercise, and turn your troubles over to God. And while you're at it, consider the following words of wisdom:

The truth is, God's strength is fully revealed when our strength is depleted.

LIZ CURTIS HIGGS

The strength that we claim from God's Word does not
depend on circumstances. Circumstances will
be difficult, but our strength will be sufficient.

CORRIE TEN BOOM

God will give us the strength and resources we need
to live through any situation in life that He ordains.

BILLY GRAHAM

Heavenly Father, I will turn to You for strength. When I am weak, You lift me up. When my spirit is crushed, You comfort me. When I am victorious, Your Word reminds me to be humble. Today and every day, I will turn to You, Father, for strength, for hope, for wisdom, and for courage. Amen.

289

READY. SET. GO!

Do not neglect the gift that is in you.
1 TIMOTHY 4:14 HCSB

God has given you talents and opportunities that are uniquely yours. Are you willing to use your gifts in the way that God intends? And are you willing to summon the discipline that is required develop your talents and to hone your skills? That's precisely what God wants you to do, and that's precisely what you should desire for yourself.

As you seek to expand your talents, you will undoubtedly encounter stumbling blocks along the way, such as the fear of rejection or the fear of failure. When you do, don't stumble! Just continue to refine your skills, and offer your services to God. And when the time is right, He will use you—but it's up to you to be thoroughly prepared when He does.

*In the great orchestra we call life, you have an instrument
and a song, and you owe it to God to play them both sublimely.*

MAX LUCADO

Lord, I praise You for Your priceless gifts. I give thanks for Your creation, for Your Son, and for the unique talents and opportunities that You have given me. Let me use my gifts that for the glory of Your kingdom, this day and every day. Amen.

290

BE SELF-DISCIPLINED

So prepare your minds for service and have self-control.
1 PETER 1:13 NCV

Proverbs 23:12 advises: "Apply your heart to discipline and your ears to words of knowledge" (NASB). And, 2 Peter 1:5–6 teaches, "make every effort to supplement your faith with goodness, goodness with knowledge, knowledge with self-control, self-control with endurance, endurance with godliness" (HSCB). Thus God's Word is clear: we must exercise self-discipline in all matters.

When we pause to consider how much work needs to be done, we realize that self-discipline is not simply a proven way to get ahead, it's also an integral part of God's plan for our lives. If we genuinely seek to be faithful stewards of our time, our talents, and our resources, we must adopt a disciplined approach to life. Otherwise, our talents are wasted and our resources are squandered.

If you're planning on becoming a disciplined person "someday" in the distant future, you're deluding yourself. The best day to begin exercising self-discipline is this one.

Action springs not from thought, but from a readiness for responsibility.
DIETRICH BONHOEFFER

Each day you must say to yourself, "Today I am going to begin."
JEAN PIERRE DE CAUSSADE

Dear Lord, I want to be a disciplined believer. Let me use my time wisely, let me obey Your commandments faithfully, and let me worship You joyfully, today and every day. Amen.

291

LET GOD SOLVE YOUR BIG PROBLEMS

But those who wait on the LORD shall renew their strength;
they shall mount up with wings like eagles,
they shall run and not be weary, they shall walk and not faint..

ISAIAH 40:31 NKJV

When times are tough, it's easy to become discouraged. And it's easy to overestimate the size of your problems. In truth, there are two kinds of problems that you should *never* worry about: the small ones that you can handle yourself and the big ones that only God can handle.

The problems that are simply too big to solve should be left in God's hands while you invest your energy on things that you have the power fix. And where can you find the courage and determination to tackle those problems? You can start by asking the Lord for His help. When you ask—and keep asking—He will give you the strength and the tools you need to repair what's broken and begin again.

Every misfortune, every failure, every loss may be transformed.
God has the power to transform all misfortunes into "God-sends."

LETTIE COWMAN

Each problem is a God-appointed instructor.

CHARLES SWINDOLL

Dear Lord, sometimes my problems are simply too big for me, but they are never too big for You. Let me turn my troubles over to You, Lord, and let me trust in You today and for all eternity. Amen.

292

DON'T BE DISCOURAGED AND DON'T LOSE HOPE

Those who trust in the LORD are as secure as Mount Zion;
they will not be defeated but will endure forever.

PSALM 125:1 NLT

When times are tough and you're feeling anxious or afraid, it's easy to become discouraged. But no problems are too big for God. Even if today is shaping up to be a very hard day, don't let your emotions be hijacked by momentary hardships. Focus, instead, on God's never-ending love for you.

Setbacks are inevitable, but your response to them is optional. So if you're experiencing tough times, don't give up and don't lose hope. Instead, remember that you and the Lord, working together, can always find a way to turn a stumbling block into a steppingstone. which means that better days will arrive, and perhaps sooner than you think.

The presence of hope in the invincible sovereignty
of God drives out fear.

JOHN PIPER

Of course you will encounter trouble. But behold a God of power
who can take any evil and turn it into a door of hope.

CATHERINE MARSHALL

Dear Lord, when I am fearful, I will turn to You. When I am discouraged, I will focus on Your promises. When I am worried about the future, I will entrust my future to You. Thank You, Father, for Your blessings, for Your love, and for Your Son. Amen.

GOD'S POWER IS YOURS

*When we were baptized, we were buried with Christ
and shared his death. So, just as Christ was raised from the dead
by the wonderful power of the Father, we also can live a new life.*

ROMANS 6:4 NCV

When you invite Christ to rule over your heart, you avail yourself of His power. And make no mistake about it: you and Christ, working together, can do miraculous things. In fact, miraculous things are exactly what Christ intends for you to do, but He won't force you to do great things on His behalf. The decision to become a full-fledged participant in His power is a decision that you must make for yourself.

In John 14:12, Christ make this promise: "I tell you the truth, whoever believes in me will do the same things that I do." So trust the Savior's promise, and expect a miracle in His name.

*Jesus gives us hope because He keeps us company,
has a vision and knows the way we should go.*

MAX LUCADO

Dear Lord, Your Son died for the salvation of all mankind, and He died for me. Through the power of Christ, I can be compassionate, courageous, and strong. Help me use that power, Father, for the glory of Your kingdom, today and forever. Amen.

294

FOCUS ON PLEASING GOD, NOT PEOPLE

Do you think I am trying to make people accept me?
No, God is the One I am trying to please. Am I trying to please people?
If I still wanted to please people, I would not be a servant of Christ.

GALATIANS 1:10 NCV

Beware of popularity contests. And beware of peer pressure if it's leading you in a direction that makes you feel uncomfortable. If the quiet inner voice that the Lord has placed in your heart says stop, listen carefully and learn.

Peer pressure can be good or bad. God wants you to seek out the good and flee from the bad. So if you encounter someone who encourages you to behave badly—or to betray your conscience—run, don't walk, in the opposite direction. And while you're deciding which direction to take, consider these insights:

Character is always lost when a high ideal is sacrificed
on the altar of conformity and popularity.

CHARLES SWINDOLL

Popularity is far more dangerous for the Christian than persecution.

BILLY GRAHAM

I don't know all the keys to success,
but one key to failure is to try to please everyone.

RICK WARREN

Dear Lord, other people may encourage me to stray from Your path, but I wish to follow in the footsteps of Your Son. Give me the vision to see the right path— and the wisdom to follow it—today and every day of my life. Amen.

295

YOUR FUTURE IS VERY BRIGHT

"I say this because I know what I am planning for you," says the LORD.
"I have good plans for you, not plans to hurt you. I will give you
hope and a good future. Then you will call my name.
You will come to me and pray to me, and I will listen to you.

JEREMIAH 29:11–12 NCV

Are you willing to place your future in the hands of a loving and all-knowing God? Do you trust in the ultimate goodness of His plan for your life? Will you face today's challenges with optimism and hope? You should. After all, God created you for a very important purpose: His purpose. And you still have important work to do: His work.

Our future may look fearfully intimidating, yet we can look up
to the Engineer of the Universe, confident that nothing escapes
His attention or slips out of the control of those strong hands.

ELISABETH ELLIOT

Seeking God first will always put us in the correct position and aim
us in the right direction to move into the future God has for us.

STORMIE OMARTIAN

Dear Lord, I thank You for the promise of an eternally bright future with You. You have given me so much, Father, and I am thankful. I know that every good thing You give me is to be shared with others. Today and every day, let me share Your blessings and Your good news with the world. Amen.

296

GOD COMFORTS US WHEN WE SUFFER

God, who comforts the downcast, comforted us.

2 CORINTHIANS 7:6 NKJV

All of us must, from time to time, endure stresses and disappointments that leave us wondering if recovery is possible. But if we commit our hearts and lives to God, we need not worry. The Creator of the universe has promised to protect us now and forever. Our responsibility, simply put, is to trust, to work, and to wait patiently for the Lord to reveal His plans.

While we are waiting for God's timetable to unfold, we can be comforted in the knowledge that our Creator can overcome any obstacle, even if we cannot. The Psalmist writes, "Weeping may endure for a night, but joy comes in the morning" (Psalm 30:5). But when we are hurting, the morning may seem very far away. It is not. God promises that He is "near to those who have a broken heart" (Psalm 34:18).

So the next time you find yourself caught up in an unfortunate situation, don't waste time or energy feeling sorry for yourself. Instead, take your concerns to the Lord and leave them there. Just do your best and leave everything else up to Him.

God is sufficient for all our needs, for every problem,
for every difficulty, for every broken heart, for every human sorrow.

PETER MARSHALL

Heavenly Father, thank You for Your love and Your protection. You lift me up when I am disappointed. You protect me in times of trouble. When I am anxious or afraid, You comfort me. Today, I will be mindful of Your love, Your wisdom, and Your grace. Amen.

297

DON'T SELL YOURSELF SHORT

I can do all things through Christ, because he gives me strength.

PHILIPPIANS 4:13 NCV

When you endure difficult times, as all of us must from time to time, you may sense that your self-confidence is slipping away. If that happens to you, slow down, collect your thoughts, and focus, not on your own weaknesses, but on God's strength. And don't make the mistake of selling yourself short.

No matter the size of your challenges, you can be sure that you and God, working together, can handle them. So the next time you're tempted to give up on yourself, remember that God will never, never, never give up on you. And with God on your side, you have nothing to fear.

Confidence in the natural world is self-reliance;
in the spiritual world, it is God-reliance.

OSWALD CHAMBERS

You need to make the right decision—firmly and decisively—
and then stick with it, with God's help.

BILLY GRAHAM

We need to recognize that lack of confidence does not equal humility. In fact,
genuinely humble people have enormous confidence because it rests in a great God.

BETH MOORE

Dear Lord, when I am faced with challenges that seem too big for me, keep me mindful that no challenge is too big for You. I have chosen to follow in the footsteps of Your Son, so I can be confident that I am protected now and forever. Amen.

298

MISTAKES HAPPEN

Have mercy on me, O God, according to your unfailing love;
according to your great compassion blot out my transgressions.
Wash away all my iniquity and cleanse me from my sin.

PSALM 51:1–2 NIV

We are imperfect people living in an imperfect world; mistakes are simply part of the price we pay for being here. But even though mistakes are an inevitable part of life's journey, *repeated mistakes* should not be. When we commit the inevitable blunders of life, we must correct them, learn from them, and pray to God for the wisdom *not* to repeat them. And then, if we are successful, our mistakes become lessons, and our lives become adventures in growth, not stagnation.

Today, like every other day, is a good day to examine your life, to face up to your shortcomings, and to begin repairing them. When you do, you'll be building a better tomorrow for yourself and your loved ones.

Lord, when we are wrong, make us willing to change;
and when we are right, make us easy to live with.

PETER MARSHALL

Lord, sometimes I make mistakes and fall short of Your commandments. When I do, forgive me, Father. And help me learn from my mistakes so that I can be a better servant to You and a better example to my friends and family. Amen.

299

PRAY, GIVE THANKS, AND REJOICE

Weeping may endure for a night, but joy comes in the morning.

PSALM 30:5 NKJV

As you go about your daily activities, remember God's instructions: "Rejoice always! Pray constantly. Give thanks in everything, for this is God's will for you in Christ Jesus" (1 Thessalonians 5:16–18 HCSB). Start praying in the morning and keep praying until you fall off to sleep at night. And rest assured: the Lord is always listening, and He always wants to hear from you.

If you're feeling anxious or fearful, slow down, say a word of thanks, and ask the Lord for courage. And while you're at it, let the following quotations encourage you to pray for God's guidance and to celebrate His love.

Prayer begins by talking to God, but it ends in listening to him. In the face of Absolute Truth, silence is the soul's language.

FULTON J. SHEEN

No man is greater than his prayer life.

LEONARD RAVENHILL

God's solution is just a prayer away!

MAX LUCADO

Heavenly Father, make me a joyful, grateful, faithful Christian. Because of my salvation through Your Son, I have every reason to celebrate life. Let me share the joyful news of Jesus Christ, and let my life be a testimony to His love and to His grace. Amen.

START EVERY DAY WITH GOD

Morning by morning he wakens me and opens my understanding to his will. The Sovereign LORD has spoken to me, and I have listened.

ISAIAH 50:4–5 NLT

A great way to prepare yourself for the rigors of everyday living is by spending a few moments with God every morning. Whether you're dealing with rollercoaster emotions, stressful circumstances, or exaggerated fears, you need God as your partner. So if you find that you're simply "too busy" for a daily chat with your Father in heaven, it's time to take a long, hard look at your priorities and your values.

Each day has 1,440 minutes—do you value your relationship with God enough to spend a few of those minutes with Him? He deserves that much of your time and more—is He receiving it from you? Hopefully so.

As you consider your plans for the day ahead, here's a tip: organize your life around the simple principle of God first. When you place your Creator where He belongs—at the very center of your day and your life—the rest of your priorities will fall into place.

Timely Tip: A regular time of quiet reflection, prayer, and Bible study will allow you to praise your Creator, to focus your thoughts, and to seek God's guidance on matters great and small. Don't miss this opportunity.

Dear Lord, I thank You for the gift of life. Today presents another opportunity to praise, to work, to love, and to serve. Thank You, Father, for this gift. Give me the wisdom to use it wisely. Amen.

301

YOU CAN DEAL WITH YOUR DOUBTS

*Immediately the father of the child cried out
and said with tears, "Lord, I believe; help my unbelief!"*

MARK 9:24 NKJV

Doubts come in several shapes and sizes: doubts about God, doubts about the future, and doubts about your own abilities, for starters. And what, precisely, does God's Word say in response to these doubts? The Bible is clear: when we are beset by doubts, of whatever kind, we must draw ourselves nearer to God through worship and through prayer. When we do so, God, the loving Father who has never left our sides, draws ever closer to us (James 4:8).

Have you ever felt your faith in God slipping away? If so, you are not alone. Every life—including yours—is a series of successes and failures, celebrations and disappointments, joys and sorrows, hopes and doubts. Even the most faithful Christians are overcome by occasional bouts of fear and doubt. But even when you feel far removed from God, God never leaves your side, not for an instant. He is always with you, always willing to calm the storms of life. When you sincerely seek His presence—and when you genuinely seek to establish a deeper, more meaningful relationship with His Son—God is prepared to touch your heart, to calm your fears, to answer your doubts, and to restore our soul.

*We never get anywhere—nor do our conditions and circumstances change—
when we look at the dark side of life.*

LETTIE COWMAN

Dear God, when doubts creep into my life, help me increase the amount of time I spend in Bible study, prayer, and worship. Thank You that the more time I spend with You, the better I feel about my my future and my faith. Amen.

302

SINCE YOU CAN'T DO EVERYTHING, YOU SHOULDN'T TRY

A simple life in the Fear-of-God is better than a rich life with a ton of headaches.
PROVERBS 15:16 MSG

You can't do everything, which means that you need to learn how to say no politely and often. Sometimes people make unreasonable requests, and when they do, you have the right to decline without feelingly guilty.

If you've been plagued by anxious thoughts—or if you find yourself running from one place to another with barely a moment to spare—it's time to begin simplifying your life by saying no more often. The following words of wisdom are intended to remind you that you can't do everything, nor should you even try.

Learn to say 'no' to the good so you can say 'yes' to the best.
JOHN MAXWELL

Prescription for a happier and healthier life: resolve to slow your pace; learn to say no gracefully; reject the temptation to chase after more pleasures, more hobbies, and more social entanglements.
JAMES DOBSON

Heavenly Father, my energy is limited and my resources are limited, which means that I simply cannot say yes to every request. Today and every day, help me say yes to the things I should do and no to everything else. Amen.

303

THE LORD HAS A PLAN FOR YOU

*But as it is written: What eye did not see and ear did not hear,
and what never entered the human mind—
God prepared this for those who love Him.*

1 CORINTHIANS 2:9 HCSB

Do you want to experience a life filled with abundance, peace, and emotional stability? If so, here's a word of warning: you'll need to resist the temptation to do things "your way" and commit, instead, to do things God's way. God has plans for your life. Big plans. But He won't force you to follow His will; to the contrary, He has given you free will, the ability to make decisions on your own. With the freedom to choose comes the responsibility of living with the consequences of the choices you make.

When you make the decision to seek God's will for your life, you will contemplate His Word, and you will be watchful for His signs. You will associate with fellow believers who will encourage your spiritual growth. And you will listen to that inner voice that speaks to you in the quiet moments of your daily devotionals.

Sometimes God's plans are crystal clear, but other times, He leads you through the wilderness before He delivers you to the promised land. So be patient, keep searching, and keep praying. If you do, then in time, God will answer your prayers and make His plans known. The Lord intends to use you in wonderful, unexpected ways. You'll discover those plans by doing things His way . . . and you'll be eternally grateful that you did.

Heavenly Father, I will earnestly seek Your will for my life. You have a plan for me that I can never fully understand. But You understand. And I will trust You today, tomorrow, and forever. Amen.

GOD WANTS YOU TO KEEP LEARNING AND GROWING

But grow in the grace and knowledge of our Lord and Savior Jesus Christ.
To Him be the glory, both now and to the day of eternity.

2 PETER 3:18 NASB

When it comes to your faith, God doesn't want you to stand still. He wants you to keep growing. And sometimes He places people along your path who, because of their personalities, can teach you lessons you could have learned in no other way. The Lord knows that spiritual maturity is a lifelong journey. You should know it too.

Each day is a glorious opportunity to serve your Creator, to learn more about His creation, and to do His will. So today, instead of focusing on the inevitable problems and challenges of everyday life, focus on God's blessings, God's love, and God's Son. View this day, and every day, as an opportunity to learn, to grow, and to serve.

Grow, dear friends, but grow, I beseech you,
in God's way, which is the only true way.

HANNAH WHITALL SMITH

The vigor of our spiritual life will be in exact proportion
to the place held by the Bible in our life and thoughts.

GEORGE MUELLER

Heavenly Father, I want to grow closer to You each day. I know that obedience to Your will strengthens my relationship with You, so help me to follow Your commandments and obey Your Word today . . . and every day of my life. Amen.

305

THE ANSWER TO SHAME IS GOD'S FORGIVENESS

Let all that I am praise the Lord; may I never forget the good things
he does for me. He forgives all my sins and heals all my diseases.

Psalm 103:2–3 NLT

If you're being victimized by shame, it's time to have a heart-to-heart talk with your Creator. If you've asked for God's forgiveness, He has given it. And because He has forgiven you, you should be quick to forgive yourself and make peace with your past. To do otherwise is to hold yourself to a different standard than God does.

The most marvelous ingredient in the forgiveness of God is that
he also forgets, the one thing a human being cannot do. With God,
forgetting is a divine attribute. God's forgiveness forgets.

Oswald Chambers

If God forgives us and we do not forgive ourselves,
we make ourselves greater than God.

Edwin Louis Cole

Just as the ancient sun rises anew every day,
so the eternal mercy of God is new every morning.

Dietrich Bonhoeffer

Dear Lord, the Bible promises that You are my loving Father. I thank You for Your love, for Your Forgiveness, and for Your Son. I will praise You, I will worship You, and I will love You, today, tomorrow, and forever. Amen.

306

WE MUST MAKE OUR ACTIONS CONSISTENT WITH OUR BELIEFS

As you have therefore received Christ Jesus the Lord, so walk in Him,
rooted and built up in Him and established in the faith,
as you have been taught, abounding in it with thanksgiving.

COLOSSIANS 2:6-7 NKJV

As Christians, we must do our best to make sure that our actions are accurate reflections of our beliefs. Our theology must be demonstrated, not only by our words but, more importantly, by our actions. In short, we should be practical believers, quick to act whenever we see an opportunity to serve God.

We may proclaim our beliefs to our hearts' content, but our proclamations will mean nothing—to others or to ourselves—unless we accompany our words with deeds that match. The sermons that we live are far more compelling than the ones we preach. So remember this: whether you like it or not, your life is an accurate reflection of your creed. If this fact gives you cause for concern, don't bother talking about the changes that you intend to make—make them. And then when your good deeds speak for themselves—as they most certainly will—don't interrupt.

If we judge our conduct by Christ and his desire to please the Father,
we will solve many decisions regarding behavior.

ERWIN LUTZER

Lord, it is so much easier to speak of the righteous life than it is to live it. Let me live righteously, and let my actions be consistent with my beliefs. May every step that I take reflect Your truth and Your love, and may I live a life that is worthy of Your love and Your grace. Amen.

307

OVERCOME THE BONDS OF PROCRASTINATION

If you do nothing in a difficult time, your strength is limited.

PROVERBS 24:10 HCSB

The habit of procrastination is often rooted in the fear of failure, the fear of discomfort, or the fear of embarrassment. Your challenge is to confront these fears and defeat them. So if unpleasant work needs to be done, do it sooner rather than later. It's easy to put off unpleasant tasks, but a far better strategy is this: do the unpleasant work first so you can enjoy the rest of the day. The sooner you face your problems—and the sooner you begin working to resolve them—the better your life will be.

Don't wait to "feel" like doing a thing to do it.
Live by decision, not emotion.

JOYCE MEYER

Do noble things, not dream them all day long; and so make life,
death, and that vast forever one grand, sweet song.

CHARLES KINGSLEY

One today is worth two tomorrows.

BEN FRANKLIN

Dear Lord, today is a new day. Help me tackle the important tasks immediately, even if those tasks are unpleasant. Don't let me put off until tomorrow what I can—and should—do today. Amen.

308

CLAIM GOD'S INNER PEACE

These things I have spoken to you, that in Me you may have peace. In the world you will have tribulation; but be of good cheer, I have overcome the world.

JOHN 16:33 NKJV

Have you found the lasting peace that can—and should—be yours through Jesus Christ? Or are you still chasing the illusion of "peace and happiness" that the world promises but cannot deliver?

The Scottish preacher George McDonald observed, "It has been well said that no man ever sank under the burden of the day. It is when tomorrow's burden is added to the burden of today that the weight is more than a man can bear. Never load yourselves so, my friends. If you find yourselves so loaded, at least remember this: it is your own doing, not God's. He begs you to leave the future to Him."

Today, as a gift to yourself, to your family, and to your friends, claim the inner peace that is your spiritual birthright: the peace of Jesus Christ. Christ is standing at the door, waiting patiently for you to invite Him to reign over your heart. His eternal peace is offered freely. Claim it today.

Peace does not mean to be in a place where there is no noise, trouble, or hard work. Peace means to be in the midst of all those things and still be calm in your heart.

CATHERINE MARSHALL

Dear Lord, when I turn my thoughts and prayers to You, I feel Your peace. But sometimes, Father, I become distracted by anxiety or sadness or fear. When I am troubled, turn my thoughts back to You. Help me to trust Your will, to follow Your commands, and to accept Your peace, today and forever. Amen.

CHOOSE KINDNESS

Talk and act like a person expecting to be judged by the Rule that sets us free. For if you refuse to act kindly, you can hardly expect to be treated kindly. Kind mercy wins over harsh judgment every time.

JAMES 2:12–13 MSG

If we believe the words of Proverbs 11:17—and we should—then we understand that kindness is its own reward. And if we obey the commandments of our Savior—and we should—we must sow seeds of kindness wherever we go.

Kindness is a choice. Sometimes, when we feel happy or generous, we find it easy to be kind. Other times, when we are discouraged or tired, we can scarcely summon the energy to utter a single kind word. But God's commandment is clear: He intends that we make the conscious choice to treat others with kindness and respect, no matter our circumstances, no matter our emotions. Kindness, therefore, is a choice that we, as Christians must make many times each day.

There are many timid souls whom we jostle morning and evening as we pass them by; but if only the kind word were spoken they might become fully persuaded.

FANNY CROSBY

Help me, Lord, to see the needs of those around me. Today, let me spread kind words in honor of Your Son. Today, let forgiveness rule my heart. And every day, Lord, let my love for Christ be demonstrated through deeds of kindness for those who need the healing touch of the Master's hand. Amen.

310

MAINTAIN A POSITIVE ATTITUDE

The LORD is my light and my salvation; whom shall I fear?
The LORD is the strength of my life; of whom shall I be afraid?

PSALM 27:1 KJV

If your inner voice is like a broken record that keeps repeating negative thoughts, you must guard your heart by training yourself to think thoughts that are more rational, more positive, more forgiving, and less destructive. Remember that negative thinking breeds more negative thinking, which leads to needless worry and anxiety.

As a Christian, you have every reason to be optimistic about your life here on earth and your eternal destiny with God in heaven. So today and every day, focus on possibilities, not stumbling blocks. And while you're at it, train yourself to count your blessings, not your hardships. It's the best way to think *and* the best way to live.

Have a sincere desire to serve God and mankind, and stop doubting.
Stop thinking negatively. Simply start living by faith, pray earnestly
and humbly, and get into the habit of looking expectantly for the best.

NORMAN VINCENT PEALE

We choose what attitudes we have right now. And it's a continuing choice.

JOHN MAXWELL

Dear Lord, today I will strive to maintain an attitude that pleases You. In every situation, I will focus on Your blessings and celebrate the life You have given me. Your gifts are priceless and eternal, and I will thank You, Father, with a grateful heart and willing hands. Amen.

311

WITH GOD, ALL THINGS ARE POSSIBLE

But Jesus looked at them and said, "With men this is impossible,
but with God all things are possible."

MATTHEW 19:26 HCSB

The Bible promises that you can do great things when you avail yourself of God's power. But how can you tap in? By allowing the Creator to work in you and through you—and by placing Him squarely at the center of your heart, that's how.

When you accept God's love and experience His power—when you trust Him to manage His world and yours—you will discover that He offers the strength to live victoriously today, tomorrow, and forever. So don't delay. Accept His strength now.

God's faithfulness and grace make the impossible possible.

SHEILA WALSH

It is wonderful what miracles God works in
wills that are utterly surrendered to Him.

HANNAH WHITALL SMITH

God is able to do what we can't do.

BILLY GRAHAM

Dear Lord, nothing is impossible for You—keep me always mindful of Your strength. Your power is limitless, so today, Father, let me expect Your blessings, let me anticipate the miraculous, and let me trust in You. Amen.

312

KEEP YOUR FOCUS ON GOD

Let us lay aside every weight and the sin that so easily ensnares us.
Let us run with endurance the race that lies before us,
keeping our eyes on Jesus, the source and perfecter of our faith.

HEBREWS 12:1–2 HCSB

The world is filled with distractions that can grab your attention and cause you forget about God. Your job is to focus on God, not the world. And while you're at it, be a discerning viewer.

Perhaps you, like so many others, have experienced anxieties and fears that are fed by the twenty-four-hour news cycle or by gratuitous violence that invades your screen when you least expect it. If so, God wants to remind you that He is here, that He is strong, and that He loves you very much. So don't focus on your fears (or, for that matter, on the fears that big media wants you to focus on). Instead, take your fears to the Lord, and leave them there.

Television is like a thief. It steals time;
it kills initiative; it destroys relationships.

EDWIN LOUIS COLE

The Christian life isn't a playground but a battlefield.

BILLY GRAHAM

Dear Lord, this world is filled with temptations and distractions; I have many opportunities to stray from Your commandments. Help me to focus, not on the things of this world, but on the message of Your Son. Let me keep Christ in my heart as I follow Him this day and forever. Amen.

313

NEVER BE ASHAMED TO ASK FOR HELP

As iron sharpens iron, so a friend sharpens a friend.
PROVERBS 27:17 NLT

To fully experience the joys and celebrations of the Christian life, you need to be spiritually and emotionally healthy. If mental health professionals can help you experience those joys—if they can help you experience God's abundance while you're following in the footsteps of His Son—then you should consider your treatment to be an integral part of the Lord's plan for your life.

Fitness is a state of body *and* a state of mind. If you're wise, you'll attend carefully to both.

It's been taboo for so long to admit you have a mental health problem. That must change.
ROSALYNN CARTER

Anything that's human is mentionable, and anything that is mentionable can be more manageable. When we can talk about our feelings, they become less overwhelming, less upsetting, and less scary.
FRED ROGERS

A diagnosis is burden enough without being burdened by secrecy and shame.
JANE PAULEY

Dear Lord, I know that You want me to experience an abundant life. And if I need medical or professional assistance to achieve a peaceful spirit, please give me the wisdom to ask for help. Amen.

314

IF YOU'RE OVERLY EMOTIONAL, PRAY ABOUT IT

The urgent request of a righteous person is very powerful.
JAMES 5:16 HCSB

Do your emotions ever rage out of control? Or do you ever feel like your emotions are simply too intense for you to manage? If so, here are the facts: God's love is real; His peace is real; His support is real; and He is always willing to help. If you pray about your challenges—if you ask for the Lord's help sincerely and often—He will answer your prayers in surprising ways.

So if you're struggling with emotional issues that seem impossible to repair, don't give up, don't stop praying, and don't be afraid to ask for help from God *and* from the people He places along your path. Then when you've done your best, step back, give thanks, and let God handle the things you can't.

Our emotions can lie to us, and we need to counter our emotions with truth.
BILLY GRAHAM

Our feelings do not affect God's facts.
AMY CARMICHAEL

A life lived in God is not lived on the plane of feelings, but of the will.
ELISABETH ELLIOT

Dear Lord, as I journey through this day, I will undoubtedly experience situations that cause me emotional distress. When I am anxious or troubled, I will turn my thoughts and prayers to You. Keep me steady, Father, and in those difficult moments, let me renew a sense of perspective and hope in Your promises, Your protection, and Your love. Amen.

315

DEVELOP A PATTERN OF GOOD WORKS

*In all things showing yourself to be a pattern
of good works; in doctrine showing integrity,
reverence, incorruptibility . . . .*

TITUS 2:7 NKJV

It has been said that character is what we are when nobody is watching. How true. When we do things that we know aren't right, we try to hide them from our families and friends. But even then, God is watching.

If you sincerely wish to walk with God, you must seek, to the best of your ability, to follow His commandments. When you do, your character will take care of itself . . . and you won't need to look over your shoulder to see who, besides God, is watching.

*Learning God's truth and getting it into our heads
is one thing, but living God's truth and getting
it into our characters is quite something else.*

WARREN WIERSBE

Dear Lord, You are my Father in heaven. You search my heart and know me far better than I know myself. May I be Your worthy servant, and may I live according to Your commandments. Let me be a person of integrity, Lord, and let my words and deeds be a testimony to You, today and always. Amen.

316

ACCEPT THE PAST AND MOVE ON

*Do not remember the past events, pay no attention to things of old.
Look, I am about to do something new; even now it is coming. Do you not
see it? Indeed, I will make a way in the wilderness, rivers in the desert.*

ISAIAH 43:18–19 HCSB

The past is past. Don't invest all your mental energy there. If you're focusing on yesterday, it's time to change your focus. If you're living in the past, move on while there's still time. If you're bearing a grudge against someone, it's time to forgive.

If you've endured a difficult past, accept it and learn from it, but don't spend too much time there. Instead, trust God's plan for your life and look to the future for God's blessings. The decision to seek God's plan and look to the future is an important decision . . . and it's the right thing to do. Don't let bitterness—or any other sin—get in the way.

*Don't waste energy regretting the way things are or thinking about what
might have been. Start at the present moment—accepting things exactly
as they are—and search for My way in the midst of those circumstances.*

SARAH YOUNG

Don't be bound by the past and its failures. But don't forget its lessons either.

BILLY GRAHAM

Dear Lord, when I am angry, bitter, or resentful, I cannot feel the peace that You intend for my life. So keep me mindful, Father, that You commanded me to forgive others, just as I have been forgiven. Today and every day, Lord, help me accept the past, treasure the present, and entrust my future to You. Amen.

317

TO COMBAT ANXIETY, STRIVE TO MAINTAIN PERSPECTIVE

*So if you're serious about living this new resurrection life with Christ,
act like it. Pursue the things over which Christ presides.*

COLOSSIANS 3:1 MSG

For most of us, life is busy and complicated. Amid the rush and crush of the daily grind, it's easy to lose perspective. But we must not let that happen. When our world seems to be spinning out of control, we must seek to regain a proper perspective by slowing down and turning our thoughts and prayers toward God.

When you focus on the world, you lose perspective. When you focus on God's promises and His love, you gain clearer perspective. To keep things in perspective, focus on God and on His plans for your life.

*Joy is the direct result of having God's perspective
on our daily lives and the effect of loving our Lord
enough to obey His commands and trust His promises.*

BILL BRIGHT

God's peace and perspective are available to you through His Word.

ELIZABETH GEORGE

Dear Lord, when the pace of my life becomes frantic, slow me down and give me perspective. Give me the wisdom to realize that the problems of today are only temporary but that Your love is eternal. When I become discouraged, keep me steady and sure, so that I might do Your will here on earth and then live with You forever in heaven. Amen.

318

BE SILENT AND
SEEK GOD'S GUIDANCE

Be silent before Me.
Isaiah 41:1 HCSB

In every stage of life, and in every circumstance, God has important things He's trying to teach you. So it pays to quiet yourself and to listen carefully for His guidance. When you do, the Lord will guide you and protect you.

From time to time, all of us encounter circumstances that test our faith. When we encounter life's inevitable tragedies, trials, and disappointments, we may be tempted to blame God or to rebel against Him. But the trials of life have much to teach us, and so does God.

Have you recently encountered one of life's inevitable tests? If so, remember that God still has lessons that He intends to teach you. So ask yourself this question: "What lesson is God trying to teach me today?"

When God speaks to us, He should have our full attention.
Billy Graham

*God's voice is still and quiet and easily buried
under an avalanche of clamor.*
Charles Stanley

Heavenly Father, I have so much to learn and You have so much to teach me. Give me the wisdom to be still and the discernment to hear Your voice, today and every day. Amen.

319

TRUST GOD AND BE JOYFUL

Rejoice in the Lord always. I will say it again: Rejoice!

PHILIPPIANS 4:4 HCSB

The joy that the world offers is fleeting and incomplete: here today, gone tomorrow, not coming back anytime soon. But God's joy is different. His joy has staying power. In fact, it's a gift that never stops giving to those who welcome His Son into their hearts.

Psalm 100 reminds us to celebrate the lives that God has given us: "Shout for joy to the LORD, all the earth. Worship the LORD with gladness; come before Him with joyful songs." (vv. 1–2 NIV). Yet sometimes, amid the inevitable complications and predicaments that are woven into the fabric of everyday life, we forget to rejoice. Instead of celebrating life, we complain about it. This is an understandable mistake, but a mistake nonetheless. As Christians, we are called by our Creator to live joyfully and abundantly. To do otherwise is to squander His spiritual gifts.

This day and every day, Christ offers you His peace and His joy. Accept it and share it with others, just as He has shared His joy with you.

When we get rid of inner conflicts and wrong attitudes toward life, we will almost automatically burst into joy.

E. STANLEY JONES

Heavenly Father, You have created a glorious universe, and You have offered me the gift of eternal life through the sacrifice of Your Son. Let me be a joyful Christian, Lord, today and every day. This day is Your gift to me. Let me use it wisely and let me honor You through my service to Your children. Amen.

320

YOU ARE ON A MISSION

But you are a chosen race, a royal priesthood, a holy nation,
a people for His possession, so that you may proclaim the praises
of the One who called you out of darkness into His marvelous light.

1 PETER 2:9 HCSB

Whether you realize it or not, you are on a personal mission for God. As a Christian, that mission is straightforward: honor God, accept Christ as your personal Savior, and serve God's children.

Of course, you will encounter impediments as you attempt to discover the exact nature of God's purpose for your life, but you must never lose sight of the overriding purposes that God has established for all believers. You will encounter these overriding purposes again and again as you worship your Creator and study His Word.

Every day offers countless opportunities to serve God and to worship Him. When you do so, He will bless you in miraculous ways. May you continue to seek God's will, may you trust His word, and may you place Him where He belongs: at the very center of your life.

Let God put you on His potter's wheel and whirl you as He likes.
OSWALD CHAMBER

If you're alive, there's a purpose for your life.
RICK WARREN

Dear Lord, I know that you have a purpose for my life, and I will seek that purpose today and every day that I live. Let my actions be pleasing to You, and let me share Your good news with a world that so desperately needs Your healing hand and the salvation of Your Son. Amen.

321

ARE YOU TRYING TO BE SELF-MADE?

*Respecting the Lord and not being proud
will bring you wealth, honor, and life.*

PROVERBS 22:4 NCV

We have heard it said on countless occasions: "He's a self-made man," or "She's a self-made woman." In truth, none of us are self-made. We all owe countless debts that we can never repay. Our first debt, of course, is to our Father in heaven—who has given us everything that we are and will ever be—and to His Son who sacrificed His own life so that we might live eternally. We are also indebted to ancestors, parents, teachers, friends, spouses, family members, coworkers, fellow believers . . . and the list, of course, goes on.

Most of us, it seems, are more than willing to stick out our chests and say, "Look at me; I did that!" But in our better moments, in the quiet moments when we search the depths of our own hearts, we know better. Whatever "it" is, God did that. And He deserves the credit.

Timely Tip: God favors the humble just as surely as He disciplines the proud. Humility leads to contentment; pride doesn't. Act accordingly.

Heavenly Father, Jesus clothed Himself with humility when He chose to leave heaven and come to earth to live and die for all creation. Christ is my Master and my example. Clothe me with humility, Lord, so that I might be more like Your Son. Amen.

322

PRAY MORE, WORRY LESS

Don't worry about anything, but in everything, through prayer and petition with thanksgiving, let your requests be made known to God.

PHILIPPIANS 4:6 HCSB

If your prayers have become more a matter of habit than a matter of passion, you're robbing yourself of a deeper relationship with God. And how can you rectify that situation? By praying more frequently and more fervently. When you do, God will give you the courage and the perspective to deal with your fears.

If you're faced with a big decision, pray about it. If there is something you're worried about, ask God to comfort you. If you're having trouble with your relationships, ask God to help you sort things out. As you pray more, you'll discover that God is always near and that He's always ready to hear from you. So don't worry about things; pray about them. God is waiting *and* listening.

When there is a matter that requires definite prayer, pray until you believe God and until you can thank Him for His answer.

HANNAH WHITALL SMITH

Prayer is the answer to every problem there is.

OSWALD CHAMBERS

Dear Lord, when I feel anxious or worried, I will turn to You for guidance and strength. And I will learn from the friends and mentors You place upon my path. Today, Father, help me focus on the things I can change—and help me work on those things—while I trust You to handle the problems that are too big for me. Amen.

OF THIS YOU CAN BE SURE: GOD KEEPS HIS PROMISES

Let us hold on to the confession of our hope without wavering,
for He who promised is faithful.

HEBREWS 10:23 HCSB

The Bible contains promises, made by God, upon which we, as believers, can and must depend. But sometimes, especially when we find ourselves caught in the inevitable entanglements of life, our faith is tested.

As you enter into the next phase of your life, you'll face many experiences: some good, and some not so good. When the sun is shining and all is well, it is easier to have faith. But when life takes an unexpected turn for the worse, as it will from time to time, your faith will be tested. In times of trouble and doubt, God remains faithful to you. You, in turn, must remain faithful to Him.

The Bible is God's book of promises, and unlike the books
of man, it does not change or go out of date.

BILLY GRAHAM

Beloved, God's promises can never fail to be accomplished, and those who
patiently wait can never be disappointed, for a believing faith leads to realization.

LETTIE COWMAN

Dear Lord, Your holy Word commands me to pray without ceasing. Let me take everything to You in prayer. When I am discouraged, let me pray. When I am lonely, let me take my sorrows to You. When I grieve, let me take my tears to You, Father, in prayer. And when I am joyful, let me offer up prayers of thanksgiving. In all things great and small, at all times, whether happy or sad, let me seek Your wisdom and Your grace through praise and prayer. Amen.

WE MUST HAVE COMPASSION FOR ONE ANOTHER

Finally, all of you be of one mind, having compassion for one another; love as brothers, be tenderhearted, be courteous.

1 PETER 3:8 NKJV

God's Word commands us to be compassionate, generous servants to those who need our support. As believers, we have been richly blessed by our Creator. We, in turn, are called to share our gifts, our possessions, our testimonies, and our talents.

Concentration camp survivor Corrie ten Boom correctly observed, "The measure of a life is not its duration but its donation." These words remind us that the quality of our lives is determined not by what are able to take from others, but instead by what we are able to share with others.

The thread of compassion is woven into the very fabric of Christ's teachings. If we are to be disciples of Christ, we, too, must be zealous in caring for others. Our Savior expects no less from us. And He deserves no less.

Our Lord worked with people as they were, and He was patient—not tolerant of sin, but compassionate.

VANCE HAVNER

Lord, make me a loving, encouraging, compassionate person. And let my love for Christ be reflected through the kindness that I show to my family, to my friends, and to all who need the healing touch of the Master's hand. Amen.

325

GOD CAN DRY YOUR TEARS

*It shall come to pass in the day the L*ORD
gives you rest from your sorrow, and from your fear.

ISAIAH 14:3 NKJV

Grief hurts, but denying your true feelings can hurt even more. With God's help—and with time—you can face your pain and move beyond it.

Perhaps you feel alone in your grief. Perhaps you feel like you've been isolated by events and circumstances from which you can never recover. If you have these feelings—and even if these feelings seem very real indeed—you're mistaken. You're never really alone because God is always with you. He is everywhere we have ever been and everywhere we will ever be.

Grief is a universal fact of life: No man or woman, no matter how righteous, is exempt. Christians, however, face their grief with the ultimate armor: God's promises. The following words of wisdom remind us that God will help heal us if we let Him into our hearts. And the time to let Him in is now.

God has enough grace to solve every dilemma you face,
wipe every tear you cry, and answer every question you ask.

MAX LUCADO

If there is something we need more than anything else during grief,
it is a friend who stands with us, who doesn't leave us. Jesus is that friend.

BILLY GRAHAM

Dear Lord, You have promised that You will not give us more than we can bear. And You have promised to lift us out of our grief and despair. Today, Father, I pray for people who are suffering, and I thank You for sustaining all of us in our days of sorrow. Amen.

326

TO MAKE WISE CHOICES, GUARD YOUR HEART

Guard your heart above all else, for it is the source of life.
PROVERBS 4:23 HCSB

Life is a series of conscious decisions and unconscious choices. Each day, we make countless decisions that can bring us closer to God, or not. When we guard our hearts—and when we live in accordance with God's command-ments—we earn His blessings. So, as followers of Christ, we must remain vigilant. Not only must we resist Satan when he confronts us, but we must also avoid the people and the places where Satan can most easily tempt us.

God wants you to guard your heart from situations or harmful emotions that would drive you away from Him. He wants the best for you, and you, of course, want the same for yourself. How do you achieve the best life has to offer? You should start by guarding your heart against the inevitable temptations and countless distractions that threaten your spiritual and emotional health.

Our fight is not against any physical enemy; it is against organizations and powers that are spiritual. We must struggle against sin all our lives, but we are assured we will win.
CORRIE TEN BOOM

Our battles are first won or lost in the secret places of our will in God's presence, never in full view of the world.
OSWALD CHAMBERS

Heavenly Father I know that you want me to guard my heart against the evils, the distractions and temptations of this world. So I will focus my thoughts on Your love, Your promises, Your blessings, and Your Son. Amen.

327

MOVING BEYOND FEELINGS OF GUILT

*If we say, "We have no sin," we are deceiving ourselves, and the truth
is not in us. If we confess our sins, He is faithful and righteous to forgive
us our sins and to cleanse us from all unrighteousness.*

1 JOHN 1:8–9 HCSB

Guilt is an emotion that can be debilitating. If you're being plagued by guilt, remember this: if you've asked for God's forgiveness, He has already given it.

Are you troubled by feelings of guilt, even after you've received God's forgiveness? Are you still struggling with painful memories of mistakes you made long ago? Are you focused so intently on yesterday that your vision of today is clouded? If so you still have work to do—spiritual work. You should ask your heavenly Father not for forgiveness (He granted that gift the very first time you asked Him!) but instead for acceptance and trust—acceptance of the past and trust in God's plan for your life.

So if the Creator has forgiven you, why are you unwilling to forgive yourself? When you answer that question honestly, you'll realize that God's forgiveness gives you permission to forgive yourself and move on.

*Guilt is an appalling waste of energy; you can't build on it.
It's only good for wallowing in.*

KATHERINE MANSFIELD

Dear Lord, when I ask for forgiveness, You give it. I am grateful for Your mercy and Your love. Today and every day, help me recognize my mistakes, help me learn from them, help me accept Your forgiveness, and help me follow more closely in the footsteps of Your Son. Amen.

328

EVEN DURING DIFFICULT DAYS, YOU CAN FIND POCKETS OF HAPPINESS AND JOY

Happy is the one whose help is the God of Jacob,
whose hope is in the LORD his God.

PSALM 146:5 HCSB

Happiness is freedom from fear—but sometimes, it's hard to live courageously. Why? Because we live in a fear-based world, a world where bad news travels at light speed and good news doesn't.

These are troubling times—times when we have legitimate fears for the future of our nation, our world, and our families. But if we trust God completely and without reservation, we can live courageously today and every day. Perhaps you, like so many others, have found your courage tested by the anxieties and fears that are an inevitable part of twenty-first-century life. If so, God wants to remind you that He is not just near; He is here.

The best day to be happy is this one. Even if you're dealing with troublesome emotions, even if you're caught up in difficult situation, you still have many reasons to celebrate. So with no further ado, let the celebration begin.

Joy comes not from what we have but what we are.

C. H. SPURGEON

Dear Lord, You are my strength and my joy. I will rejoice in the day that You have made, and I will give thanks for the countless blessings that You have given me. Let me be a joyful Christian, Father, as I share the good news of Your Son, and let me praise You for all the marvelous things You have done. Amen.

329

FEELING LONELY?
FIND FRIENDS WHO NEED HELP

A friend loves you all the time, and a brother helps in time of trouble.
PROVERBS 17:17 NCV

The philosopher William James observed, "Human beings are born into this little span of life, and among the best things that life has to offer are its friendships and intimacies. Yet, humans leave their friendships with no cultivation, letting them grow as they will by the roadside." James understood that when we leave our friendships unattended, the resulting harvest is predictably slim.

If you're feeling lonely, it's a signal that you need to reach out. Remember that God is close by, and so is someone who needs your help. If you find someone to help, you won't be lonely for long.

Friendship is one of the sweetest joys of life. Many might have failed beneath the bitterness of their trial had they not found a friend.
C. H. SPURGEON

I cannot even imagine where I would be today were it not for that handful of friends who have given me a heart full of joy. Let's face it: friends make life a lot more fun.
CHARLES SWINDOLL

Dear Lord, thank You for the gift of friendship. Help me be a loyal friend to others. Let me be ready to listen, ready to encourage, and ready to offer them a helping hand. Today, I will pray for my friends, and I will praise You, Father, for all Your gifts. Amen.

330

TRUST GOD AND GET BUSY

Are there those among you who are truly wise and understanding?
Then they should show it by living right and doing
good things with a gentleness that comes from wisdom.

JAMES 3:13 NCV

Can you place your future into the hands of a loving and all-knowing God? Can you live amid the uncertainties of today, knowing that God has dominion over all your tomorrows? Can you summon the faith to trust God in good times and hard times? If you can, you are wise and you are blessed.

Once you've made the decision to trust God completely, it's time to get busy. The willingness to take action—even if the outcome of that action is uncertain—is an effective way to combat hopelessness. When you decide to roll up your sleeves and begin solving your own problems, you'll feel empowered, and you may see the first real glimmer of hope.

So today and every day, ask God for these things: clear perspective, mountain-moving faith, and the courage to do what needs doing. After all, no problem is too big for God. Through Him, all things are possible.

Timely Tip: If you're worried about dealing with a difficult situation, don't give up hope, and don't stop looking for a better solution to your problem. Instead of procrastinating, tackle the problem now. You and God, working together, can do amazing things. So be hopeful and get busy.

Heavenly Father, help me identify the most important things on my to-do list today. And let my actions be pleasing to You. I will praise You, Lord, by following in the footsteps of Your Son and acting accordingly. Amen.

331

BE A FEARLESS WOMAN

Teach me Your way, O Lord; I will walk in Your truth.
PSALM 86:11 NKJV

The book of Judges (chapters 4 and 5) tells the story of Deborah, the fearless woman who helped lead the army of Israel to victory over the Canaanites. Deborah was a judge and a prophetess, a woman called by God to lead her people. And when she answered God's call, she was rewarded with one of the great victories of Old Testament times. Like Deborah, all of us are called to serve our Creator. And like Deborah, we may sometimes find ourselves facing trials that can bring trembling to the very depths of our souls. As believers, we must seek God's will and follow it.

As this day unfolds, seek God's will for your own life and obey His Word. He will give you the strength to meet any challenge, the courage to face any trial, and the wisdom to live in His righteousness and in His peace.

*Anxiety is the natural result when our hopes are centered
in anything short of God and His will for us.*
BILLY GRAHAM

Lord, let Your will be my will. When I am confused, give me maturity and wisdom. When I am worried, give me courage and strength. Let me be Your faithful servant, Father, always seeking Your guidance and Your will for my life. Amen.

332

ASK GOD FOR THE THINGS YOU NEED

The effective prayer of a righteous man can accomplish much.

JAMES 5:16 NASB

God has promised that when you ask for His help, He will not withhold it. So ask. And when you pray, listen carefully to the quiet voice of your heavenly Father. Seek His guidance; watch for His signs; and listen to the wisdom that He shares through the reliable voice of your own conscience.

God loves you, and you deserve all the best that He has to offer. You can claim His blessings today by being faithful to Him. When you genuinely and humbly seek His instruction, the Lord will lead you on the path of His choosing. Today and every day, the Lord will bless you and keep you. All you must do is ask.

*We honor God by asking for great things
when they are a part of His promise. We dishonor Him
and cheat ourselves when we ask for molehills
where He has promised mountains.*

VANCE HAVNER

Heavenly Father, Your Word promises that when I ask for Your help, You will give it. I thank You, Lord, for Your love, for Your help, and for Your Son. Amen.

333

JUST SAY NO TO PESSIMISM

The LORD is my light and my salvation; whom shall I fear?
The LORD is the strength of my life; of whom shall I be afraid?

PSALM 27:1 NKJV

Pessimism is emotional poison. And negativity has the power to harm your heart if you let it. So if you've allowed negative thoughts to creep into your mind and heart, here's your assignment: start spending more time thinking about your blessings and less time fretting about your hardships.

God has promised to protect us, and He intends to fulfill His promise. In a world filled with dangers and temptations, God is the ultimate armor. In a world filled with misleading messages, God's Word is the ultimate truth.

This day, like every other, is a gift from above, filled to the brim with possibilities. But persistent pessimistic thoughts can rob you of the energy you need to accomplish the most important tasks on your to-do list. So today, be careful to direct your thoughts toward things positive. And while you're at it, take time to thank the Giver of all things good for gifts that are, in truth, far too numerous to count.

The best preparation for the future is the present
well seen to, and the last duty done.

GEORGE MACDONALD

Heavenly Father, as I focus on the day ahead, I will focus on Your love, Your protection, and Your Son. Whatever this day may bring, I thank You, Lord, for the opportunity to live abundantly. I will praise You, Father—and trust You—this day and forever. Amen.

334

DON'T KEEP RELIVING YOUR PAST

Forget about what's happened; don't keep going over old history. Be alert, be present. I'm about to do something brand-new. It's bursting out! Don't you see it? There it is! I'm making a road through the desert, rivers in the badlands.

ISAIAH 43:18–19 MSG

Do you invest more time than you should reliving the past? Are you troubled by feelings of anger, bitterness, envy, or regret? Do you harbor ill will against someone you can't seem to forgive? If so, it's time to get serious about putting the past in its proper place: behind you.

Perhaps there's something in your past that you deeply regret. Or maybe you've been scarred by a trauma that you simply can't seem to resolve. If so, it's time to ask for God's help—sincerely, prayerfully, and often—as you decide, once and for all, to move beyond yesterday's pain so you can more fully savor the precious present.

Of course, it's perfectly natural to fret over the injustices you've suffered and to hold grudges against the people who inflicted them. But God has a better plan: He wants you to live in the present, not the past, and He knows that even when you can't forget, you can forgive and, by doing so, move on. It's the right thing to do and the right way to live.

God does not wish us to remember what he is willing to forget.

GEORGE A. BUTTRICK

Heavenly Father, free me from anger, resentment, and envy. When I am bitter, I cannot feel the peace that You intend for my life. Keep me mindful that forgiveness is Your commandment, and help me accept the past, treasure the present, and trust the future . . . to You. Amen.

335

WHEN YOU FEEL ANXIOUS, PRAY

Are any of you suffering hardships? You should pray.
Are any of you happy? You should sing praises.

JAMES 5:13 NLT

If you're feeling trapped by anxiety, fear, or any other negative emotion, God wants you to talk to Him about it. The Lord is always with you, always listening to your prayers, always ready to lead you in a direction of His choosing. Your challenge, of course, is to pray about the things that are on your heart and to listen carefully for His responses.

Prayer is of transcendent importance. Prayer is the mightiest
agent to advance God's work. Praying hearts and hands
only can do God's work. Prayer succeeds when all else fails.

E. M. BOUNDS

Time spent in prayer will yield more than that given to work.
Prayer alone gives work its worth and its success. Prayer opens
the way for God Himself to do His work in us and through us.

ANDREW MURRAY

Before prayer changes others, it first changes us.

BILLY GRAHAM

Heavenly Father, when I am anxious or fearful, I will turn to You for strength, and perspective, and courage. I know that You are my shepherd, and that You have promised to care for me now and forever. I thank You, Lord, for all your blessings, and I will trust You to manage the challenges that are simply too big for me. Amen.

336

HE REWARDS DISCIPLINE AND OBEDIENCE

The one who follows instruction is on the path to life,
but the one who rejects correction goes astray.
PROVERBS 10:17 HCSB

Wise men and women understand the importance of discipline. In Proverbs 28:19, God's message is clear: "Those who work their land will have abundant food, but those who chase fantasies will have their fill of poverty" (NIV). When we work diligently and consistently, we can expect a bountiful harvest. But we must never expect the harvest to precede the labor.

Thoughtful Christians understand that God doesn't reward laziness or misbehavior. To the contrary, God expects His children (of all ages) to lead disciplined lives . . . very disciplined lives.

The Bible calls for discipline and a recognition of authority.
Children must learn this at home.
BILLY GRAHAM

The alternative to discipline is disaster.
VANCE HAVNER

Lord, I want to be a disciplined person. Let me use my time wisely, and let me teach others by the faithfulness by my conduct, today and every day. Amen.

337

FOLLOW THE GUIDEBOOK

There's nothing like the written Word of God for showing you the way to salvation through faith in Christ Jesus. Every part of Scripture is God-breathed and useful one way or another—showing us truth, exposing our rebellion, correcting our mistakes, training us to live God's way. Through the Word we are put together and shaped up for the tasks God has for us.

2 Timothy 3:15–17 MSG

God has given us a guidebook for righteous living called the Holy Bible. It contains thorough instructions which, if followed, lead to fulfillment, righteousness, and salvation. But if we choose to ignore God's commandments, the results are as predictable as they are tragic.

God has given us the Bible for the purpose of knowing His promises, His power, His commandments, His wisdom, His love, and His Son. As we study God's teachings and apply them to our lives, we live by the Word that shall never pass away. Today, let us follow God's commandments, and let us conduct our lives in such a way that we might be shining examples to our families, and, most importantly, to those who have not yet found Christ.

Reading news without reading the Bible will inevitably lead to an unbalanced life, an anxious spirit, a worried and depressed soul.

Bill Bright

Dear Lord, as I journey through this life, help me always to consult the true road map: Your holy Word. I know that when I turn my heart and my thoughts to You, Father, You will lead me along the path that is right for me. Today, let me know Your will and study Your Word so that I might know Your plan for my life. Amen.

338

DRAW CONFIDENCE FROM GOD

Let us hold tightly without wavering to the hope we affirm,
for God can be trusted to keep his promise.

HEBREWS 10:23 NLT

Are you confident about your future, or do you live under a cloud of anxiety and doubt? If you trust God's promises, you have every reason to live comfortably and confidently. But despite God's promises, and despite His blessings, you may, from time to time, find yourself being tormented by negativity and fear. If so, it's time to redirect your thoughts and your prayers.

Even the most optimistic men and women may be overcome by occasional bouts of fear and anxiety. You are no different. But even when you feel discouraged—or worse—you should remember that God is always faithful, and you are always protected.

Timely Tip: If negative emotions have caused you to doubt your abilities or your opportunities, it's time for a complete mental makeover. God created you for a purpose, and He has important work specifically for you. So don't let anxious feelings or irrational fears steal your joy, your self-confidence, or your faith in God. Because the Lord is faithful, you can be confident that you are protected and your future is secure.

Heavenly Father, give me confidence and courage for the day ahead. When I am fearful, let me feel Your strength. Let me always trust in Your promises, Lord, and let me draw strength from those promises and from Your unending love. Amen.

339

FORGIVENESS IS THE GIFT YOU GIVE TO YOURSELF

All bitterness, anger and wrath, shouting and slander must be removed from you, along with all malice. And be kind and compassionate to one another, forgiving one another, just as God also forgave you in Christ.

EPHESIANS 4:31–32 HCSB

Forgiveness is a gift of great value, but ironically it's a gift that is often worth more to the giver than to the recipient. You simply cannot give the gift of forgiveness without receiving an important blessing for yourself.

From a psychological perspective, the act of forgiving relieves you of some very heavy mental baggage: persistent feelings of hatred, anger, and regret. More importantly, the act of forgiveness brings with it a spiritual blessing, a knowledge that you have honored your heavenly Father by obeying His commandments.

Simply put, forgiveness is a gift that you give yourself by giving it to someone else. When you make the choice to forgive, everybody wins, including you.

Timely Tip: Forgiveness is its own reward. Bitterness is its own punishment. Bitter thoughts are bad for your spiritual and emotional health. Guard your words and thoughts accordingly.

Heavenly Father, give me the wisdom to forgive others quickly and completely. When I forgive others, I also free myself from bitterness and regret. You have instructed me to forgive others, Lord, just as You have forgiven me. So today, I will honor You by forgiving others, even when it's hard. Amen.

340

DEAL WITH DISAPPOINTMENTS

Do not be afraid or discouraged, for the Lord will personally go ahead of you. He will be with you; he will neither fail you nor abandon you.

DEUTERONOMY 31:8 NLT

Sometimes the seas of life are calm, and sometimes they are not. When we find ourselves beset by the inevitable storms of life, we may sense that all is lost—but if we imagine, even for a moment, that all hope is gone, we are mistaken.

The Bible is unambiguous: it promises that God will remain steadfast, even during our darkest hours. God's Word makes it clear that He is with us always, on good days and bad days. He never leaves our side, and He never stops loving us.

So if you're feeling buffeted by the winds and the waves of life, don't despair. God is not just near; He is here. He has promised to protect you now and forever. And upon that promise, you can always depend.

We all have sorrows and disappointments, but one must never forget that, if commended to God, they will issue in good. His own solution is far better than any we could conceive.

FANNY CROSBY

Dear Lord, when I am discouraged, give me perspective and faith. When I am weak, give me strength. When I am fearful, give me courage for the day ahead. I will trust in Your promises, Father, and I will live with the assurance that You are with me not only for this day, but also throughout all eternity. Amen.

341

YOU CAN TRUST GOD'S PROMISES

God blesses those who patiently endure testing and temptation. Afterward they will receive the crown of life that God has promised to those who love him.

JAMES 1:12 NLT

Throughout the seasons of life, we must all endure life-altering personal losses that leave us breathless. When we do, we may be overwhelmed by fear, by doubt, or by both. Thankfully, God has promised that He will never desert us. And God keeps His promises.

Life is often challenging, but as Christians, we must trust the promises of our heavenly Father. God loves us, and He will protect us. In times of hardship, He will comfort us; in times of sorrow, He will dry our tears. When we are troubled or weak or sorrowful, God is with us. His love endures, not only for today, but also for all of eternity.

Timely Tip: Remember that tough times are simply opportunities to trust God completely and to find strength in His promises. And remember: tough times can also be times of intense personal growth.

Dear Lord, when I face the inevitable disappointments of life, give me perspective and faith. When I am discouraged, give me the strength to trust Your promises and follow your will. Then when I have done my best, Father, let me live with the assurance that You are firmly in control, and that Your love endures forever. Amen.

342

LIVE IN BLESSED OBEDIENCE

When you and your children return to the LORD your God
and obey him with all your heart and with all your soul according
to everything I command you today, then the LORD your God
will restore your fortunes and have compassion on you and
gather you again from all the nations where he scattered you.

DEUTERONOMY 30:2–3 NIV

We live in a world filled with temptations, distractions, and countless opportunities to disobey God. But as believers who seek to be godly role models for our families, we must turn our thoughts and our hearts away from the evils of this world. We must turn instead to God.

Today, take every step of your journey with God as your traveling companion. Read His Word and obey His commandments. Support only those activities that further God's kingdom and your spiritual growth. Be an example of righteous living to your friends, to your neighbors, and to your loved ones. Then reap the blessings that God has promised to all those who live according to His will and His Word.

Timely Tip: Obedience is one of the ways you can express your gratitude to God for the countless blessings He has given you. And remember: it's not enough to understand God's rules; you must also live by them or face the inevitable consequences.

Dear Lord, when I am tempted to disobey Your commandments, correct my errors and guide my path. Make me a faithful steward of my talents, my opportunities, and my possessions so that Your kingdom may be glorified, now and forever. Amen.

343

MAKE CHANGES IN DISCOURAGING RELATIONSHIPS

Don't make friends with quick-tempered people or spend time with those who have bad tempers. If you do, you will be like them. Then you will be in real danger.

PROVERBS 22:24–25 NCV

In a perfect world filled with perfect people, our relationships, too, would be perfect, and our anxieties would be few and far between. But none of us are perfect and neither are our relationships . . . and that's okay. As we work to make our imperfect relationships a little happier and healthier, we grow as individuals and as families. But if we find ourselves in relationships that are debilitating or dangerous, then changes must be made, and soon.

If you find yourself caught up in a personal relationship that is bringing havoc into your life, and if you can't seem to find the courage to do something about it, don't hesitate to consult your pastor. Or you may choose to seek the advice of a trusted friend or a professionally trained counselor. But whatever you do, don't be satisfied with the status quo.

We must meet our disappointments, our malicious enemies, our provoking friends, our trials of every sort, with an attitude of surrender and trust. We must rise above them in Christ so they lose their power to harm us.

HANNAH WHITALL SMITH

Dear Lord, help me choose my friends wisely. And help me establish lasting relationships with likeminded believers who give me spiritual and emotional strength. Amen.

344

CLAIM GOD'S ABUNDANT PEACE

And the peace of God, which surpasses every thought,
will guard your hearts and your minds in Christ Jesus.

PHILIPPIANS 4:7 HCSB

Are you the kind of person who accepts God's spiritual abundance without reservation? If so, you are availing yourself of the peace and the joy that He has promised. Do you sincerely seek the riches that our Savior offers to those who give themselves to Him? Then follow Him. When you do, you will receive the love and the abundance that Jesus offers to those who follow Him.

Seek first the salvation that is available through a personal, passionate relationship with Christ, and then claim the joy, the peace, and the spiritual abundance that the shepherd offers His sheep.

The only way you can experience abundant life
is to surrender your plans to Him.

CHARLES STANLEY

Heavenly Father, You have promised an abundant life through Your Son Jesus. Thank You, Lord, for Your abundance and Your peace. Your blessings endure forever, Lord, and I will praise You today, tomorrow, and throughout eternity. Amen.

345

HE IS ALWAYS FAITHFUL

*God is faithful, by whom you were called into
the fellowship of His Son, Jesus Christ our Lord.*

1 CORINTHIANS 1:9 NKJV

God is faithful to us even when we are not faithful to Him. God keeps His promises to us even when we stray far from His will. He continues to love us even when we disobey His commandments. But God does not force His blessings upon us. If we are to experience His love and His grace, we must claim them for ourselves.

Are you tired, discouraged, or fearful? Be comforted: God is with you. Are you confused? Listen to the quiet voice of your heavenly Father. Are you bitter? Talk with God and seek His guidance. Are you celebrating a great victory? Thank God and praise Him. He is the Giver of all things good. In whatever condition you find yourself, trust God and be comforted. The Father is with you now and forever.

God is always sufficient in perfect proportion to our need.

BETH MOORE

*It is a joy that God never abandons His children.
He guides faithfully all who listen to His directions.*

CORRIE TEN BOOM

Lord, Your faithfulness is everlasting. You are faithful to me even when I am not faithful to You. Today, let me serve You with my heart, my soul, and my mind. And then let me rest in the knowledge of Your constant love for me. Amen.

346

FIND PEACE AMID THE NOISE AND CONFUSION

I wait quietly before God, for my victory comes from him.
PSALM 62:1 NLT

Sometimes peace can be a scarce commodity in this noisy, complicated world. You live in a high-information society where time-gobbling distractions leave scarcely a moment for contemplation, reflection, or prayer.

Thankfully, God's peace is always available. Even when you're struggling with the inevitable demands and complexities of twenty-first-century life, the Lord will comfort you when you turn to Him in prayer. Your heavenly Father is ready to calm your fears, renew your strength, and give you peace of mind if you let Him. The rest is up to you.

When something robs you of your peace of mind, ask yourself if it is worth the energy you are expending on it. If not, then put it out of your mind in an act of discipline. Every time the thought of "it" returns, refuse it.
KAY ARTHUR

Deep within the center of the soul is a chamber of peace where God lives and where, if we will enter it and quiet all the other sounds, we can hear His gentle whisper.
LETTIE COWMAN

Heavenly Father, amid the confusion of everyday life, let me accept the peace and abundance that You offer through Your Son Jesus. You have blessed me in so many ways, Lord, and You give me peace when I draw close to You. Help me to trust Your will, to follow Your commands, and to accept Your peace, today, tomorrow, and every day of my life. Amen.

347

KEEP PRAYING, KEEP WORKING, AND DON'T GIVE UP

Let us not become weary in doing good, for at the proper time
we will reap a harvest if we do not give up.

GALATIANS 6:9 NIV

In Hebrews 10:36, we are taught that, "Patient endurance is what you need now, so that you will continue to do God's will. Then you will receive all that he has promised" (NLT). But when tough times arrive, we are inevitably faced with a powerful temptation: the temptation to give up, or give in, or quit before we reach the finish line.

When we face disappointments or unfortunate circumstances, the Lord stands ready to protect us. Our responsibility, of course, is to pray for His help and ask for His protection. And while we are waiting for God's plans to unfold, we can be comforted in the knowledge that our Creator can overcome any obstacle, even if we cannot.

Today, ask the Lord God for the courage to step beyond the boundaries of your self-doubts. Ask Him for the wisdom to trust and the confidence to persevere. Keep praying, keep working, and leave everything else up to Him. And then, watch in amazement as He helps you face your fears, tackle your problems, and live victoriously for Him.

Dear Lord, sometimes this life is difficult indeed. Sometimes I am fearful. Sometimes I cry tears of frustration and loss, but even then, You never leave my side. Today, Lord, let me be a finisher of my faith. Let me persevere—even if the day is difficult—and let me follow in the footsteps of Your Son Jesus this day and forever. Amen.

348

TRUST HIM COMPLETELY

I will be your God throughout your lifetime—
until your hair is white with age.
I made you, and I will care for you.
I will carry you along and save you.

ISAIAH 46:4 NLT

The Lord has promised to lift you up and guide your steps if you let Him. God has promised that when you entrust your life to Him completely and without reservation, He will give you the strength to meet any challenge, the courage to face any trial, and the wisdom to live in His righteousness.

God's hand uplifts those who turn their hearts and prayers to Him. Will you count yourself among that number? Will you accept God's peace and wear His armor against the temptations and distractions of our dangerous world? If you do, you can live courageously and optimistically, knowing that you have been forever touched by the loving, unfailing, uplifting hand of God.

Timely Tip: Whatever your weaknesses, God is stronger. And His strength will help you measure up to His tasks.

Dear Lord, as I face the challenges of this day, You protect me. I thank You, Father, for Your love and for Your strength. I will lean upon You today and forever. Amen.

349

OBEDIENCE LEADS TO JOY AND PEACE

God's righteousness is revealed from faith to faith,
just as it is written: The righteous will live by faith.

ROMANS 1:17 HCSB

The Bible promises that the Lord will teach us how to live wisely and well. And one of the tools He uses to instruct us is His holy Word. God's Word is the ultimate guidebook for life here on earth and for life beyond the grave. The Bible is, therefore, a treasure beyond measure, and we must treat it that way.

This day, like every other, is filled to the brim with opportunities, challenges, and choices. But no choice that you make is more important than the choice you make concerning your heavenly Father. Today, you will either place Him at the center of your life—or not—and the consequences of that choice have implications that are both temporal and eternal.

Sometimes we don't intentionally neglect God; we simply allow ourselves to become overwhelmed with the demands of everyday life. And then, without our even realizing it, we gradually drift away from the One we need most. Thankfully, God never drifts away from us; He remains always present.

As you begin this day, place God and His Son where they belong: in your head, in your prayers, on your lips, and in your heart. And then, with God as your guide and companion, let the journey begin . . .

When we do what is right, we have contentment, peace, and happiness.

BEVERLY LaHAYE

Dear Lord, I ask for the strength, the wisdom, and the courage to live a life that pleases You. You love me and protect me, heavenly Father. Let me be grateful, and let me live for You today, tomorrow, and throughout eternity. Amen.

350

HELP ME NOT TO JUDGE

When they persisted in questioning Him,
He stood up and said to them,
"The one without sin among you
should be the first to throw a stone at her."

John 8:7 HCSB

The warning of Matthew 7:1 is clear: "Judge not, that ye be not judged" (KJV). Yet even the most devoted Christians may fall prey to a powerful yet subtle temptation—the temptation to judge others. But as obedient followers of Christ, we are commanded to refrain from such behavior.

As Jesus came upon a young woman who had been condemned by the Pharisees, He spoke not only to the crowd that was gathered there, but also to all generations when He warned, "He that is without sin among you, let him first cast a stone at her" (John 8:7). Christ's message is clear, and it applies not only to the Pharisees of ancient times, but also to us.

Christians think they are prosecuting attorneys or judges,
when, in reality, God has called all of us to be witnesses.

Warren Wiersbe

Dear Lord, sometimes I am quick to judge others. But You have commanded me not to judge. Keep me mindful, Father, that when I judge others, I am living outside of Your will for my life. You have forgiven me, Lord. Let me forgive others, let me love them, and let me help them . . . without judging them. Amen.

351

LEARN FROM FAILURE

Though a righteous man falls seven times,
he will get up, but the wicked will stumble into ruin.

PROVERBS 24:16 HCSB

As we go about the business of learning life's lessons, we can either do things the easy way or the hard way. The easy way can be summed up as follows: when God tries to teaches us something, we learn it . . . the first time! Unfortunately, too many of us learn much more slowly than that.

When we resist God's instruction, He continues to teach, whether we like it or not. Our challenge, then, is to discern God's lessons from the experiences of everyday life. Hopefully, we learn those lessons sooner rather than later because the sooner we do so, the sooner He can move on to the next lesson and the next and the next.

Setbacks are inevitable, but your response to them is optional. You and the Lord, working together, can always find a way to turn stumbling blocks into steppingstones, so don't give up, don't abandon hope, and don't be afraid. Better days will arrive, and perhaps sooner than you think.

No matter how badly we have failed, we can always get up
and begin again. Our God is the God of new beginnings.

WARREN WIERSBE

Failure is one of life's most powerful teachers. How we handle our failures
determines whether we're going to simply "get by" in life or "press on."

BETH MOORE

Heavenly Father, when I encounter failures and disappointments, keep me mindful that You are in control. Let me persevere—even if my soul is troubled—and let me follow Your Son, Jesus Christ, this day and forever. Amen.

352

JESUS IS THE BREAD OF LIFE

"I am the bread of life," Jesus told them.
"No one who comes to Me will ever be hungry,
and no one who believes in Me will ever be thirsty again."

JOHN 6:35 HCSB

He was the Son of God, but He wore a crown of thorns. He was the Savior of mankind, yet He was put to death on a rough-hewn cross made of wood. He offered His healing touch to an unsaved world, and yet the same hands that had healed the sick and raised the dead were pierced with nails.

Jesus Christ, the Son of God, was born into humble circumstances. He walked this earth, not as a ruler of men, but as the Savior of mankind. His crucifixion, a torturous punishment that was intended to end His life and His reign, instead became the pivotal event in the history of all humanity.

Jesus is the bread of life. Accept His grace. Share His love. And follow His in footsteps.

The crucial question for each of us is this: What do you think of Jesus,
and do you yet have a personal acquaintance with Him?

HANNAH WHITALL SMITH

Dear Jesus, You give me peace. Thank You, Lord, for the gift of eternal life and for the gift of eternal love. May I be ever grateful, and may I share Your good news with a world that so desperately needs Your healing grace. Amen.

353

REPLACE PESSIMISM WITH OPTIMISM

*For God has not given us a spirit of fear and timidity,
but of power, love, and self-discipline.*

2 Timothy 1:7 NLT

Negative self-talk breeds negative results. Positive self-talk breeds positive results. So as you monitor your thoughts, stay positive. And whatever you do, please don't let chronic negativity shape your future. As a follower of God's only begotten Son, you have every reason to break the chains of negativity. And that's precisely what you should do, as the following words of wisdom clearly attest.

*Occupy your minds with good thoughts, or your enemy will
fill them with bad ones; unoccupied they cannot be.*

St. Thomas More

*Developing a positive attitude means working continually
to find what is uplifting and encouraging.*

Barbara Johnson

*Find the good. It's all around you. Find it,
showcase it, and you'll start believing in it.*

Jesse Owens

Heavenly Father, today, I ask You to give me optimism and hope. I will expect the best from the day ahead, and I will look for the best in others. Make me Your faithful servant with praise on my lips and hope in my heart. Amen.

354

GOD CAN RESTORE YOUR STRENGTH

You are being renewed in the spirit of your minds;
you put on the new self, the one created according to
God's likeness in righteousness and purity of the truth.

EPHESIANS 4:23–24 HCSB

On occasion, the demands of daily life can drain us of our strength and rob us of the joy that is rightfully ours in Christ. When we find ourselves anxious, discouraged, or worse, there is a source from which we can draw the power needed to recharge our spiritual batteries. That source is God. When we genuinely lift our hearts and prayers to Him, He renews our strength and restores our confidence.

Are you troubled or anxious? Take your anxieties to God in prayer. Are you weak or worried? Delve deeply into God's holy Word and sense His presence in the quiet moments of the early morning. Are you spiritually exhausted? Call upon fellow believers to support you, and call upon Christ to renew your spirit and your life. The Lord will never let you down. To the contrary, He will always lift you up if you ask Him to. And the best moment to ask for His help is always the present one.

God is not running an antique shop! He is making all things new!

VANCE HAVNER

Dear Lord, You have the power to make all things new. When I grow weary, let me turn my thoughts and my prayers to You. When I am discouraged, restore my faith in You. Renew my strength, Father, and let me draw comfort and courage from Your promises and from Your unending love. Amen.

355

ALWAYS PUT GOD FIRST

You shall have no other gods before Me.

EXODUS 20:3 NKJV

For most of us, these are very busy times. We have obligations at home, at work, at school, or at church. From the moment we rise until we drift off to sleep at night, we have things to do and people to contact. So how do we find time for God? We must *make* time for Him, plain and simple. When we put God first, we're blessed. But when we succumb to the pressures and temptations of the world, we inevitably pay a price for our misguided priorities.

In the book of Exodus, God warns that we should put no gods before Him. Yet all too often, we place our Lord in second, third, or fourth place as we focus on other things. When we place our desires for possessions and status above our love for God—or when we yield to the countless frustrations and distractions that surround us—we forfeit the peace that might otherwise be ours.

In the wilderness, Satan offered Jesus earthly power and unimaginable riches, but Jesus refused. Instead, He chose to worship His heavenly Father. We must do likewise by putting God first and worshiping Him only. God must come first. Always first.

Jesus Christ is the first and last, author and finisher, beginning and end, alpha and omega, and by Him all other things hold together. He must be first or nothing. God never comes next!

VANCE HAVNER

Dear Lord, keep me mindful of the need to place You first in every aspect of my life. You have blessed me beyond measure, Father, and I will praise You with my thoughts, my prayers, my testimony, and my service, this day and every day. Amen.

356

LIVE AS AN ENTHUSIATIC DISCIPLE

Don't work only while being watched,
in order to please men, but as slaves of Christ,
do God's will from your heart. Serve with
a good attitude, as to the Lord and not to men.

EPHESIANS 6:6–7 HCSB

With whom will you choose to walk today? Will you walk with shortsighted people who honor the ways of the world, or will you walk with the Son of God? Jesus walks with you. Are you walking with Him? Hopefully, you will choose to walk with Him today and every day of your life. Jesus has called upon believers of every generation (and that includes you) to follow in His footsteps. And God's Word promises that when you follow in Christ's footsteps, you will learn how to live freely and lightly (Matthew 11:28–30).

Jesus doesn't want you to be a run-of-the-mill, follow-the-crowd kind of person. Jesus wants you to be a "new creation" through Him. And that's exactly what you should want for yourself too. Jesus deserves your extreme enthusiasm; the world deserves it; and you deserve the experience of sharing it.

His voice leads us not into timid discipleship but into bold witness.

CHARLES STANLEY

Dear Lord, You have called me not to a life of mediocrity, but to a life of passion. Today, I will be an enthusiastic follower of Your Son, and I will share His good news—and His love—with all who cross my path. Amen.

357

THIS DAY IS A NEW BEGINNING

Do not remember the former things, nor consider the things of old. Behold, I will do a new thing.

ISAIAH 43:18–19 NKJV

Each new day offers countless opportunities to serve God, to seek His will, and to obey His teachings. But each day also offers countless opportunities to stray from God's commandments and to wander far from His path.

Sometimes we wander aimlessly in a wilderness of our own making, but God has better plans for us. And whenever we ask Him to renew our strength and guide our steps, He does so.

Consider this day a new beginning. Consider it a fresh start, a renewed opportunity to serve your Creator with willing hands and a loving heart. Ask God to renew your sense of purpose as He guides your steps. Today is a glorious opportunity to serve your Father in heaven. Seize that opportunity while you can; tomorrow may indeed be too late.

Timely Tip: God can make all things new, including you. If you're feeling burned out or emotionally distraught, slow down, say a silent prayer, and focus on God's promises. And while you're at it, remember that the Lord can renew your spirit and restore your strength. Your job, of course, is to let Him.

Dear Lord, conform me to Your image. Create in me a clean heart, a new heart that reflects Your love for me. When I need to change, change me, Lord, and make me new. Amen.

358

CHANGE IS ALWAYS AN OPPORTUNITY FOR GROWTH

For You, O God, have tested us; You have refined us as silver is refined. You brought us into the net; You laid affliction on our backs. You have caused men to ride over our heads; we went through fire and through water; but You brought us out to rich fulfillment.

PSALM 66:10–12 NKJV

If you're going through major changes, or if you're experiencing a spiritual growth spurt, don't be surprised if you experience a few growing pains. Why? Because real transformation begins on the inside and works its way out from there. And sometimes the process of working things out can be painful. Painful, but necessary.

Lasting change doesn't occur "out there"; it occurs "in here." It occurs, not in the shifting sands of your own particular circumstances, but in quiet depths of your own obedient heart. So if you're in search of a new beginning—or, for that matter, a new you—don't expect changing circumstances to miraculously transform you into the person you want to become. Transformation starts with God, and it starts in the silent center of a humble human heart—like yours.

God specializes in giving people a fresh start.

RICK WARREN

What saves a man is to take a step. Then another step.

C. S. LEWIS

Dear Lord, You have the power to make all things new. Renew my strength, Father, and renew my hope for the future. Today and every day, Lord, let me draw comfort and courage from Your promises and from Your unending love. Amen.

359

EVERY DAY IS AN OPPORTUNITY TO FOLLOW IN CHRIST'S FOOTSTEPS

"Follow Me," He told them, "and I will make you fish for people!"
Immediately they left their nets and followed Him.

MATTHEW 4:19–20 HCSB

Each day, as we awaken from sleep, we are confronted with countless opportunities to serve God and to follow in the footsteps of His Son. When we do, our heavenly Father guides our steps and blesses our endeavors.

As citizens of a fast-changing world, we face challenges that sometimes leave us feeling overworked, overcommitted, and overwhelmed. But God has different plans for us. He intends that we slow down long enough to praise Him and to glorify His Son. When we do, He lifts our spirits and enriches our lives.

Today provides a glorious opportunity to place yourself in the service of the One who is the Giver of all blessings. May you seek His will, may you trust His word, and may you walk in the footsteps of His Son.

Be assured, if you walk with Him and look to Him,
and expect help from Him, He will never fail you.

GEORGE MUELLER

Jesus gives us hope because He keeps us company,
has a vision and knows the way we should go.

MAX LUCADO

Dear Jesus, My life has been changed forever by Your love and sacrifice. Today I will praise You, I will honor You, and I will walk with You. Amen.

360

TRUST GOD'S WISDOM

*For the LORD gives wisdom; from His mouth
come knowledge and understanding.*

PROVERBS 2:6 HCSB

In today's information-driven world, facts, figures, and opinions are just a click away. But real wisdom doesn't come from a search engine, from talk radio, from the evening news or from social media. Searching for genuine nuggets of wisdom in the endless stream of modern-day media messages is like panning for gold without a pan—only harder. Why? Because real wisdom doesn't come from the world; it comes from God. And it's up to you to ask Him for it: "Ask, and it will be given to you; seek, and you will find; knock, and it will be opened to you. For everyone who asks receives, and he who seeks finds, and to him who knocks it will be opened" (Matthew 7:7–8 NKJV). Jesus made it clear to His disciples that they should petition God to meet their needs. So should you.

Genuine, heartfelt prayer produces powerful changes in you and in your world. When you lift your heart to God, you open yourself to a never-ending source of divine wisdom and infinite love. Yet too many folks are too timid or too pessimistic to ask God for help. Please don't count yourself among their number.

God will give you wisdom if you have the courage to ask Him (and the determination to keep asking Him). If you call upon Him, He will give you guidance and perspective. If you make God's priorities your priorities, He will lead you along a path of His choosing. If you study God's teachings, you will be reminded that God's reality is the ultimate reality.

Dear Lord, when I depend upon the world's wisdom, I make many mistakes. But when I trust in Your wisdom, I build my life on a firm foundation. Today and every day I will trust Your Word and follow it, knowing that the ultimate wisdom is Your wisdom and the ultimate truth is Your truth. Amen.

361

A HEALTHY LIFESTYLE CAN REDUCE STRESS

*Therefore, I urge you, brothers and sisters, in view of God's mercy,
to offer your bodies as a living sacrifice, holy and pleasing to God—
this is your true and proper worship.*

ROMANS 12:1 NIV

In the book of Romans, Paul encourages us to make our bodies "holy and pleasing to God." Paul adds that to do so is "true and proper worship." For believers, the implication is clear: God intends that we take special care of the bodies He has given us. But it's tempting to do otherwise.

We live in a fast-food world where unhealthy choices are convenient, inexpensive, and tempting. And we live in a digital world filled with modern conveniences that often rob us of the physical exercise needed to maintain healthy lifestyles. As a result, too many of us find ourselves glued to the television, with a snack in one hand and a clicker in the other. The results are as unfortunate as they are predictable.

When you combine sensible exercise with a nutritious diet, you'll feel better and you'll discover the stress-reducing effects of a healthy lifestyle. So if you're being victimized by your own unhealthy habits, today is the perfect day for a change. You can start by taking personal responsibility for the body that God has given you. Then make the solemn pledge to yourself that you will begin to make the changes that are required to enjoy a longer, healthier, happier life. No one can make those changes for you; you must make them for yourself. And with God's help, you can do it. With Him, all things are possible.

Heavenly Father, You have given me the gift of life. And I know that my body is, indeed, a priceless gift from You. Guide my steps, Lord, and help me treat my body with care and respect, today and every day of my life. Amen.

362

DEAL WITH CHANGE

A sensible person sees danger and takes cover;
the inexperienced keep going and are punished.

PROVERBS 27:12 HCSB

In our fast-paced world, everyday life has become an exercise in managing change. Our circumstances change; our relationships change; our bodies change. We grow older every day, as does our world. So it's no wonder that so many of us feel anxious and afraid. Thankfully, God does not change. He is eternal, as are the truths that are found in His holy Word.

Are you facing one of life's inevitable "mid-course corrections"? If so, you must place your faith, your trust, and your life in the hands of the One who does not change: your heavenly Father. He is the unmoving rock upon which you must construct this day and every day. When you do, you are secure.

Conditions are always changing; therefore, I must not be dependent upon conditions. What matters supremely is my soul and my relationship to God.

CORRIE TEN BOOM

Timely Tip: Change is inevitable. Growth is not. God will come to your doorstep on countless occasions with opportunities to learn and to grow, and He will knock. Your challenge, of course, is to open the door.

Dear Lord, change in my life is inevitable. I can see change all around me, and I am thankful that You never change and keep me secure. Amen.

363

DON'T LOSE YOUR ENTHUSIASM

Whatever you do, do it enthusiastically,
as something done for the Lord and not for men.

COLOSSIANS 3:23 HCSB

Do you see each day as a glorious opportunity to serve God and to do His will? Are you enthused about life, or do you struggle through each day giving scarcely a thought to God's blessings? Are you constantly praising God for His gifts, and are you sharing His good news with the world? And are you excited about the possibilities for service that God has placed before you, whether at home, at work, at church, or at school? You should be.

You are the recipient of Christ's sacrificial love. Accept it enthusiastically and share it fervently. Jesus deserves your enthusiasm; the world deserves it; and you deserve the experience of sharing it.

Timely Tip: Look upon your life as an exciting adventure because that's precisely what it can be and should be. Today and every day, your challenge is to maintain your enthusiasm for life, even when times are tough. So ask God to help you focus on His blessings, and don't let anybody or anything steal your joy.

Dear Lord, You have called me not to a life of mediocrity, but to a life of passion. Today, I will be an enthusiastic follower of Your Son, and I will share His good news—and His love—with all who cross my path. Amen.

364

GOD'S GIFT OF ETERNAL LIFE IS AVAILABLE TO YOU

For God so loved the world, that he gave his only begotten Son,
that whosoever believeth in him should not perish, but have everlasting life.

JOHN 3:16 KJV

The Bible makes this promise: when you believe in Jesus and give your heart to Him, you will receive an incredible gift—the gift of eternal life. This promise is unambiguous, and it's the cornerstone of the Christian faith.

Jesus is not only the light of the world; He is also its salvation. He came to this earth so that we might not perish, but instead spend eternity with Him. What a glorious gift; what a priceless opportunity. As mere mortals, we cannot fully understand the scope, and thus the value, of eternal life. Our vision is limited but God's is not. He sees all things; He knows all things; and His plans for you extend throughout eternity.

If you haven't already done so, this moment is the perfect moment to turn your life over to God's only begotten son. When you give your heart to the Son, you belong to the Father—today, tomorrow, and for all eternity.

God has promised us abundance, peace, and eternal life.
These treasures are ours for the asking; all we must do is
claim them. One of the great mysteries of life is why on earth
do so many of us wait so very long to lay claim to God's gifts?

MARIE T. FREEMAN

Dear Lord, my life here on earth is brief. But You have offered me the priceless gift of eternal life through Your Son. I accept Your priceless gift, Father, with praise and thanksgiving. Today, give me the courage to share the good news of my salvation with those who need Your healing touch. Amen.

365

WE ARE COMMISSIONED TO WITNESS

Go, therefore, and make disciples of all nations, baptizing them in the name of the Father and of the Son and of the Holy Spirit, teaching them to observe everything I have commanded you. And remember, I am with you always, to the end of the age.

MATTHEW 28:19–20 HCSB

After His resurrection, Jesus addressed his disciples. As recorded in Matthew 28, Christ instructed His followers to share His message with the world. This "Great Commission" applies to Christians of every generation, including our own.

As believers, we are called to share the good news of Jesus with our families, with our neighbors, and with the world. Christ commanded His disciples to become fishers of men. We must do likewise, and we must do so today. Tomorrow may indeed be too late.

Witnessing is not something that we do for the Lord; it is something that He does through us if we are filled with the Holy Spirit.

WARREN WIERSBE

Heavenly Father, every man and woman, every boy and girl is Your child. You desire that all Your children know Jesus as their Lord and Savior. Father, let me be part of Your Great Commission. Let me give, let me pray, and let me go out into this world so that I might be Your worthy disciple, today and every day. Amen.

RECOGNIZING COMMON MOOD AND ANXIETY DISORDERS

COMMON ANXIETY AND MOOD DISORDERS

An anxiety disorder is a condition that causes exaggerated emotions to interfere with a person's ability to lead a normal life. All of us feel anxious from time to time, but a person who experiences an anxiety disorder is faced with overwhelming, debilitating feelings of fear, dread, or panic. Obsessive behaviors—characterized by recurrent, unwanted thoughts (obsessions) or undesirable repetitive behaviors (compulsions)—are also considered to be anxiety-related conditions.

A mood disorder is a mental health condition that has an adverse effect on a person's emotional state. The two most common mood disorders are depression and bipolar disorder. Both of these conditions are further divided into sub-categories based, in part, on the severity and duration of the person's symptoms.

Mood and anxiety disorders are quite common. The National Institute of Mental Health (NIMH) estimates that almost 10 percent of U.S. adults will experience a mood disorder during a given year and that over 20 percent of adults will experience a mood disorder sometime during their lifetime.

Anxiety disorders are even more common than mood disorders. In fact, the NIMH calls anxiety disorders "the most common mental health concern in the United States." They estimate that currently about 40 million adults (almost 20 percent of the adult population) suffer from some type of anxiety-related condition. Common anxiety disorders include, but are not limited to: generalized anxiety disorder, obsessive-compulsive disorder, panic disorder, post-traumatic stress disorder, and social anxiety disorder.

Both mood and anxiety disorders tend to run in families, which means that they can be inherited from one or both parents. Additionally, environmental factors—such as a traumatic event, a serious illness, or a significant life-changing situation—can be causal factors.

Clearly mood and anxiety disorders pose serious problems for individual sufferers and for the loved ones who care for them. Thankfully, these disorders are, in most cases, readily treatable with therapy or medication—or a combination of the two—combined with self-care.

The following descriptions provide a brief introduction to the above-mentioned disorders. Should you need to learn more, detailed information is readily available. And if you suspect that you or someone you care about may be impacted by one of these disorders, or by a mental illness not mentioned here, don't wait to seek treatment. Mental health problems can evolve into serious, debilitating, life-threatening conditions. So it's always better to seek professional guidance sooner, rather than later.

THE MOST COMMON ANXIETY DISORDERS

Generalized Anxiety Disorder (GAD): This condition is characterized by chronic anxiety, by exaggerated worry, tension, and apprehension even when there is no discernable cause for those feelings.

GAD, which often begins in the teen years or early adulthood, develops slowly. According to NIMH, symptoms of GAD include:

- Being excessively worried about everyday things
- Having trouble controlling worries or feelings of nervousness
- Knowing that one's worries are exaggerated and excessive
- Feeling restless; having trouble relaxing
- Having difficulty concentrating
- Being easily startled
- Having trouble falling asleep or staying asleep
- Feeling tired most or all the time
- Experiencing physical symptoms such as headaches, muscle aches, stomach aches, or unexplained pains;
- Experiencing difficulty swallowing
- Experiencing twitches or tremors
- Being irritable or feeling "on edge"
- Sweating profusely, feeling lightheaded or out of breath

Children and teens with GAD often worry excessively about:

- Performances in school, sports, or other public activities

- Catastrophes such as earthquakes or wars

Adults with GAD are often highly nervous about everyday circumstances, such as:

- Job security or performance
- Health
- Finances
- The health and well-being of their children
- Being late
- Completing household chores and other responsibilities

Post-traumatic Stress Disorder (PTSD): This disorder develops in some people who have either experienced or witnessed a terrifying, life-threatening, or life-altering event. PTSD symptoms may start within one month of the traumatic event, but for many individuals, symptoms may not appear until years later. These symptoms create significant problems in social settings, work-related environments, and relationships. PTSD symptoms are generally grouped into four categories: intrusive memories, avoidance, negative changes in thinking and mood, and changes in physical and emotional reactions.

Obsessive-Compulsive Disorder (OCD): This anxiety disorder is characterized by recurrent, unwanted thoughts (obsessions) and/or repetitive behaviors (compulsions). Repetitive behaviors such as hand washing, counting, checking, or cleaning are often performed with the hope of preventing obsessive thoughts or making those thoughts go away. Performing these rituals, however, provides only temporary relief. Not performing the aforementioned repetitive behaviors causes psychological discomfort and a marked increase in anxiety.

Panic Disorder: This anxiety disorder is characterized by unexpected and repeated episodes of intense fear (panic attacks) accompanied by physical and psychological symptoms that include:

- Sudden and repeated panic attacks that result in overwhelming feelings of anxiety and fear
- The feeling of being out of control
- The fear of death or impending doom during a panic attack
- Physical symptoms during a panic attack, such as a pounding or racing heart, sweating, chills, trembling, breathing problems, weakness or dizziness, tingly or numb hands, chest pain, stomach pain, or nausea
- An intense worry about when the next panic attack will occur
- A fear or avoidance of places where panic attacks have occurred in the past

Social Anxiety Disorder (also knowns as Social Phobia): This disorder is characterized by excessive self-consciousness and overwhelming anxiety resulting from social or performance situations in which the person is exposed to unfamiliar people or to possible scrutiny by others. A person with social phobia fears that he or she may act in a way—or may display anxiety-related symptoms—that will cause embarrassment or humiliation. In extreme cases, the phobia may be so broad that the sufferer experiences symptoms almost anytime he or she interacts with other people.

THE MOST COMMON MOOD DISORDERS

Major Depression (also known as Major Depressive Disorder or Clinical Depression): Major depression is a common, serious mood disorder. It causes severe symptoms that affect how one feels, thinks, and manages daily activities such as sleeping, eating, or working. To be diagnosed with depression, symptoms must be present for at least two weeks. Symptoms include, but are not limited to:

- Feelings of sadness, hopeless, or despondency
- Feelings of guilt, worthlessness, or helplessness
- Difficulty sleeping, early-morning awakening, or oversleeping

- Having noticeably less interest in usual pleasurable activities
- Decreased energy level
- Appetite or weight changes
- Feeling that life no longer has meaning
- Irritability
- Moving or talking more slowly
- Feeling restless or having trouble sitting still
- Difficulty concentrating, remembering, or making decisions
- Thoughts of death or suicide, or suicide attempts
- Aches or pains, headaches, cramps, or digestive problems that have no clear physical cause

Bipolar Disorder (also known as Manic-Depressive Disorder). According to NIMH, bipolar disorder is, "a brain disorder that causes unusual shifts in mood, energy, activity levels, and the ability to carry out day-to-day tasks." People suffering with this condition experience episodes of depression alternating with periods of mania.

There are four basic types of bipolar disorder, all of which involve demonstrable changes in mood, energy, and activity levels. These moods vacillate between periods of extreme energy and/or irritability (known as manic episodes) followed by periods of extreme sadness, hopelessness, or despair (known as depressive episodes). According to NIMH, people experiencing manic episodes may exhibit some or most of the following symptoms:

Manic Symptoms in Bipolar Disorder

- Feeling very "up," "high," or elated
- Feeling extremely energetic
- Experiencing increased activity levels
- Feeling jumpy or "wired"
- Having trouble falling asleep or staying asleep
- Exhibiting pressured speech patterns, i.e. talking faster than normal
- Feeling agitated, irritable, or "touchy"

- Racing thoughts
- Attempting to do many things at once

According to NIMH, bipolar patients experiencing depressive episodes may exhibit some or most of the following symptoms:

Depressive Symptoms in Bipolar Disorder

- Feeling very sad, down, empty, or hopeless
- Having very little energy
- Exhibiting decreased activity levels
- Having trouble sleeping (either too little sleep or too much)
- Feeling unable to enjoy anything
- Feeling worried and empty
- Having trouble concentrating
- Exhibiting forgetfulness
- Eating too much or too little
- Feeling tired or "slowed down"
- Thinking about death or suicide

OTHER COMMON MOOD DISORDERS

Persistent Depressive Disorder (also known as Dysthymia). This is a chronic, low-grade mood disorder in which symptoms of depression or irritability last for at least two years. A person diagnosed with persistent depressive disorder may experience episodes of major depression along with periods of less severe symptoms. But for a diagnosis of persistent depressive disorder, the depressive symptoms—both major symptoms and less severe ones—must last, in total, for at least two years.

Postpartum Depression: Many women are mildly depressed or anxious after the birth of a child. These symptoms, if they occur at all, typically clear within two weeks after delivery. Postpartum depression is a much more serious condition. Women with postpartum depression experience full-blown major depression after delivery. Feelings of extreme sadness, anxiety, and exhaustion are common, thus making it difficult for mothers to care for themselves and their babies.

Seasonal Affective Disorder (SAD): This is a form of depression that occurs during certain seasons of the year. Typically SAD begins in the late autumn or early winter and lasts until spring or summer. Less commonly, SAD episodes may begin during the late spring or summer. Symptoms of winter seasonal affective disorder often resemble those of major depression.

A FINAL NOTE

For previous generations, mental illness was often spoken about in whispers. For many sufferers and their families, emotional disorders were a source of embarrassment or shame. Thankfully, this is no longer the case. Today, mental health is a top-of-mind priority for medical professionals who are keenly aware that most mental disorders have both medical as well as psychological origins. As such, most emotional disorders are now imminently treatable. Thanks to advances in medical science, healing is available through counseling, through medication, or through a combination of the two.

If you suspect that you—or someone you care about—may be experiencing a mood disorder, an anxiety disorder, or any other psychiatric condition, don't hesitate to seek professional help. To fully experience God's abundance, you need to be spiritually and emotionally healthy. If mental health professionals can help you achieve the emotional stability you need to experience God's abundance here on earth, you should consider your treatment to be part of God's plan for your life.